Mega-Events and Globalization

Since the turn of the twenty-first century, there has been a trend for urban "mega-events" to be awarded to cities and nations in the East and Global South. Such events have been viewed as economic stimulants as well as opportunities to promote national identity, gain greater international recognition, and exercise a form of "soft power." However, there has also been ongoing controversy about the value, impact, and legacy of global mega-events in these cities and nations.

This book provides a critical examination of the ambition for spectacle that has emerged across the East and Global South. The chapters explore the theoretical and conceptual issues associated with mega-events and new forms of globalization, from the critical political economy of mega-events in a changing world order to the contested social and economic legacies of mega-events and the widespread opposition that increasingly accompanies these events. The book also explores questions of urban development and governance, the role of new communications technologies in global economic expansion, the high security state, and the growing global influence of international non-governmental organizations.

This book offers a rich collection of original theoretical contributions and global case studies from leading international scholars of the social sciences and humanities. It offers a fresh and unique interdisciplinary perspective that synthesizes cutting-edge research on mega-events and urban spectacles while simultaneously contributing to a broader understanding of the dynamics of global capitalism and international political power in the early twenty-first century.

Richard Gruneau is Professor of Communication at Simon Fraser University, Vancouver, Canada.

John Horne is Professor of Sport and Sociology in the School of Sport and Wellbeing at the University of Central Lancashire, Preston, UK.

Routledge Research in Sport, Culture and Society

Mega-Events and Globalization

Capital and spectacle in a changing world order

Edited by Richard Gruneau and John Horne

Routledge
Taylor & Francis Group

LONDON AND NEW YORK

First published 2016
by Routledge
2 Park Square, Milton Park, Abingdon, Oxon OX14 4RN

and by Routledge
711 Third Avenue, New York, NY 10017

Routledge is an imprint of the Taylor & Francis Group, an informa business

British Library Cataloguing in Publication Data
A catalogue record for this book is available from the British Library

Library of Congress Cataloging in Publication Data
A catalogue record for this book has been requested

ISBN: 978-1-138-80561-3 (hbk)
ISBN: 978-1-315-75217-4 (ebk)

Typeset in Times New Roman
by Swales & Willis Ltd, Exeter, Devon, UK

Contents

Contributors

Michael Borowy is a researcher at the Centre for Policy Research on Science and Technology (CPROST) at Simon Fraser University, Vancouver, British Columbia, Canada. His current research focuses on the video and computer games industry, digital policy, and "eSport."

Hyun Bang Shin is Associate Professor of Geography and Urban Studies at the London School of Economics in the UK. His recent work focuses on "speculative urbanism" in the Global South, gentrification, and human rights and housing issues.

Jules Boykoff is Associate Professor and Chair of the Department of Politics and Government, Pacific University, in Portland, Oregon, USA. His current research focuses on social movements, media, political dissent, and the state.

Anne-Marie Broudehoux is Professor at the School of Design, University of Quebec at Montreal, Quebec, Canada. Her research focuses upon urban image construction associated with mega-event preparations and the socio-spatial impacts of mega-events on urban built environments.

James Compton is Associate Professor in the Faculty of Information and Media Studies at the University of Western Ontario in London, Ontario, Canada. His research interests lie in the areas of journalism, university governance, and the political economy of communications.

Simon Darnell is Assistant Professor in the Faculty of Kinesiology and Physical Education at the University of Toronto in Toronto, Ontario, Canada. His research focuses on critical sociology, sport, and social development.

Ashwin Desai is Professor of Sociology at the University of Johannesburg, South Africa. His research interests include contemporary South African politics, inequality and poverty, social movements, race, and sport.

Grant Farred is Professor of Africana Studies and English at Cornell University, Ithaca, NY, USA. His research interests include postcolonial theory, race, formation of intellectuals, sports theory, cultural studies, and literary studies.

Kevin Fox Gotham is Professor of Sociology and Associate Dean of Academic Affairs in the School of Liberal Arts (SLA) and Director of the Social Policy and Practice Program at Tulane University in New Orleans, LA, USA. He has research interests in real estate and housing policy, urban redevelopment policy, post-disaster rebuilding, and the political economy of tourism.

Christopher Gaffney is Senior Research Fellow in the Geographisches Institut, Universität Zürich, Zürich, Switzerland. His work focuses on sports stadia, mega-events, popular cultures, and popular struggles.

Richard Gruneau is Professor of Communication at Simon Fraser University, Vancouver, British Columbia, Canada. His research interests include social theory, the political economy of communication, media studies, sport, and popular cultures.

John Horne is Professor of Sport and Sociology in the School of Sport and Wellbeing, University of Central Lancashire, Preston, UK. His research interests include the sociology of sports mega-events, sport, and globalization, and consumer culture.

Rob Millington is a doctoral candidate in the School of Kinesiology and Health Studies, Queen's University, Kingston, Ontario, Canada. He is currently undertaking research on the history of Sport for Development and Peace (SDP) at a UN-policy level and its implementation in the Global South through SDP programs and sport mega-events.

Carlos Vainer is Professor in the Institute of Urban and Regional Planning and Research at the Federal University of Rio de Janeiro (IPPUR/UFRJ) in Rio de Janeiro, Brazil. His work focuses on regional and urban policies, migrations, social and environmental impacts of large urban projects, urban conflicts, and social movements in the context of globalization.

Dal Yong Jin is Associate Professor in the School of Communication at Simon Fraser University, Vancouver, British Columbia, Canada. His research interests include social media and convergence, mobile technologies and game studies, globalization and media, transnational cultural studies, and the political economy of media and culture.

1 Mega-events and globalization

A critical introduction

Richard Gruneau and John Horne

Over the past two decades, academic writing about large-scale, highly visible, urban events has become a growth industry. There are now conferences all over the world devoted to discussions of the meaning and importance of the Olympics, or football World Cups, and to debates about their risks and potential legacies.[1] The burgeoning interest in events doesn't stop with these obvious mega-events; it extends to include a range of other high-profile entertainment events and urban festivals. In recent years, there have been special issues of academic journals devoted to the study of these events and it has become difficult to keep up with the sheer number of books that address the topic in some way or another.[2] Commenting on the recent upsurge of writing on mega-events, Martin Polley notes wryly that if "the motto of London 2012 was 'inspire a generation' for hundreds of authors this was easily recast as inspire a publication."[3] Prominent publishers such as Routledge, Elsevier and John Wiley have started book series in "event management" and there are a growing number of university programs devoted to preparing students for careers managing and hosting major events.

Definitions of "mega-events," and of "event studies" more broadly, vary across different theoretical understandings and disciplines and there are a number of roughly equivalent phrases in both academic and popular writing, such as "Hallmark" or "Marquee" events. Writing in 2000, Maurice Roche offered one of the earliest definitions of mega-events: "large-scale cultural (including commercial and sporting) events, which have a dramatic character, mass popular appeal and international significance."[4] This definition has the virtues of simplicity and inclusiveness. Still, it seems almost modest by today's standards, when the world's most prominent mega-events command such unprecedented public visibility and popularity, now not just "mass popular appeal," but mass appeal on a truly global scale. In recent years, scholarly researchers and university administrators have recognized just how much mega-events *matter* to hundreds of millions of enthusiasts: as vital civic occasions; celebrations of identity, nation and community and welcome opportunities for distraction. Because they are recurring events held according to an expected schedule, Olympics and men's football World Cups, in particular, have become normalized as seemingly natural features of the rhythms of modern life, an unfolding horizon of festivals of modernity anticipated like the changes of the seasons.

A handful of other regularly scheduled major events, such as the Superbowl in the US, can reach similar levels of prominence and, in Roche's words, there is a "dense social-ecosystem" of second- and third-tier mega-events vying for public and media attention on the global stage, such as the Commonwealth, Pan American, or Asian Games, Youth Olympics, and "other" World Cups in sports such as rugby, cricket, track and field athletics and Formula 1 car races.[5] These sporting events jostle for space in international, national and local civic calendars with large-scale political gatherings, such as G8 Summits and IMF or World Bank conferences, as well as prominent art, film and music festivals, and a wide range of "heritage" or historical celebrations. In many parts of the world, civic life and leisure in the early twenty-first century are strongly influenced by the rhythms of these events. In this context, it shouldn't be surprising to find that the academic study of events, has become regularized and normalized too, often connecting to institutions outside the academy to promote new ways of thinking about events, and new conceptual or organizational skills, all geared to a fast-growing economy of events and intense experiences.

Economy is the operant term here, because the world's most prominent mega-events have become economic monsters, sucking in huge amounts of public investment while generating global audiences whose attraction for cities, and value to advertisers and sponsors, has inflated dramatically since the 1980s. Bent Flyvbjerg suggests that we should probably distinguish between "mega" (million), "giga" (billion), and "tera" (trillion) dollar (USD), projects depending on their scale.[6] But the point is that civic and national ambitions for mega-events—for recognition, visibility, political leverage, tourism, foreign investment, or economic development—now underwrite the production of spectacles that are increasingly significant nodal points of global communications and capitalist accumulation. As a result, it has become more difficult than ever to conceive of such events as stand-alone occasions with political, economic, or cultural autonomy; rather mega-events in the twenty-first century reveal themselves as deeply and profoundly *relational*. In this sense, all mega-events today are inherently global. They necessarily connect the local to the global because their very existence requires a sustained engagement between national and local authorities, supporters and critics, with global networks of capital accumulation and circulation, culture and communications, international governmental relations, international non-governmental organizations (INGOs), and international flows of migration and tourism.

Mega-events, academic writing, and the project of this book

These relational networks and flows include the writing of academics, the organizations that fund research, the agencies that hire academic consultants and the publishers of scholarly work. The growing academic interest in mega-events has not only developed in conjunction with the escalating scale, visibility and cost of mega-events, it has also been influenced by a strengthening entrepreneurial culture in many universities since the late 1980s.[7] Diminishing state investments in Western universities have been accompanied by greater demands for quality assurance, accountability and, in some jurisdictions, the establishment of competitive "merit-based" funding models. Swept up in this competitive market logic, universities have worked harder to measure and improve "productivity" while simultaneously promoting their "brands" in national and international markets for research funding, investment, and student and faculty recruitment. In a world driven by university and departmental rankings, citation counts, impact indices, and sizes of research grants, academic writers have been pushed to be more entrepreneurial in their day-to-day professional lives.

The academic study of mega-events has taken off in this context, not just because of the prestige by association that can accrue to individual researchers and their universities through the study of these events, but also because mega-events offer rich opportunities for collaboration with consultants, planners, marketers, business organizations, INGOs, BINGOs (business-oriented, international non-governmental organizations) and governments. Such collaborations often bring the entrepreneurial agendas of university-based researchers into a (largely) harmonious relationship with the entrepreneurial ambitions of the cities and nations which host mega-events, as well as those of the INGOs and corporations which sanction the events, promote them, profit from them, or use them as platforms to achieve other agendas.

Consider just two examples. First, during the 2010 Shanghai World Expo—whose theme was "Better City, Better Life"—academic researchers and consultants played a prominent role in congresses and forums examining issues of urban development and environmental sustainability. This resulted in a joint United Nations/International Bureau of Expositions "Guide for Sustainable Urban Development in the 21st Century."[8] Academics literally became part of the exhibition through their contribution to the "social responsibility" framing of the event. There is nothing particularly new in this. From the time of their origins in nineteenth-century Europe, international expositions have often involved prominent academics in event organization and have hosted congresses and public lectures that attracted researchers and practitioners from a wide range of disciplines.[9] The growth of social responsibility themes in the branding of World Expos since the 1970s represents a continuation of this older pedagogical tradition and expands it in a progressive contemporary direction, thereby opening up opportunities for collaborations with academic researchers in newer fields of global relevance, such as environmental sustainability and social marketing.

A second example is the role played by academics over the past twenty years in the international promotion of sport for development and peace, variously working in conjunction with United Nations agencies, the International Olympic Committee (IOC), Commonwealth Games Committees, the Fédération Internationale de Football Association (FIFA) and advocacy groups, such as the INGO "Right to Play." As Bruce Kidd has noted, a late twentieth-century shift towards market-oriented solutions to global problems ushered in a "new focus on entrepreneurship" that saw growing interest in the use of sport as a strategy for social development, largely driven by a spirit of humanitarian intervention.[10]

Bringing international sport organizations such as the IOC or FIFA into such endeavors underlined the notion that sporting mega-events can promote socially progressive and positive outcomes, including the opening-up of sporting opportunities for women and people with disabilities, championing human rights and using sport as a tool in international economic development.[11]

These examples demonstrate how academic collaborations with agencies involved in the staging of mega-events in recent years have been important both in the promotion of broader social objectives and of more immediate "legacies." In the latter case, it is well established that the legacies of mega-events can be tangible in nature; that is, related in some way to improvements in the material infrastructure or, more controversially, to the economies of a city or nation. Tangible legacies typically involve such things as major investments in mass transportation, the redevelopment of waterfront communities, or the building of iconic sports stadiums. In addition, mega-events can also leave intangible legacies related to the rich lived experiences they often provide. As Roche has noted, mega-events can provide audiences and participants with popular memories and cultural resources for the construction of "a meaningful life" and for reflecting upon identity and enacting agency.[12] Sporting mega-events, in particular, Roche suggests, provide important opportunities for the creation of a global sense of "co-presence" among the world's populations. In contrast to such things as disasters, wars and VIP funerals, Roche argues, "the planned and positive (celebratory) character" of sporting mega-events "provide cultural realizations of 'the global village' that are otherwise unmatched as global cultural forms."[13]

There is no question that academic work focused on identifying and weighing the tangible and intangible legacies of mega-events, or on how mega-events might promote socially progressive agendas, has provided important information and significant insights. But, in our view, much of this literature—even when it appears progressive in intent—tends to downplay the negative or contradictory features of these events, especially in respect to considerations of injustice, inequality, social polarization and domination. At its worst, this can lend itself to uncritical evangelism in mega-event studies or a blind rush to cash in on them in various ways. For example, despite its joint sponsorship by the United Nations, the *Shanghai Manual* produced at the 2010 World Expo 2010 reads more like a promotional brochure for its sponsoring body, the Bureau of International Exhibitions, than a measured academic assessment of mega-events and issues of environmental sustainability.[14] The claim that "investment in mega-events is an investment for the public good" is treated throughout the document as an axiomatic principle.[15] This leaves no room to consider more controversial aspects of mega-events, such as the slum clearances and displacements of poor citizens that occurred in the years before the Shanghai World Expo, displacements masked by the self-professed commitment to environmental sustainability.[16]

Similarly, much of the writing on sport for development and peace (although certainly not all of it) has failed to address the possibility that some of its sponsoring organizations may be implicated in the exacerbation of economic inequality and social polarization, issues that the movement is arguably committed to address. In other instances—the case of FIFA-sponsored initiatives is especially notable here—there has been insufficient scholarly attention to the possibility that sport and development projects may be implicated in intra-organizational crony-ism, corruption and clientalism. In some cases, the involvement of academics with major sporting INGOs can lead to significant conflicts of interest; for exam-ple, as Helen Lenskyj suggests, when the participation of academics in research institutes subsidized by the International Olympic Committee (IOC) can blur "the lines between Olympic cheerleading and scholarly debate."[17]

These lines are easily blurred because well-established organizations that sponsor sporting mega-events, such as the IOC or FIFA, have a taken-for-granted global presence through their long-standing roles as sport regulatory bodies and their histories of partnership with governments, powerful corporations and other international organizations. Moreover, since the 1990s, the increased wealth of these organizations has heightened their capacities for largesse on a variety of fronts, including support to projects of interest to academic researchers. At the same time, intense competition between nations and cities for sporting mega-events has created greater possibilities for scandal, including, most recently, a number of indictments and arrests of prominent FIFA officials for allegations of bribery and corruption made by US authorities. The long-term consequences of these indictments and arrests remain to be seen but, like the IOC, FIFA has shown itself to be exceptionally adroit in the past at circumventing challenges to its authority and influence. Both organizations have worked hard, often using public relations specialists—experts in the art of "spin"—to deflect criticism and promote themselves as non-profit entities with a socially progressive mission: expanding sporting opportunities for *all* on a global scale.[18]

The seductive romanticism of this image, matched with the economic and geo-political ambitions of hosts and sponsoring organizations, and the global popu-larity of events such as the Olympics or men's World Cup, have tended to give a Teflon character to organizations such as the IOC or FIFA. Criticism can be frequent, and in the case of the IOC has led to modest reforms, but few of the most trenchant criticisms seem to stick. To complicate things further, in a world charac-terized by what David Harvey calls "the commodification and commercialization of everything," even highly critical analyses of mega-events can be subsumed and subverted by commercial and promotional forces.[19] For example, activist criti-cisms of mega-events can readily find places in non-critical university courses in event studies, adding just enough criticism to bolster a claim to comprehen-siveness or social relevance while simultaneously inoculating students against the dangers of political radicalism. The critique of mega-events can also contribute to what Thomas Kemple calls "new ways of knowing and doing capitalism," where the targets of criticism learn from their critics and adapt accordingly. In such cir-cumstances, criticism can simply become part of the "stocks" of commercial and political acumen that find their way into the "portfolios" of the very organizations that are being criticized.[20]

Furthermore, the lines between the sales objectives of mega-event promoters and sponsors, and those of publishers who sell academic discourses about such events—even critical ones—can sometimes be very thin. This book, whose contributors take a largely critical view of mega-events, is no exception. Such are the contradictions in a world where images and video clips of urban protests in Brazil during the Confederation Cup in June of 2013 were posted on YouTube and used by newspapers to sell audiences to advertisers, or, as James Compton states in his chapter in this volume, where digitally shared narratives and videos of Cossacks whipping members of the activist group, Pussy Riot, at the 2014 Sochi Winter Olympics were readily incorporated into "the promotional machinery of the global marketing of events and experiences."

Still, despite the powerful conformist tendencies and pressures noted above, the contradictions surrounding mega-events today don't always result in the neutralizing sale of criticism or the containment of its oppositional energy. The more economically monstrous and spectacular that mega-events have become over the past two decades, the more opposition they appear to have generated. Because mega-events are inherently relational in a more broadly global sense than ever before, the nations, cities and INGOs which typically award and license these events must now engage with an international cacophony of dissenting voices, with the unlikely prospect that these voices can be completely silenced in the age of global media. As Kevin Fox Gotham observes later in this book: "Unlike the past, where opposition to mega-events was often muted or exceptional, today we witness an explosion of unrest and protests led by opposition coalitions dedicated to drawing global attention to the inequities and anti-democratic nature of spectacles."

Sporting mega-events have become especially notable focal points for social criticism and unrest because they provide internationally visible opportunities for critics to protest perceived inequalities, corruption, or social injustice by "seizing the platform" that the events provide.[21] Depending on the social and political context of the event in question, criticism can variously be found in large public demonstrations, street art, graffiti and popular literature, in addition to news reporting, investigative journalism and opinion columns in both mainstream and alternative news media, as well as in a considerable body of academic work. Criticism can also circulate globally in digital form, in blogs, tweets and on activist websites, creating new social and intellectual resources and new networked possibilities for opposition. The critique of sporting mega-events has become an important aspect of globalization because it provides a transnational social and political space for public discussion that exceeds the boundaries of nation states. This lends itself to greater opportunities to evaluate mega-events from multiple standpoints of global justice, postcolonial aspirations and other important ethical, social, political and ecological issues of our time.[22]

Our goal in this collection is to map the main lines of criticism directed towards mega-events in the early twenty-first century, while exploring theoretical explanations of the increasing prominence of mega-events in contemporary life, especially in non-Western contexts, such as East Asia, the so-called BRICS countries (Brazil, Russia, India, China, South Africa) and areas of the world often designated as "the Global South."[23] The widespread hosting of mega-events in Asian and Southern nations is a comparatively recent phenomenon. For example, throughout the first half of the twentieth century, the Olympics were exclusively hosted by cities in Western (now often called "Northern") nations. There was greater global variation in host cities for men's football (soccer) World Cups, largely due to the intensity of support for football in South America, as well as FIFA's policy of spreading the event to its regional associations. Still, between the inception of the World Cup in 1930 and the end of the twentieth century, the event was held in Western nations ten times in comparison to only five times in countries in either the East or South.

The geographical distribution of host cities for World's Fairs and major international expositions reveals a roughly similar spatial trajectory. There were numerous "international" expositions in the nineteenth century, ranging in scale and public visibility, hosted in major European cities. Major industrial exhibitions were also staged frequently throughout the colonies of the World Powers during the nineteenth century—in cities such as Buenos Aires, Calcutta, Rio de Janeiro, Bogotá, Sao Paulo and Bombay (Mumbai). As Armand Mattelart points out, among major nations of the era, only China and Japan proved initially resistant to the emergence of this "new form of contact among nations via industry."[24] However, in the years between the end of the First World War and the 1990s, the process of awarding International Exhibitions became more regulated and host cities were more likely to be located in the West. However, by the end of the twentieth century, World's Fairs, or "Expos" began to be awarded to cities in the East and South in greater numbers. We have already noted that Shanghai was host to the "World Expo" in 2010. Yeosu, South Korea, hosted the ensuing World Expo in 2012 and World Expo events are scheduled for Kazakhstan in 2017 and Dubai in 2020.

A similar globalizing trend is evident in the case of sporting mega-events. The BRICS nations have been especially notable in this regard, with the summer or winter Olympics awarded to Beijing in 2008, Sochi in 2014, Rio de Janeiro in 2016, the youth Olympics to Nanjing in 2014 and the Commonwealth Games to Delhi in 2010.[25] Since 2000, the men's football World Cup was held in South Africa in 2010, in Brazil in 2014 and is scheduled for Russia in 2018. Outside the BRICS nations, since the late 1990s, prominent sporting events have been held, or are scheduled, for many other cities and nations in the East and South. Examples include Japan (Winter Olympics in Nagano in 1998, the 2002 men's football World Cup in multiple cities and the Summer Olympics in Tokyo in 2020); South Korea (the 2002 men's football World Cup and the 2018 Winter Olympics in Pyeongchang); Qatar (the 2022 men's football World Cup).

In compiling the chapters in the book we had a number of central organizing questions in mind. What are the factors that have made mega-events so important in cities and nations around the world and in particular why has the hosting of mega-events become so attractive to cities in the BRICS nations and the Global South? What are the economic, political and social risks and benefits of hosting such events? What implications, if any, can be drawn from analyses of recent spectacular events in the BRICS and South for a broader understanding of changing relations of economic and political power on a global scale? To what extent do such events promote or deform concepts of local and global citizenship or shape conditions of governance at local, national and international levels? To what extent do mega-events contribute to global social inequalities or provide opportunities for challenging them? What do such events tell us about the significance or the effectiveness of various forms of popular resistance to global power networks?

Key issues in the critical analysis of contemporary mega-events

The chapters that follow do not offer definitive answers to these questions but, taken collectively, they highlight a number of important issues in the critical analysis of mega-events and globalization. In addressing these issues, many of our contributors take their inspiration from the "alter-globalization" struggles against social polarization, economic inequality and injustice that became prominent around the world over the past two decades. In our view, the nature and scale of these struggles, and the social conditions that appear to have generated them, are leading greater numbers of researchers to re-engage with critical political economy perspectives that fell out of fashion in academic writing on globalization and mega-events during the 1990s and early 2000s.

Consider just a few examples of critical political economy's fall from grace in the late twentieth century. Roland Robertson's influential sociological work on globalization in the 1990s is particularly notable here, as is Roche's early work on mega-events. Both writers position their projects as an attempt to go beyond the limitations of critical political economy perspectives such as the Marxian analysis of imperialism, Latin American dependency theories, and the World Systems Theory of writers such as Immanuel Wallerstein or Giovanni Arrighi. In Robertson's words, it was necessary to go beyond the economistic focus of these theories to emphasize "*culture* and the *agency* aspect of the making of the global system."[26] Roche takes a similar view in arguing for a more "complex" analysis of how mega-events can be associated with globalization, and especially with the formation of "global culture."[27] In addition, albeit with a different and more critical focus, many late twentieth-century theorists of "postcolonialism" challenged what they saw as the Eurocentrism and economic determinism of Marxian-inspired theories of imperialism, dependency, or capitalist globalization.[28]

These were extremely important and compelling interventions that introduced a much-needed sensitivity to issues of human self-creation, gendered, racial and national *differences* and hybridities in academic writing on globalization. But, over the past twenty years the increasing prominence of alter-globalization movements at WTO, IMF and G8 meetings, the US-centered "Occupy" movement, struggles over "structural adjustments" in South America and over "austerity" in the Eurozone, and the struggles of dissident indigenous and other subaltern groups across Latin America, Africa and Asia have all suggested a need to reconsider the value of critical political economy. One common theme that emerged from such struggles was a growing awareness by academic critics of the extraordinary impact of the late twentieth-century neoliberal ideological turn in international economic relations, with accompanying policies that accelerated the mobility of capital around the world while generating increasing social inequality and environmental destruction in its wake. The global financial crisis of 2007–08 in particular invited a political economic analysis of the irrationalities and contradictions of unregulated capitalist globalization. By the middle of the first decade of the twenty-first century, notable Marxian critics, such as David Harvey, had become influential in international academic networks in many disciplines and there were a number of conferences and special editions of journals making a plea for the return to critical political economy perspectives on globalization.[29]

Taking up this challenge, we argue that one of the most important critical issues in the study of mega-events is to assess the role they play in expanding the realm of capitalist exchange on a global scale. The centerpiece of industrial capitalism has always been the making of tangible objects for consumption—items such as machines, clothing, knives or forks. However, as long as industrial capitalist production is concentrated on the production of tangible objects, "it faces chronic problems of overproduction due to the tendency for markets to be become satiated."[30] For financial expansion to occur, the lifetime of consumer products must ideally be shortened and dependencies on new products must be developed. The push for new products in the postwar era—new forms of commodification—led to the growth of economies built around the production of immaterial goods such as services, knowledge, experiences and events. By the final two decades of the twentieth century, the production of events in many parts of the world was beginning to rival the more traditional making of things.[31]

As early as the 1940s, Max Horkheimer and Theodor Adorno commented on the striking development of "cultural industries" in Western societies.[32] There has been a significant and consistent growth in the scale and value of cultural commodities in the world since then and mega-events have been a constituent part of this process. The essential political-economic points here are twofold. The first is the degree to which the growth and commodification of events has facilitated economic growth by expanding the sphere of exchange—the universalization of the market. The second is the way that ephemeral commodities and the peripheral activities they stimulate have provided a way for capital that is launched into circulation to be recuperated quickly. As David Harvey argues, echoing Marx: "the faster the capital launched into circulation can be recuperated, the greater the profit will be."[33] With their fixed and short time frames, the recuperation of capital investments in mega-events is noticeable faster than, say, in the automobile, electronic, or aerospace industries.

This partially explains the extent to which mega-events have acted historically as constitutive features of the rationalization of space and time associated with the global market system. The spatial rationalization of many of the world's most prominent cities has involved numerous programs of "creative destruction," for example, through massive population displacements and dispossessions, the destruction of older communities and of the natural environment, the replacement of low-rise communities by high-rise buildings, and the broad-scale redesign of urban space to facilitate the easier movement of people and commerce. But the last forty years have witnessed an unprecedented boom in the urbanization of economic life around the world, resulting in hundreds of millions of people streaming from rural areas into the world's largest cities, and most often into slums, barrios and favelas.[34] At the same time, many urban areas have developed to become what John Hannigan calls "fantasy cities": homes to spectacular architecture, vast entertainment complexes of theatres, upmarket stores, museums and sports stadia, along with substantially gentrified downtown populations.[35] The "fantastic" aspect of life in these cities, or at least in their core entertainment and gentrified residential zones, derives from their heavy reliance on spaces of spectacle.

This raises the question of exactly who has benefited most from the programs of creative destruction associated with the intensified global production of spaces of spectacle. There are usually clear borders between slum dwellers and the residents of gentrified spaces in fantasy cities. However, an important part of the creative destruction that often accompanies mega-events is the transgression of these borders by opening up favelas, ghettos and slums to the combined interventions of real-estate investment and finance capital.[36] On the one hand, these areas can be emptied of their residents in the run-up to staging mega-events, sometimes forcibly, in order to open geographically desirable slum spaces for financial speculation and gentrification. On the other hand, mega-events can also act as stimulants to open slums to the sale of internationally branded products by inundating poor communities with the advertising of event sponsors, encouraging a loosening of credit restrictions to encourage consumption and providing a rationale for a police clampdown on black-market activities.

The use of cities to promote accumulation in this way has led to a sometimes bizarre mix of market volatility and gentrification in the wake of hosting mega-events. In economically strong economies, such as the US, some European societies, as well as *some* of the BRICS and East Asian nations, mega-events provide a way of absorbing surplus capital while simultaneously providing additional stimulants to local economies by multiplying and accelerating connections to global circuits of capitalist production and circulation. However, huge capital investments in spectacle have tended to hyper-inflate the importance of real estate not only in "global cities" but in many aspiring cities as well. For example, unprecedented rural in-migration to Chinese cities has made the construction of residential apartments a major factor in an economy that in turn has become "the main driver of the global economy since the world-wide crisis that began in 2007."[37] When you add in expenditure for creating factory, warehouse and office spaces, along with investment in gentrified shopping and entertainment districts and large-scale infrastructure projects—including mega-events such as the Beijing Olympics, the Asian Games in Guangzhou, or the Shanghai World Expo—the scale of investment in Chinese cities over the past two decades has simply been overwhelming. In this regard, Harvey points to a *Financial Times* report noting how "in just two years, from 2011 to 2012, China produced more cement than the United States did in the entire twentieth century."[38] Along with this urban boom, real-estate values in the "desirable" areas of many Chinese cities—Shanghai and Hong Kong provide obvious examples—have increased significantly, while also being subject to volatile swings in market prices.

At least in China a socialist legacy has meant there have been attempts (although rarely at market rates) to compensate the stunningly large populations that have been displaced by mega-projects and mega-events.[39] As the regulatory climate in international economic development has shifted in a neoliberal direction in many other parts of the world, there has been greater reliance on privatization in place of older state-centered models that operated on the notion that progressive taxation and rational planning could provide vital *public* amenities and services. Today, many self-defined "world-class" or "global" cities struggle with problems of homelessness and reduced public services while taxation rates for corporations and wealthy individuals continue to fall. Urban elites often view mega-events as vital strategies of wealth creation, but there is little evidence to suggest that the wealth they create trickles down to urban underclasses who face an erosion of public services and the challenge of finding affordable housing, health services and transportation. In many of the world's "global cities" a combination of gentrification and land speculation has lent itself to shortages in affordable housing frequently combined with surpluses of properties that sit empty as investors wait for property values to increase.

If mega-events are often associated with programs of creative destruction, gentrification, social polarization and property speculation, they have also been important manifestations of significant financialization in late twentieth and early twenty-first-century capitalism. A sweeping deregulation of the international financial system in the 1970s, matched with technological developments in communications and computing, a neoliberalization of monetary policy in a number of the world's major economies, and a parallel neoliberal turn within the World Bank and the International Monetary Fund had the effect of shifting the nexus between states and international finance from the 1970s through the 1990s.[40] Two key aspects of late twentieth-century globalization arose from these circumstances. The first was a dramatic increase in the number of corporations that began to organize their profit taking across state boundaries. The second was a rapid integration of previously globalized national and regional markets into a single, largely unregulated, global market.[41] As Samir Amin argues: "whereas a few decades ago the large corporations still waged their competitive battles essentially on national markets, the market size now required for victory in the first round of matches is approaching 500–600 million consumers."[42]

Few circumstances in the world can mobilize these mega-markets of potential consumers like contemporary mega-events and especially major international sporting events such as the Olympics and the men's football World Cup. At the risk of only slight exaggeration, you can make the argument that sporting mega-events have increasingly become a terrain where much of the world does business. Moreover, their escalating scale in recent years has effectively made them institutions that promote intense financialization and speculative investment. Most notably, the production of mega-events is typically dependent upon a parallel production of often staggering debt. The world's bankers and well-capitalized investors are the inevitable winners. The losers are cities and nations not yet sitting at the world's financial head table, but who are tempted to borrow heavily to finance their ambitions for an invitation to the dinner. As Greece found out in 2004, the turn to mega-event capitalism as a solution to slow economic growth, let alone as an expression of national pride and regional political ambition, can be an immense financial trap.

The capacity of digital media to provide new opportunities for broadening and valorizing audience attention is another significant issue in the critical analysis of mega-events and globalization in the twenty-first century. The commodification of new audiences in online platforms creates enhanced capacities for an expansion—a further pushing back—of capital's frontiers. Social media such as Facebook and Twitter have become unprecedented vehicles for creating new markets, commodities, synergies, forms of marketing, networks of publicity and, some argue, even new forms of immaterial labor.[43] They also play a key role in the acceleration of the recovery time of digital investments. But, as noted earlier, they simultaneously provide enhanced means to criticize the very markets, synergies and networks they create. This invites the question whether the possibilities for reflexivity and opposition that social media create can offer *effective* challenges to capitalist accumulation or whether, as Jodi Dean argues, these challenges are likely to be little more than democratic or participatory "fantasies."[44]

Amin raises an important point for debate when he argues that the highly mediated global politics of the twenty-first century—or as he calls it, "low intensity democracy"—has a tendency to devolve into populist positions that are as likely to move in socially conservative directions as progressive ones. Insofar as the criticisms of low intensity democracy largely focus on local, regional, or national issues—such as transportation costs and housing availability—Amin suggests, they tend not to grasp the dynamics of the current stage of international market-centered imperialism.[45] Mezzadra and Neilson take the analysis further, arguing that the challenge is one of "translatability," of implementing effective articulations between local and global criticisms based on shared understandings of "the processes of dispossession and exploitation that crisscross the operations of capital."[46] This may mean linking up or coordinating criticism raised at different types of mega-events, for example of WTO summits and men's football World Cups or the Olympics. The ultimate goal is the attempt to build "new transnational forms of democratic political organization capable of combining struggles and multiplying their affirmative aspects."[47]

Democratic governance is another significant issue surrounding mega-events and globalization in the twenty-first century. Mega-events not only require creative destruction, they require it on a fixed schedule, with little room for error. Transportation infrastructure must be well in place by the start of the event and land redevelopment completed, with pavilions, stadiums, arenas and other venues finished to required standards. For these reasons, the run-up to staging mega-events is often put on an emergency footing, with an accompanying relaxation of normal democratic oversight. In this sense, and virtually from the point at which bids from hosting nations or cities are accepted, mega-events occur as "states of exception," where normal rules of governance become suspended in deference to the "needs" of local organizing committees, sponsors and the INGOs that have given them their blessing.[48] INGOs in sport, such as FIFA and the IOC, wield considerable power due to their ability to select between cities or nations with competing bids, insisting on certain event standards and pressuring governments about where to put what venues. This increases the democratic deficit associated with mega-events because these INGOs are not accountable to any electorate, as FIFA's numerous bribery and corruption scandals have graphically demonstrated. Furthermore, the power of the largest sporting INGOs has accelerated since the 1980s, as their own capacities to accumulate capital have grown through increased media and advertising revenues, sponsorships and the aggressive defense of copyright associated with their brands. In 2010, FIFA reported "reserves" of US$1,280 million, with a substantial portion of that generated after 2000. The IOC earned a record US$8 billion between 2009 and 2013.[49]

A state of exception intensifies during the actual staging of mega-events, largely due to security concerns, forcing citizens to endure higher levels of security and surveillance than they might normally accept. Fear of the threat of terrorism drives these concerns and provides a powerful rationale for increased security, with the largest mega-events now spending billions of dollars on highly militarized security and surveillance regimes. Research has shown that sports mega-events above all provide unique opportunities to deploy and test new technologies and strategies, with the lessons learned at one sports mega-event readily transferred to other events in a developing model of "best practices" in security.[50] In recent years this has sometimes involved contracts with private security companies, for example, Brazil's multi-billion-dollar retention of Israeli security companies to assist government and police agencies during the 2014 men's football World Cup.[51] While the official rationale for high security is based on meeting the threat of terrorism, enhanced security forces and technologies can be deployed in response to a much broader range of "security challenges" deemed to potentially threaten the event, including the militarized "management" of legitimate protests.

Once a highly militarized security apparatus is put in place, it is hard to roll it back. As one security official told US journalist Dave Zirin before the 2012 London Olympics, if you buy a drone, you are not going to "just put it back in the box."[52] More broadly, we might say that the world's apparent addiction to mega-events (and to related urban mega-projects) in the twenty-first century is strongly implicated in an increasing *normalization of states of exception.* In many parts of the West that means the normalization of conditions where traditions of democratic governance are under revision, where the formerly "exceptional" is becoming increasingly routine. However, the militarization of mega-event security is only one coordinating dimension of an intensified focus on quasi-military "logistics" as a normal state of planning in states of exception. Mezzadra and Neilson define logistics as "the art and science of building networked relations" in order to "organize capital . . . to make every step of its 'turnover' productive."[53] As mega-events have grown in scale and economic value over the past half-century, we can observe a subtle historical shift in their organizational dynamics and management—from comparatively amateur approaches to management at the mid-point of the twentieth century, to more professionalized approaches through the end of the century, to today's highly coordinated, networked, logistical approaches dominated by an underlying "code" which introduces "the social relation of capital into the most minute and detailed operations."[54]

Still, and despite its omnipresence, this code is subtly mediated by national specificities associated with the histories and ambitions of hosting nations. The character of networked operational logistics at the Summer Olympics in Beijing in 2008 was not precisely the same as in the 2012 London Olympics in London, nor in the 2014 Winter Olympics in Sochi, Russia. This is an important point because it seems somewhat at odds with the terms of globalization that are now so often set by transnational actors. For example, the European Union can dictate monetary policy to member states—the situation in Greece in 2015 is an obvious example; organizations such as the G8 provide platforms for a dense web of international agreements; transnational organizations such as the IMF or World Bank dictate economic terms to many nations, and, while not on the same scale of importance, highly capitalized INGOs such as the IOC and FIFA have delegations from nation states regularly begging at their doorsteps.

Nonetheless, states still matter. If there was a focus on the decline of state power in much of the writing on globalization during the 1990s, in recent years there has been a more subtle reconsideration of the role states play in global capitalism and in the assertion of neo-imperial ambitions. This point seems obvious enough given the success of Chinese "state capitalism" and there is no doubt that the United States continues to be a significant force in framing many of the rules that govern international trade and financial institutions. But, more broadly, states have always had an ambivalent but *necessary* relationship to the transnational corporations (TNCs) which are in the forefront of capitalist globalization. As Immanuel Wallerstein points out, TNCs:

> have always needed states and fight states. They need states to guarantee their global attempt at monopolization and hence high profit levels, as well as to help limit the demands of workers. They fight the states insofar as the states act as protections of antiquated interests or are over responsive to workers (or popular) pressures.[55]

Mega-events can provide dramatic forums where these tensions are played out. On the one hand, they are staged to promote economic interests associated with the attempt to revalorize urban spaces, as well to attract investments, skilled or affluent immigrants and tourists, as well as priming local consumer markets. But, on the other hand, their promoters seek legitimacy by referencing sometimes "antiquated" interests and representations, such as civic or national pride, citizenship and "popular" sovereignty. The contradiction can lend support to opposition when mega-events are seen to promote actions running contrary to local traditions and values, when they appear to oppose hard-won democratic victories, or fail to live up to their own rhetorics of legitimation. For example, Mezzadra and Neilson argue that mass protests in Brazil during the 2013 Confederation Cup and 2014 men's World Cup could mobilize around "the political legitimacy acquired in the years of the Lula governments and the social power manifest in an unprecedented access to consumer opportunities" deriving from previous income redistribution policies.[56]

It goes without saying that the lure of mega-events in nations and cities around the world is driven by much more than purely economic rationales, even if those rationales are now inescapable dimensions of any nation's or city's decision to launch a bid. Rationales for bidding on mega-events in the East and South, for example, are often similar to those of cities in the West or North, but are differentially inflected based on particularities of the nations and cities in question, many of which have histories of Western colonization. As several of the contributors to this volume suggest, mega-events are widely understood across the East and Global South to offer both economic and political opportunities for formerly peripheral nations and cities to demonstrate entrepreneurialism, organizational competence and technical expertise, all with a view to improving their civic and national images and achieving a more central position in global circuits of investment, finance, communications and tourism. However, they are also seen to provide opportunities for nations and cities in the East and South to stake a claim to something more: recognition, respect, and full fledged participation on the "world-class" stage of twenty-first century modernity, not only in economic, social and political terms but also in the cultural realms of art and architecture.

Earlier, we referred to mega-events as "festivals of modernity" and, as Arif Dirlik argues, there can be little doubt that if "globalization means anything, it is the incorporation of societies globally into a capitalist modernity."[57] But today, capitalist modernity has become far more complex and variegated than in the early twentieth century when it was dominated by a singularly colonial and Western sensibility. The Second World War and its decolonization aftermath, in Dirlik's words: "restored the voices of the colonized, and opened the way to recognition of the spatial and temporal co-presence of those whom a Eurocentric modernization discourse had relegated to invisibility and backwardness."[58]

By participating in mega-events, formerly colonized countries can showcase their economic and technological "development" and make their own claims on modernity. In doing this, they have typically juxtaposed memories and representations of their own pasts and hopes for the future with dominant Eurocentric strands of late twentieth-century modernity. Today, as Dirlik argues:

> intensified and accelerated interactions between societies—that justify the discourse of globalization—are surely signs of the modern. Yet these very same relationships render modernity into a site of conflict and contention, raising fundamental questions about its historical and ethical meaning (or meaninglessness).[59]

So, the presence of formerly colonial societies as hosts and participants in today's mega-events is at once an affirmation of their inclusion in a global system of capitalist modernity and an ongoing source of reflexivity about fissures and fractures in the ways that global modernity can be promoted and experienced.

This raises additional questions about the role that mega-events in non-Western societies might play as manifestations of global power shifts, and most notably in the erosion of the power of the "global triad" of economic powers that became dominant after the Second World War: the United States, Europe and Japan. China, in particular, emerged during the late twentieth century as a returning power in the global economy, suggesting the re-emergence of an increasingly multi-polar economic system. Yuezhi Zhao points out that China's striking economic growth was accompanied by a number of significant "soft-power" initiatives in the early 2000s.[60] Examples include the establishment of Confucius Institutes all over the world and "state funding to official media outlets with an explicit objective to expand their global reach, as well as increased interest in issues of global media governance, among many other initiatives designed to improve China's image abroad."[61] Bids for mega-events such as the 2008 Summer Olympics, or for second-tier events such as the Asian Games, are fully consistent with these broader initiatives. They are also consonant with international development policies that have seen Chinese financial aid and engineering expertise involved in constructing more than fifty sports stadiums across Africa, South America, Latin America and other parts of Asia.[62] At the same time, as Huyn Bang Shin points out in his chapter in this volume, the quest for mega-event hosting in China has also been influenced by *internal* power dynamics associated with rising inter-city competition made possible after the economic reforms of the 1990s.

If there is a distinctively Chinese approach to capitalist modernity that portends a more geographically multi-polar international economic and political order, there are also influential variants emerging in many other parts of the world. For example, the Sochi Olympics and the 2018 Russian men's football World Cup were clearly pursued for the promotion of Russian identity as well as an assertion of the virtues of Russian capitalist modernity. Similarly, elites in the oil-rich Middle East are seeking to use mega-events to promote their brands of (Islamic) modernization, despite that region's internal struggles with sectarian differences and resurgent "tradition" in the form of fundamentalist political movements. The spectacular real-estate, construction and sporting mega-projects scheduled for cities such as Doha and Dubai in the next decade demonstrate a way to absorb surplus capital in the region.[63] But they are also part of a self-conscious strategy of international public relations operating along many fronts, including participation in leadership roles in sporting INGOs and investments in major sporting events and franchises outside the Middle East, such as ownership of iconic European sports teams and significant investments in European sports stadiums or sponsorships.[64]

Still, critical discussions of mega-event hosting as exercises in soft power—the "politics of attraction"—are one sided unless they are situated in a parallel analysis of the instabilities and stubborn regularities that run through these various capitalist modernities.[65] Peter Dicken describes the emerging twenty-first-century global economy as increasingly "volatile," with "short lived surges of economic growth punctuated by periods of downturn or even recession" and centered on a handful of global cities rather than nations.[66] In William Robertson's view, it is a complex, disorderly and highly uneven system that appears to have no coherent center because of "the transnational geographic dispersal of the full range of world production processes" and because digitized "financial circuits allow wealth to be moved around the world instantaneously."[67] However, at the same time, and in a seemingly contradictory way, the world has also become a densely "unified field for global capitalism."[68] For example, economic growth in East Asia continues to be heavily reliant on the health of its major export markets in North America. This is just one example of how the late twentieth-century triad, especially the United States, continues as a vitally significant nodal point in the field.

Indeed, even though the power of the triad (including US protectorates such as South Korea and Taiwan) is now highly refracted through international agencies, the old late twentieth-century axis continues to have substantial control over what Amin calls the "five monopolies": international technological development, international financial flows, communications, access to the world's resources, and production of weapons of mass destruction.[69] Elsewhere, other than the BRICS nations, a relatively small number of "developing" societies have experienced significant economic growth. But, even here, as Dicken concludes, some are "in deep financial difficulty while others are at, or even beyond, the point of survival."[70] For elites in these societies, hosting mega-events can fuel intoxicating dreams of "catching up" or "modernizing," and if the world's major mega-events are out of reach economically there is strong incentive to host one of the lesser mega-events, such as the Asian Games, Commonwealth Games, or a World Bank International Conference.[71] The attraction of these second- and third-tier mega-events for ambitious cities and nations, not only in the East and South, but globally, has driven up the costs of these events and has inflated their imagined significance.

Concern is sometimes raised in the popular press that there is a growing trend for the world's most prominent mega-events to be staged in countries that lack democratic traditions and oversight, and that the future of many mega-events may lie primarily in countries where militarization and repression are *non-exceptional*. In this view, the combinations of cost, security demands, and surveillance will make these events less attractive in Western liberal democracies, leading to greater likelihood of the largest global spectacles gravitating to authoritarian environments. By the same token, there is an implicit suggestion that INGOs such as the IOC and FIFA are being seduced by the ability of wealthy authoritarian regimes to insure the orderly staging of their events.

It is worth noting here that there is often considerable ethnocentrism, even racism, in the treatment of such topics in the Western press, a point that Grant Farred addresses in his chapter in this volume. For example, Western writers have been quick to criticize human rights abuses in China, or in Qatar, but typically ignore or downplay the history of "freely negotiated" labor in their own societies, its long-standing connections to racism, displacement and enslavement and to ongoing inequities and modes of domination in sweatshops, in the toil of migrant workers and in the trafficking of sex workers.[72] An international division of labor has been characteristic of capitalism for hundreds of years, but Mezzadra emphasizes the heterogeneity and mobility of contemporary global labor relations today, suggesting "a different sort of globalization, what we could call a subaltern globalization, which accompanies capitalist globalization."[73]

The migratory character of work in the early twenty-first century is an indication of this "subaltern globalization," indicating that the critical analysis of "labor migration control regimes" is a vitally important topic in studies of globalization. It is only a short step from this general point to the argument that the critical analysis of mega-events must also engage with how the staging of mega-events is connected to these regimes of control, where what is at stake is not simply a wage, but often the biopolitical control over life itself. The horrific case of quasi-enslaved migrant workers building World Cup stadia in Qatar springs immediately to mind, but the globalization of subalternity is by no means limited to the Middle East and it is necessary to extend this kind of analysis to other spaces and places and, especially, to the way that global capitalist modernity itself produces inequality on a dramatic and increasing scale.[74]

Saskia Sassen has recently referred to this production of accelerating global inequality as a "savage sorting of winners and losers."[75] As countries advance national agendas in pursuit of a geographically multi-polar capitalist modernity, we face the challenge of imagining what a truly multi-polar world order might look like. Amin argues that some think of this as "restoring balance in the Atlantic Alliance," to allow the European Union and Japan to have a position "similar to that of the United States in running the world." Others see a world where the BRICS nations, "perhaps even some emerging nations in the South, will join and achieve balance in the concert of the major powers."[76] The dream of freedom from what Makarand Paranjape calls the "bear hug of the West" continues to have a strong resonance in many of these societies and is reflected throughout a great deal of postcolonial theory.[77]

However, others see the dream of multi-polarity as a better balance between dominant and subaltern groups within global capitalism *without* the assumption that the decolonizing agendas of formerly peripheral or semi-peripheral states will necessarily achieve this. Amin considers himself among this group and argues that the most meaningful prospect of progress through globalization must not be thought of with respect to the geopolitical advantage of states so much as the provision of a "reliable and robust basis for democratization" on a global scale.[78] Zhao makes a similar argument in the case of China, suggesting that *unless* China's "awakening" follows a "post-capitalist and post-consumerist, sustainable, developmental path, or is at least reflective of both internal and external debates and struggles between dominant and alternative visions of the global order," China will become just another home to a dominating transnational capitalist class, with accompanying inequality, domination and social unrest throughout the country.[79] It should be evident by now that our own views lean towards a similar conception of *social* multi-polarity, which gives priority to struggles for justice and equality among the world's people's through the immanent critique of global systems of accumulation, dispossession and domination. We see the critical analysis of capitalist spectacle as an important and necessary aspect of this broader political project.

The structure and organization of this book

In keeping with the range of issues described above, we have organized chapters into three broad thematic areas: (1) creative destruction, modernization and spectacular capitalism, (2) states of exception, and (3) economies of events and experiences. In his chapter in the first section, Kevin Fox Gotham expands on the concept of creative destruction to theorize ways in which the planning and staging of mega-events reflect geographically uneven and politically volatile trajectories of urban development. He pays particular attention to the ways in which capital seeks to destabilize and undermine inherited institutions and social structures that impede capital accumulation in order to facilitate new forms of investment and profit making. His analysis reiterates some of the points we have made in this introduction: mega-event preparations typically anticipate and work toward the revalorization of space through displacement, rezoning, and the conversion of unprofitable land-uses into spaces of profit making via consumption-based entertainment experiences. But such perspectives are also deeply contradictory and produce widespread social reaction and opposition to these tendencies.

James Compton follows this with a discussion of ways that sports mega-events are implicated in the general acceleration of media in global sporting cultures. He argues that the study of mega-events has paid insufficient attention to the political economy of global media, the construction of global audience commodities, and the politics of cultural performance. His chapter addresses these issues with specific reference to the proliferation and growing importance of sports mega-events in global capitalism. In particular, he explains the role that global sporting spectacles play in capitalism's need to accelerate the processes of production, circulation and consumption. Using the concept of the "integrated spectacle," outlined over fifty years ago by the French Situationist critic, Guy Debord, Compton also examines contradictions that emerge between "concentrated" and "diffuse" forms of spectacularized sports mega-events.

In the next chapter, Simon Darnell and Rob Millington examine the hosting of sports mega-events as a specific dimension of the relationship between sport and development. They offer a comparative analysis of two significant sports mega-events in Latin America: the 1968 Summer Olympics in Mexico City and the 2016 Summer Olympic Games in Rio de Janeiro, Brazil. They synthesize scholarly analyses of Mexico '68 and Rio '16 alongside media reports and show how supporters of sports mega-events have consistently traded on development rhetoric in order to justify the expenses of hosting such events and the benefits they accrue. Despite some important differences between Mexico '68 and Rio '16, particularly in the context of political economy, there are consistencies in the *kind* of development promises attached to them. Sports mega-events continue to signify and support traditionally dominant ideas of development attached to the promises of modernization. Rather than a shift away from modernization, and in parallel with development thinking more broadly, hosting sports mega-events has moved towards a more fully integrated relationship between sport, development, corporatization and "celebration capitalism." In turn, the advent of neoliberal globalization and the corporatization of the Olympic spectacle have only heightened the development stakes of hosting, and increased the seductive promises of modernity ascribed to sports mega-events.

Ashwin Desai begins the next chapter by noting that Nelson Mandela's years as the first democratically elected President of South Africa often seemed like a series of spectacles. Nothing epitomized this more than the sporting fields of the country. The 1995 winning of the rugby World Cup and the winning of soccer's African Cup of Nations helped develop the idea of *Madiba* (Mandela) *Magic* that caught the public imagination in South Africa. It also signaled a time when those who suffered under apartheid would take their place as full-fledged citizens, under a new flag and new national anthem, guided by a new constitution in a new South Africa. But, if Mandela marked the closure of one history, defined by colonial dispossession and racial oppression, he also signaled an opening to potential exploitation under the banner of spectacular capitalism, creating a future of economic crisis and endless cycles of debt. Desai points out how mega-events become like an addiction, where the only cure to the ongoing crisis in South African capitalism comes to be understood as "more capitalism," and in a spectacular form.

The next section's chapters, loosely organized around the theme of "states of exception," commence with reference to the recent experience of Brazil in hosting sports mega-events. In the opening chapter in the section, Carlos Vainer argues that residents of Rio de Janeiro ("Carioca") are experiencing a complex and contested formation of a new coalition able to propose, and impose to the "city in crisis," a new hegemonic project. He identifies the concepts of the city that underlie this process, the make-up of the coalition that now runs the city, and the ways that mega-events have induced a state of exception that is becoming increasingly normalized, not only in Rio but, on a smaller scale, in other host cities around Brazil. In an environment of exception, urban policy gives priority to "flexible negotiation" through the pursuit of "flexible accumulation" and reveals the "true nature and meaning of neoliberal governance." But, at the same time, this "direct democracy of capital" has crated widespread movements of resistance.

In the following chapter, Anne-Marie Broudehoux explores how mega-events are entrenched in the politics of urban image construction. Not only do such events play a role in the spectacularization of the urban landscape, they also impose a particular worldview, shaped by the interests, desires and aspirations of local economic and political elites, international sporting federations and their global sponsors. Broudehoux demonstrates how hosting mega-events exerts pressure upon host cities to transform their urban environment to fit imagined global expectations of modernity. Cities invest in spectacular urban projects that will attest to their economic performance, organizational efficiency and cultural sophistication, while aspects of urban reality that suggest backwardness or decline are left out or often hidden, because they may tarnish the city's carefully constructed image. Broudehoux goes on to suggest how mega-events seek to exclude specific members of society from urban image construction as well as working to hide, beautify and discipline the poor and their material manifestations.

The chapter also investigates how groups have mobilized against such exclusionary policies and it examines multiple and creative forms of radicalization and resistance in host cities.

In discussing the 2014 Winter Olympic Games held in Sochi, Russia, Jules Boykoff assesses the dialectic between state repression and activist mobilization. He argues that repression does not automatically quell dissent. Sometimes state suppression can galvanize activism. In the case of Sochi 2014, the coercive structure slotted into place in advance of the Games severely constricted the possibilities for expressing political dissent during the Olympic event itself. However, despite these structural barriers, a number of activists did use the Sochi 2014 Olympics as a platform for expressing political dissent. Some of these were athlete-activists, but most were non-athletes attempting to use the Olympics spotlight to illuminate issues that mattered to them.

In the ensuing chapter, Grant Farred explores the interplay between civic and national ambitions, the continued growth of the high-security state and issues of colonial and racial difference, drawing examples from the 2014 World Cup in Brazil, the South African World Cup in 2010 and future World Cups in Russia in 2018 and Qatar in 2022. In Farred's view, there is a primary contradiction in all sports mega-events: they are "autoimmune," by which he means they "contain within themselves the very condition of their own destruction." In the quest for acceptance, every host nation not only risks cultivating negative images, they also invite the presence of forces aiming to attack the state. An ever-escalating round of militarization is the manifestation of a game that can never ultimately be won. Through a comparison of the South African men's World Cup in 2010, and the forthcoming men's World Cup in Qatar in 2022, Farred goes on to discuss the significance of colonialism and race in discourses surrounding each event, suggesting that race is a "floating signifier" ironically emptied of much of its potency in the case of discourses surrounding South Africa, yet mobilized powerfully in ideological ways in respect to considerations of the World Cup in Qatar. At the same time, however, Qatar's own preparation for the event necessitates criticism based on the abuses of migrant workers.

While Carlos Vainer focuses on the politics of urban planning in one Brazilian city, Chris Gaffney's chapter explores the socio-economic impacts of hosting the 2014 FIFA World Cup throughout Brazil, and introduces the third main research area of this collection: economies of events and experiences. Gaffney's analysis stems from substantive observations developed during extensive engagement with scholars, activists and media in Brazil as well as a longitudinal study that dealt with the urban impacts of the World Cup in all twelve of the host cities. Gaffney explores subtle regional variations between host cities but argues that a condition of permanent crisis, emergency and exception led to a weakening of Brazilian democratic institutions, the deterioration of public spaces, and the increased socio-economic polarization of Brazilian society.

Hyun Bang Shin's chapter brings together analysis of the event-led development experiences of Guangzhou, China, and Incheon, South Korea, in hosting the 2010 and 2014 Asian Games respectively. The Asian Games developed after a conference held during the 1948 Olympics in London when several Asian countries, recently independent from colonial rule, sought a regional forum to display the improving level of achievement in Asian sport while showcasing developing unity in the region. The first Asian Games was held in India in 1950 and the Games have been held every four years since. Shin points out that the political significance of recent Asian Games may have been less prominent than recent Olympic Games in the region (for example, the 1988 Seoul Olympic Games and 2008 Beijing Olympic Games), but the two Asian Games had remarkable impacts on the host cities. The juxtaposition of these two sports mega-events reveals how mega-event preparation entails the spatial manifestation of longer-term developmental aspirations held by entrepreneurial local states, and how resulting speculative and debt-driven booster projects can be detrimental to host cities by incurring a heavy financial burden.

In the final chapter, Borowy and Jin speculate about the possibility of "eSport" developing as a platform for staging "mega-events of the future." In so doing, they analyze the growth and development of eSport events as public spectacles on a global scale. More specifically, they demonstrate how South Korea, in particular, has played a major role in the "sportification" of digital gaming, not coincidentally due to a unique conjuncture of social and technological developments associated with Korea's hosting of the 1988 Summer Olympics in Seoul. During the 1990s, Korea formally recognized digital gaming as an official national sport. By examining the evolution of eSport from arcade games, and private forms of amusement, into larger-scale sport-like events held in concert halls, arenas and stadiums, they outline the transition of a competitive digital play activity into a form of global capitalist spectacle. They suggest this transition is usefully situated in a broader discussion of the growth of "the experience economy" around the world. In their view, the rise of public gaming spectacles has had the effect of repositioning players and fans within new promotional chains that organize synergies between competitive play, public events, spectating, marketing and business strategy. In their view, the spectacularization of gaming (built literally on devices constructed by a new digital proletariat) is at the forward edge of change in the development of high-technology capitalism.

We began this "critical" introduction with a reference to Maurice Roche's definition of mega-events and, noting Roche again, we acknowledged the contributions that mega-events can play both in the creation of meaningful human experiences and the making of global culture. But our goal in this collection is to explore issues that go beyond Roche's analysis and in this introduction we have made a case for a revived political economy perspective on mega-events with a focus on how mega-events may expand the operational scopes of global capitalism and the high security state, with their systematic sorting of urban, national and transnational "winners" from local and global subaltern losers. In conclusion, we not only want to make a plea for the critical analysis of mega-events, we also hope this collection demonstrates the value of multidisciplinary standpoints for criticism. The contributors to this book work in a variety of disciplines and research areas including sociology, communications, urban studies, political studies, geography, kinesiology, architecture and literary studies. In bringing an international group of contributors together from a variety of disciplinary backgrounds, we hope to offer a unique range of critical angles of vision on mega-events and globalization. It will be up to the book's readers to decide if we have succeeded.

Acknowledgments

We would like to acknowledge the assistance of Katherine Reilly and Yuezhi Zhao for providing helpful bibliographic sources and Jeong-Wan Hong for research assistance early in the project. We also want to thank Ben Carrington, Brian Wilson and Shawn Forde for their comments on an early draft of this chapter.

Notes

1 Recent examples include: "Mega-Events and the City II," International Conference, Universidade Federal do Rio de Janeiro, Rio de Janeiro, April 2014; "Metropolitization and mega-events: the impacts of the 2014 World Cup and 2016 Olympics," International Conference, Observatorio das Metropoles, Universidade Federal do Rio de Janeiro, Rio de Janeiro, December 2013; Conference on "Local legacies and sports mega-events," Mulier Institute, University of Utrecht, The Netherlands, April 2013; Conference on "Impacts of hosting sports mega-events," Waseda University, Tokyo, Japan, February 2013.
2 For recent journal issues devoted to a focus on mega-events see: *Leisure Studies,* Volume 31, Number 3, July 2012; *British Journal of Sociology,* Volume 63, Issue 2, 2012. *International Journal of Sport Policy and Politics,* Volume 4, Number 3, November 2012. *Contemporary Social Science,* Volume 9, Number 2, June 2014. *Sport in Society,* 2013. Some recent books include: Grix, *Leveraging Legacies*; Girginov, *Handbook*; Tzanelli *Olympic Ceremonialism,* and Hayes and Karamichas, *Olympic Games.*
3 Polley, "Inspire A Publication," 255.
4 Roche, *Mega Events and Modernity,* 1.
5 Roche, *Mega Events,* 3.
6 Flyvbjerg, "What You Should Know."
7 For example, see Collini, *What are Universities For?*; Docherty, *Universities at War*; and Hearn, "Through the Looking Glass."
8 United Nations et. al., *Shanghai Manual.*
9 Mattelart, *The Invention of Communication,* 112–32.
10 Bruce Kidd, "A New Social Movement," 374.
11 A critical analysis of such arguments can be found in Gruneau, "Sport, Development."
12 Roche, *Mega-Events and Modernity,* 225.
13 Roche, "Olympic and Sport Mega Events," 6.
14 The Bureau of International Expositions (BIE), formed in Paris in 1928, is the organization that sanctions "World" Expos. In 2014, the BIE was made up of 168 member nations, all of which agree to be bound by BIE controls over event hosting. While the BIE has no mechanism to limit the ambition of countries or cities outside the organization that are determined to stage urban trade fairs of exhibitions, all BIE members agree only to participate in BIE-sanctioned expos. See the BIE "official site": http://www. bie-paris.org/site/en/

15 United Nations et. al., *Shanghai Manual*, 34.

16 On urban displacements in Shanghai in the early 2000s, see Huang, *Spectacular Post Colonial Cities*. Useful discussions of tension between urban entrepreneurialism and environmental sustainability can be found in Jonas and While, "Greening the Entrepreneurial City."

17 Lenskyj, *Olympic Industry Resistance*, 10.

18 Payne, *Olympic Turnaround*; Corporate Watch, "Hill and Knowlton;" Jennings, "Journalists?".

19 Harvey, *Rebel Cities*, 109.

20 Kemple, "The I/eye of Capital," 20. Also see Raco, "Delivering Flagship Projects."

21 Price, "On Seizing the Olympic Platform," and Timms, "The Olympics as a Platform."

22 For some examples, see Harvey et. al., *Sport and Social Movements*.

23 Labeling using terms such as "East" and "West," or "North" and "South" can be misleading because the categories overlap in complicated ways. For example, there are significant cultural and economic differences between an "eastern" country such as Japan or South Korea, and "western" countries in Europe and North America. These western countries are also typically designated as falling in the "Global North." But, in the second half of the twentieth century, Japan, in particular, formed an important part of an economic axis (a triad) with the United States and Europe, suggesting closer affiliation economically with the Global North than the South. To acknowledge this tension, we adopt the convention of referencing both East/West and North/South divisions.

24 Mattelart, *The Invention of Communication*, 113.

25 On the BRICS nations and mega-events see: Horne, "Building BRICs by building stadiums," and Curi et al., "The Pan American Games."

26 Robertson, "Mapping the Global Condition," 28, original emphasis.

27 Roche, "Olympic and Sport Mega-Events."

28 A more developed discussion can be found in Rao, "New Imperialisms, New Imperatives."

29 For example, in communications see Fuchs and Mosco, "Marx is Back."

30 Harvey, "The Enigma of Capital."

31 Harvey, *The Condition of Postmodernity*.

32 Horkheimer and Adorno, *Dialectic of Enlightenment*.

33 Harvey, *The Condition of Postmoderntiy*, 179.

34 On global rural-urban migration, see UN HABITAT, *The Challenge of Slums* and Davis, *Planet of Slums*.

35 Hannigan, *Fantasy Cities*.

36 Mezzadra and Neilson, "Extraction, Logistics, Finance," 12.

37 Harvey, "The Crisis of Planetary Urbanization."

38 Cited in ibid.

39 See Ying Fen Huang's discussion in *Spectacular Post Colonial Cities*.

40 Some of these issues are summarized in Harvey, *A Brief History of Neoliberalism*.

41 This point is explored in greater depth in Arrighi, "Globalization and Historical Sociology."

42 Amin, *Beyond U.S. Hegemony*, 4.

43 For example, see Fuchs, *Digital Labour and Karl Marx*.

44 Dean, *Democracy*.

45 Amin, "Capitalism, Imperialism, Globalization."

46 Mezzadra and Neilson, "Extraction, Logistics, Finance," 17.

47 Ibid.
48 The German philosopher Carl Schmitt first popularized the phrase "state of exception," but it is more recently associated with Giorgio Agemben's book, *State of Exception.*
49 FIFA, 61st FIFA Congress, Financial Report, 2010, 14; Lubin and Delevigne, "Olympics Inc."
50 For example see, Boyle and Hagerty, "Spectacular Security," and Cornelissen, "Mega Event Securitisation."
51 For a more detailed discussion of security in Brazil see, Zirin, *Brazil's Dance with the Devil.*
52 Zirin, "Exporting Gaza."
53 Mezzadra and Neilson, "Extraction, Logistics, Finance," 13.
54 Ibid.
55 Wallerstein, cited in Arrighi, "Globalization and Macrosociology."
56 Mezzadra and Neilson, "Extraction, Logistics, Finance," 12.
57 Dirlik, "Global Modernity?," 275.
58 Ibid., 276.
59 Ibid.
60 Zhao, "China's Quest," 19.
61 Ibid., 20.
62 On Chinese "stadium diplomacy," see Will, *China's Stadium Diplomacy.*
63 Hanieh, *Capitalism and Class.*
64 See Hann, "Middle East and Asia."
65 We've taken this phrase from Grix and Lee, "Soft Power."
66 Dicken, *Global Shift,* 68.
67 Robinson, "Global Capitalism Theory," 12.
68 Ibid., 5.
69 Amin, *Beyond U.S. Hegemony,* 4. Our view here follows Amin's argument more than Robertson's emphasis on a shift from "world" to "global" economic relations where states have become less significant. See Robertson, "Global Capitalism Theory."
70 Dicken, *Global Shift,* 68.
71 For example, see Greene, "Staged Cities."
72 On this point, see Chakravartty and de Silva, "Accumulation, Dispossession and Debt."
73 Mezzadra, "How Many Histories of Labour?" 166.
74 Amin,"Capitalism, Imperialism, Globalization," 158.
75 Sassen, "A Savage Sorting"; also see Bauman, *Wasted Lives.*
76 Amin, *Beyond U.S. Hegemony,* 2.
77 Paranjape, "The End of Postcolonial Studies."
78 Amin, *Beyond U.S. Hegemony,* 2.
79 Zhao, "China's Quest," 28.

Bibliography

Adorno, T. and Horkheimer, M. *Dialectic of Enlightenment.* London: Verso/NLB, 1979.
Agemben, G. *State of Exception.* Trans. by Kevin Attell. Chicago, IL: University of Chicago Press, 2005.
Amin, S. "Capitalism, Imperialism, Globalization." In R.M. Chilcote (ed.) *The Political Economy of Imperialism.* Kluwer Academic Publishers, 1999.
———. *Beyond U.S. Hegemony: Assessing the Prospects of a Multipolar World.* London: Zed Books, 2006.

Arrighi, G. "Globalization and Historical Macrosociology" In J. Abu-Lughod (ed.) *Sociology for the Twenty-first Century: Continuities and Cutting Edges*. Chicago, IL: University of Chicago Press, 2000: 117–33.

Bauman, Z. *Wasted Lives: Modernity and its Outcasts*. Cambridge: Polity, 2003.

Boyle, P. and K.D. Haggerty. "Spectacular Security: Mega-Events and the Security Complex." *International Political Sociology* 3, no. 3 (2009): 257–74.

Chakravartty P., and da Silva, D.F. "Accumulation, dispossession, and debt: The racial logic of global capitalism—an introduction." *American Quarterly*, 64, no. 3 (2012): 361–85.

Collini, S. *What are Universities For?* London: Penguin, 2012.

Cornelissen S. "Mega Event Securitisation in a Third World Setting: Global Processes and Ramifications during the 2010 FIFA World Cup." *Urban Studies*, 48 (2011): 3221–40.

Corporate Watch. "Hill & Knowlton: Corporate Crimes": http://www.corporatewatch.org.uk/content/corporate-watch-hill-knowlton-corporate-crimes.

Curi M, J. Knijnik and G. Mascarenhas. "The Pan American Games in Rio de Janeiro 2007: Consequences of a sport mega-event on a BRIC country." *International Review for the Sociology of Sport,* 46, no. 2 (2011): 140–56.

Davis, M. *Planet of Slums*. London: Verso, 2006.

Dean, J. *Democracy and Other Neoliberal Fantasies: Communicative Capitalism and Left Politics.* Chapel Hill, NC: Duke University Press, 2009.

Dicken, P. *Global Shift: Mapping the Changing Contours of the World Economy*. 5th edn. Thousand Oaks, CA: Sage, 2005.

Dirlik, A. "Global Modernity? Modernity in An Age of Global Capitalism." *European Journal of Social Theory*. 6, no. 3 (2003): 275–92.

Docherty, T. *Universities at War*. London: Sage, 2015.

FIFA, 61st *FIFA Congress, Financial Report, 2010*, May 31–June 1, 2011: http://www.fifa.com/mm/document/affederation/administration/01/39/20/45/web_fifa_fr2010_eng[1].pdf.

Flyvbjerg, B. "What You Should Know About Megaprojects and Why: An Overview." *Project Management Journal* 45, no. 2 (2014): 6–19.

Fuchs, C. *Digital Labour and Karl Marx*. London: Routledge, 2014.

——— and V. Mosco. "Introduction—Marx is Back: The Importance of Marxist Theory and Research for Critical Communications Study Today." *Triple C* (special issue), 10, no. 2 (2012).

Girginov, V. (ed.). *Handbook of the London 2012 Olympic and Paralympic Games.* Volume 1: *Making the Games.* London: Routledge, 2013.

Greene, S.J. "Staged Cities: Mega-events, Slum Clearance and Global Capital." *Yale Human Rights and Development Journal*, 6, no. 1 (2003): 161–87.

Grix, E. and D. Lee, "Soft Power, Sports Mega-Events and Emerging States: The Lure of the Politics of Attraction." *Global Society*, 27, no. 4 (2013).

Grix, J. (ed.). *Leveraging Legacies from Sports Mega-Events*. Basingstoke: Palgrave, 2014.

Gruneau, R. "Sport, Development and the Challenge of Slums." In Russell Field (ed.), *Playing for Keeps: The Continuing Struggle for Sport and Recreation.* Toronto: University of Toronto Press, 2015.

Hann M. "Middle East and Asia Boost Investment in Top Level Sports," *Reuters*, January 11, 2015: http://www.reuters.com/article/2015/01/12/us-sport-investment-mideast-asia-idUSKBN0KL00F20150112.

Hanieh, A. *Capitalism and Class in the Gulf Arab States*. London: Palgrave Macmillan, 2011.

Hannigan, J. *Fantasy City: Pleasure and Profit in the Postmodern Metropolis*. New York: Routledge, 1998.

Harvey, D. *The Condition of Postmodernity*. Oxford: Basil Blackwell, 1989.

———. *A Brief History of Neoliberalism*. Oxford: Oxford University Press, 2005.

———. *Rebel Cities*. London: Verso, 2008.

———. "The Enigma of Capital and the Crisis This Time." Paper prepared for American Sociological Association Meetings, Atlanta, August 16, 2010: http://davidharvey.org/2010/08/the-enigma-of-capital-and-the-crisis-this-time/.

———. "The Crisis of Planetary Urbanism." In Pedro Gadanho (ed.) *Uneven Growth: Tactical Urbanisms for Expanding Cities*. New York: Museum of Modern Art, 2014: http://post.at.moma.org/content_items/520-the-crisis-of-planetary-urbanization.

Harvey, J., J. Horne, P. Safai, S. Darnell and S. Courchesne-O'Neill. *Sport and Social Movements: From the Local to the Global*. London: Bloomsbury, 2014.

Hayes, G. and J. Karamichas (eds.). *Olympic Games, Mega-Events and Civil Societies: Globalization, Environment, Resistance*. Basingstoke: Palgrave Macmillan, 2012.

Hearn, A., "Through the Looking Glass: The Promotional University 2.0." In Melissa Aronczyk and Devon Powers (eds.), *Blowing Up the Brand: Critical Perspectives on Promotional Culture*. New York: Peter Lang, 2010.

Horne, J. "Building BRICs by building stadiums. Preliminary reflections on recent and future sports mega-events in four emerging economies": http://www.bl.uk/ sportandsociety/exploresocsci/sportsoc/mega/buildingbricks.pdf.

Huang, Ying-Fen. *Spectacular Postcolonial Cities: Markets, Ideology and Globalization in the Making of Shanghai and Hong Kong*. Ph.D. Dissertation, School of Communication, Simon Fraser University, 2008: http://summit.sfu.ca/item/9072.

Jennings, A. "Journalists? They're media masseurs," *British Journalism Review* 23, no. 2 (2013): 25–31 http://www.bjr.org.uk/data/2012/no2_jennings.

Jonas, A.E. and A. While. "Greening the Entrepreneurial City?: Looking for Spaces of Sustainability Politics in the Competitive City." In R. Krueger and D. Gibbs (eds.), *The Sustainable Development Paradox: Urban Political Economy in the United States and Europe*. New York: Guilford Press, 2007: 123–59.

Kemple, T, M. "The I/eye of Capital: Classical Theoretical Perspectives on the Spectral Economies of Late Capitalism." In T. Dufresne and C. Sacchetti (eds.). *The Economy as a Cultural System*. New York: Bloomsbury, 2013.

Kidd, B. "A New Social Movement: Sport for Development and Peace," *Sport in Society: Cultures, Commerce, Media, Politics*. 11, no. 4 (2008).

Lenskyj, J.H., Helen Jefferson. *Olympic Industry Resistance: Challenging Olympic power and propaganda*. Albany NY: SUNY Press, 2008.

Lubin, G. and Delevigne, L. "Olympics Inc.: The Secretive 6 Billion Dollar World of the International Olympic Committee." *Business Insider*, February 17, 2010.

Mattelart, A. *The Invention of Communication*. Minneapolis, MN: University of Minnesota Press, 1996.

Mezzadra, S. "How Many Histories of Labour? Toward a Theory of Postcolonial Capitalism." *Postcolonial Studies*, 14, no. 2 (2011): 151–72.

———, and Brett Neilson, "Extraction, Logistics, Finance: Global Crisis and the Politics of Operations." *Radical Philosophy*, 178, March/April (2013): 8–18.

Paranjape, M. "The End of Postcolonialism." In Paranjape, M., A. Sarwal and A. Rajendran (eds.), *English Studies: Indian Perspectives*. Delhi: Mantra, 2000.

Payne, M. *Olympic Turnaround: How the Olympic Games Stepped Back from the Brink of Extinction to Become the World's Best Known Brand*. Westport, CT: Praeger, 2006.

Polley, M. "Inspire A Publication. Books, journals, and the 2012 Olympic and Paralympic Games." In V. Girginov (ed.). *Handbook of the London 2012 Olympic and Paralympic Games.* Volume 2: *Celebrating the Games.* London: Routledge, 2014: 255–65.

Price, M. "On Seizing the Olympic Platform." In M. Price and D. Dayan (eds.). *Owning the Olympics: Narratives of the New China.* Ann Arbor: University of Michigan Press, 2008.

Raco, M. "Delivering Flagship projects in an Era of Regulatory Capitalism: State-led Privatization and the London Olympics 2012." *International Journal of Urban and Regional Research* 38, no. 1 (2014): 176–97.

Rao, N. "New Imperialisms, New Imperatives: Taking Stock of Postcolonial Studies." *Postcolonial Text*, 2, no. 1 (2006): http://postcolonial.org/index.php/pct/article/view Article/386/816.

Robertson, R. "Mapping the Global Condition: Globalization as the Central Concept." *Theory, Culture and Society*, 7, no. 2/3 (1990): 15–30.

Robinson, W. "Global Capitalism Theory and the Emergence of Transnational Elites." Working Paper No. 2010/02, *UNU-WIDER, World Institute for Development Economics Research*, January (2010): 1–16.

Roche, M. *Mega-Events & Modernity: Olympics and Expos in the Growth of Global Culture.* London: Routledge, 2000.

———. "Olympic and Sport Mega-Events as Media-Events: Reflections on the Globalisation paradigm", *Sixth International Symposium for Olympic Research* (2002): 1–12: http://library.la84.org/SportsLibrary/ISOR/ISOR2002c.pdf.

Sassen, S. "A Savage Sorting of Winners and Losers: Contemporary Versions of Primitive Accumulation." *Globalizations*, March–June, 7, no. 1–2 (2010): 23–50.

Timms, J. "The Olympics as a Platform for Protest: a case study of the London 2012 'ethical' Games and the Fair Play campaign for worker's rights." *Leisure Studies*, 31, no. 3, (2013): 355–72.

Tzanelli, R. *Olympic Ceremonialism and the Performance of National Character: From London 2012 to Rio 2016.* Basingstoke: Palgrave Macmillan, 2013.

United Nations, The Bureau of International Expositions, and the Shanghai World Exposition Executive Committee. *Shanghai Manual: A Guide for Sustainable Urban Development in the 21st Century*: https://sustainabledevelopment.un.org/content/documents/shanghaimanual.pdf.

UN-HABITAT, *The Challenge of Slums: Global Report on Human Settlements*. London: 2003

Will, R. *China's Stadium Diplomacy. World Policy Journal*, Summer, 2012 http://www.worldpolicy.org/journal/summer2012/chinas-stadium-diplomacy.

Zhao, Y. "China's Quest for Soft Power: Imperatives, Impediments and Irreconcilable Tensions?" *Javnost—The Public*, 20, no. 4 (2013): 17–30.

Zirin, D. *Brazil's Dance with the Devil: The World Cup, The Olympics and The Fight for Democracy.* Chicago, IL: Haymarket Books, 2014.

———. "Exporting Gaza: The Arming of Brazil's World Cup Security." *The Nation*, June 30, 2014.

Part I

Creative destruction, modernization, and spectacular capitalism

2 Beyond bread and circuses

Mega-events as forces of creative destruction

Kevin Fox Gotham

Introduction

In this chapter, I use the concept of *creative destruction* to theorize the ways in which the planning and staging of mega-events reflect geographically uneven and politically volatile trajectories of urban development. Scholars such as David Harvey, Neil Smith and Neil Brenner have emphasized how the creative and destructive forces of capital have an impact on the built environment at various scales.[1] The concept draws our attention to the ways in which capital seeks to destabilize and undermine inherited institutions and social structures that impede capital accumulation in order to facilitate new forms of investment and profit making. Creating and parceling out spaces for mega-events and associated urban redevelopment is tantamount to devaluing spaces in order to infuse them with value-producing potential. New transportation networks, water and energy infrastructures, information and communication technologies, and brick-and-mortar projects for entertainment and consumption represent institutional efforts to enhance commodity exchange, create and diversify flows of investment, and promote the circulation of people, culture, and capital. Mega-event preparation activities typically anticipate and actively plan for the *revalorization of space* through displacement, rezoning, and the conversion of unprofitable land-uses into spaces of profit making via consumption-based entertainment experiences.

For years, scholars have assailed mega-events as instruments of hegemonic power designed to mollify popular opinion, win public support and provide legitimacy for imperialist policies, and neutralize opposition to pro-growth agendas.[2] The intent is to shift attention away from everyday social problems in the city and pacify local people, a form of ideological manipulation referred to as "bread and circuses."[3] This metaphoric phrase suggests that if oppressed people receive food and entertainment they will forget their problems and believe in the beneficence of the system. Generally, the phrase implies the manufacturing of public approval and consent through diversion, distraction, or a soothing and anesthetic entertainment experience. In Peter Eisinger's oft-cited article, the notion of bread and circuses expresses the trend toward building cities as entertainment venues rather than accommodating quality-of-life interests and concerns of residents.[4]

My argument is that mega-events have become strategically crucial arenas that express the contradictory dynamics of creative destruction. Joseph Schumpeter coined the term "creative destruction" in 1942 to refer to capitalism's tendency to simultaneously promote innovation and obsolescence within the spheres of economic production, technological development and industrial organization. Building on the polemical work of Karl Marx and Friedrich Engels,[5] Schumpeter argued that the incessant drive for profit motivates capitalists to create and adopt new labor-saving technologies and constantly expand markets which then contribute to capital accumulation. At the same time, the process of innovation that "incessantly revolutionizes the economic structure" destroys existing economic activity whose viability depended on innovations from an earlier economic regime.[6] Having lost the ability to compete, displaced firms and emerging new firms strive to produce new innovations, thus perpetuating the cycle of "creative destruction." In Schumpeter's classic formulation, creative destruction is the source of capitalism's revolutionary dynamic in which the simultaneous production of wealth and surplus coincides with the production of poverty and misery. In addition, creative destruction intimates capitalism as a contradictory totality shot through with dysfunctional features—e.g., alienation of workers, destruction of the environment, cut-throat competition, recurrent economic crises—that serve as cause as well as effect of the accumulation and development process.

In a series of works spanning nearly two decades, David Harvey brings a spatial dynamic and logic to the ongoing process of creative destruction, arguing that capitalism represents itself "in the form of a physical landscape created in its own image."[7] According to Harvey, creative destruction expresses the fundamental tension between spatial fixity and motion that define the turbulent production, circulation, and consumption of commodities and capital. On the one hand, capital must be fixed in place, set within a "structured coherence" of a particular location that anchors routines, networks of activity, and investment flows. On the other hand, capital must always be on the move, incessantly creating new markets and more thoroughly exploiting old markets by shifting investment from high-wage to low-wage regions of the world and from less profitable to more profitable sectors. As a contradictory process of often conflict-riven socio-spatial restructuring, capitalist development constantly vacillates between preserving the fixed social relations and institutions that supported past capital investments in the built environment and destroying these relations and institutions in order to create new opportunities for investment.[8] As a consequence, according to Harvey, we "witness a perpetual struggle in which capitalism builds a physical landscape appropriate to its own condition at a particular moment in time, only to have to destroy it, usually in the course of a crisis, at a subsequent point in time."[9]

The emphasis on capitalism's creative propensities and destructive tendencies is the central conceptual framework that I adopt in this chapter to understand the dysfunctional and contradictory nature of mega-events. I use the notion of destruction to refer to the destabilization of extant social relationships, institutions, and structural arrangements through various socio-legal regulations, statutes, and reform initiatives. I use the notion of creation to refer to the establishment of new institutions, infrastructures, and tourist-oriented spectacles (including mega-events) for economic growth and development. Importantly, creation and destruction are not conceptually separate and analytically distinct from one another. Rather, they are dialectical, interconnected, and mutually constitutive processes of change. Moreover, the creative destruction of social structural arrangements and territorial organization is always unpredictable, often highly contradictory, and deeply contested. The notion of creative destruction reveals the paradoxes and ambiguities of urban spectacles and sheds light on the ways in which they are imposed from the top down and yet can be contested and transformed from the bottom up. From this perspective, one should avoid one-sided and reductive explanations in favor of a view that theorizes mega-events as battlefields of contention in which individuals and groups compete for access to and control over material and cultural resources.

Mega-events and the political economy of urban development

Mega-events are major expressions of global tourism and motivators for cities to redevelop themselves as places of spectacle, entertainment, and consumption. They also act as inducements for development designed to attract affluent professionals in the media, design, computer programming, and other high-tech industries. While the roles and impacts of mega-events as a form of development aimed at stimulating consumption have been well documented, less attention has been devoted to theorizing and empirically examining why and how mega-events and other urban spectacles provoke intense conflict, antagonism, and political struggle. The global spread of development schemes aimed at attracting tourists and affluent professionals to cities is one of the most hotly debated issues of the present era. For proponents, tourism and related spectacles such as mega-events are a continuation of modernization and a force of progress, cosmopolitanism, increased wealth, freedom, democracy, and happiness.[10] Supporters typically present development through investment in expanded opportunities for consumption and urban spectacle as beneficial, generating fresh economic opportunities, political democratization, and cultural diversity. In contrast, critics have condemned such forms of investment for imposing the logic of capital and market rationality on ever more regions of the world and spheres of life through various forms of state power and economic domination.[11] In addition, critics assert that mega-events and other expensive urban spectacles undermine democracy, promote cultural homogenization, and accelerate ecological destruction by destroying natural species and the environment.[12]

Today, critical urban theorists confront the challenge of theorizing the emergent forms of development in the present era constructed by syntheses of technology and capital in the production or urban mega-events. Since the 1970s, governments in North America and Europe have implemented a variety of neoliberal policies and regulatory strategies geared towards enhancing urban competitiveness through strategies of privatization and deregulation, and the use of spatially targeted tax incentives and other tax deductions and exemptions for corporations.[13] Examples of neoliberal policies and strategies include public-private partnerships, enterprise zones, empowerment zones, urban development corporations, entertainment and tourist destinations, and the proliferation of tax subsidies such as tax abatements, industrial revenue bonds, and tax increment financing (TIF). These neoliberal economic development tools reflect a wholesale shift in the priorities of local governments, which are increasingly less concerned with issues of social redistribution, provision of public services, and so forth, and are more concerned with promoting economic competitiveness, attracting investment capital, and creating a favorable "business climate."[14] Over the past three decades, the production, consumption, and socio-legal regulation of mega-events has developed in a context of neoliberal economic ideology and globalization.

Mega-events such as the Olympics or a World's Fair are now characterized by highly rationalized event planning and preparation, sophisticated urban re-imaging and re-branding campaigns, and new legal tools and tax incentives. The international attention that mega-events attract has been considered by elites as a potential source of new tax revenue and private investment. For elites in a host locality, attracting a mega-event provides international recognition, global prestige, and unique opportunities for place promotion, thereby enticing corporate investment.[15] Mega-events and other specialized events that include festivals, celebrations, sports events, and business conventions have become crucial for cities in re-imaging themselves to both potential investors and consumers. Across North America, all major cities now possess convention and exhibition facilities, along with specialized agencies devoted to selling space and bidding on events.[16] As David Harvey notes, "Imaging a city through the organization of spectacular urban spaces became a means to attract capital and people (of the right sort) in a period (since 1973) of intensified inter-urban competition."[17]

Moreover, advances in communication and information technologies combined with increased inter-urban competition have been significant drivers of the growth of corporate and government interest in hosting mega-events. As C. Michael Hall notes, the globalization of media, communication, and information via new technologies has "meant that 'market reach' of a mega-event has become greater than ever before," since images of the mega-event and related advertising can be beamed around the world instantaneously.[18]

Today, mega-events confront us as volatile forces of creative destruction that are empowering some groups, disempowering others, and spawning a host of irrational effects and negative consequences. I argue that the double-pronged conceptualization of creative destruction can illuminate the complex and highly contradictory trajectories of institutional change that have been generated through the deployment of the mega-event strategy in cities and countries around the world. Consequently, my intention is to present mega-events as contested, contradictory, and open to collective resistance and transformation, not just monolithic juggernauts of domination, or vehicles of progress or beneficial economic development, as in many discourses. Crucial to articulating the contradictions of mega-events and avoiding one-sided and reductive conceptions is to recognize that mega-events are highly versatile, embrace many agendas, amalgamate new ideas and priorities, and adapt to changing times and social conditions. Because mega-events are constituted by relations of domination and subordination, they express the volatile currents of resistance and struggle associated with the creative-destructive tendencies of tourism development.

Contradictions of mega-events

Scholars and researchers have dramatically disclosed the ways that the planning and staging of mega-events can have destructive effects, provoke intense collective protest, and undermine democratic governance.[19] Much research has noted that mega-events exacerbate gaps between the rich and poor within host cities through various urban revitalization activities such as forced evictions, mass demolition of low-income housing, and widespread displacement.[20] Displacement can be explicit and overt, or indirect and ancillary. In a study of the potential impacts of the 2000 Olympic Games in Sydney, Australia, Cox and colleagues concluded that previous Olympic-related development often pushed out public and private lower-cost housing through increased land prices, and higher property taxes and construction costs.[21] Davis's analysis of residential redevelopment in Seoul for the 1988 Olympic Games found that "there is incontrovertible evidence of a causal link between event hosting and forced evictions."[22] Extensive research on the 2008 Beijing Olympics found that evictions and displacement contributed to a significant loss of affordable housing stock for urban poor families and migrants.[23] The Geneva-based human rights group, the Centre on Human Rights and Evictions (COHRE), estimated a total of 1.5 million Beijing residents were displaced by mega-event redevelopment. This number dwarfed the 720,000 evicted for the 1988 games in Seoul.[24] As the COHRE report concluded:

> forced evictions, discrimination against minorities, targeting homeless persons, and the many other effected we noted, are in complete contradiction to the very spirit and ideals of the Olympic Movement, which aims to foster peace, solidarity, and respect of universal fundamental principles.[25]

The reality of and motivation for forced evictions and displacement is not difficult to understand. Since mega-events bring increased visibility to host cities, they often inspire political and economic elites to banish negative urban imagery including poverty, disinvestment, and slum housing. Under the logic of mega-event planning and redevelopment, the visibility of poverty and other urban problems becomes a major stigma for cities. The eradication of urban stigma and the attendant denigration of slum housing and urban disinvestment operate to assert the viability and incipient power of elite versions of urban space and reality. Not surprisingly, as with virtually all Olympics, we see "accumulation by dispossession,"[26] in which efforts to create profit through mega-event redevelopment results in intense exploitation, displacement, and harm to low-income people. The displacement of people and destruction of housing becomes the *sine qua non* for both erecting new and spectacular spaces of consumption. Thus, in many cities, we see fierce contests being fought over images and counter-images of places, a process that suggests that struggles over representations of space are fundamental to mega-event planning debates.

Mega-events represent contradictory amalgams of capitalism and democracy in which neoliberal strategies are increasingly adopted by cities around the world, even as democracy spreads and mega-events themselves are being contested by democratic demands and forces. Due to international protest and demonstration against the negative impacts of the Olympics on host populations, the International Olympic Committee (IOC) has begun to require host cities to address a much wider range of local impacts of the "global Games," and to undertake planning initiatives to ensure maximum local social inclusion.[27] Interestingly, as Vanwynsberghe and collaborators point out in their study of Vancouver's successful bid for the 2010 Winter Olympic and Paralympic Games, the mega-event planning process has "become [an] even more powerful instrument for the promotion of liberal philosophies"—e.g., inclusion, accountability, individual freedom and voluntary participation—through neoliberal local governance regimes. They point out that social inclusion is promised through the proliferation of ever more institutionally diffused public-private partnerships, though such efforts to promote and ensure social inclusion have met with limited success. They conclude, "it appears clear that the fusion of transnationally mobile mega-events and prevailing doctrines of neoliberal entrepreneurialism has become a significant new framework for local urban social policy."[28]

In an analysis of the 2012 London Olympics, Mike Raco describes the development of the "London Olympic model" in which democratic imperatives, such as those around sustainability and employment rights, have been institutionally replaced and converted into contractual requirements on firms, a form of state-led privatization that was also being incorporated into the planning of the Rio Olympics of 2016. The trade-off is that as legal and technical arrangements become more complex, democratic accountability is lost, since it becomes more difficult to identify the location of power and decision making. Moreover, "traditional representative democracy, and even participative representation as understood in recent proclamations of good governance, may be becoming less significant as the location of politics shifts to ever more technocratic domains."[29]

This private sector-led model could dramatically increase the costs of planning and hosting a mega-event, since state agencies must spend money to enforce the new regulatory requirements that are imposed on private developments. At the same time, this model creates new institutional conditions for elite firms and investors to use public resources for what essentially are private gains. In this model, the state becomes a service purchaser and arranger, a manager and coordinator of services delivered by private contractors. The problem is that inadequate contract oversight and lack of cost controls could increase the potential for fraud and waste. Lack of accountability can also create openings and provide opportunities for private contractors to siphon public resources and exploit government agencies to further their profiteering interests and accumulation agendas.

Mega-events as contested terrain

Researchers have long argued that the goal of the mega-event planning process is to placate people through promises that the mega-event will bring wealth and abundance to the host community. For example, in a series of oft-cited works, Helen Lenskyj argues that attempts to "manufacture consent" to an Olympic bid are made by controlling mega-event related news in the media.[30] Strategies to control mega-event news include efforts by pro-hosting organizations to "reach out" and "engage" local residents in the bid, framing tourism-related development as a major benefit to the entire community, and deploying claims that the mega-event will create new jobs, enhance public services, and generate abundant revenue for host city.[31] In an analysis of the Cape Town 2004 Olympic bid, Harry Hiller contends that while "there was no simple carte blanche acceptance of all aspects of the Olympic idea," local residents harbored a "widespread buy-in to the Olympic ideology. Supporting the bid became an ideological position because it was based on a belief that the Olympics would indeed foster economic growth."[32] Anne-Marie Broudehoux's critical review of Beijing's redevelopment for the 2008 Olympics argues that event preparations "acted as a propaganda tool and an instrument of pacification to divert attention from the shortcomings of China's rapid economic development."[33]

While the intent of most mega-events and tourist-oriented spectacles is to pacify people and constitute them as atomized spectators, the actual effect and outcome can be far different as people can often appropriate dominant images and symbols and use them to challenge the status quo. That is, people are not passive dupes easily seduced, distracted, or mollified by spectacular imagery and patriotic slogans produced by mega-event producers and marketers. Rather, as active agents, people are dynamically involved in the construction of meaning and, indeed, produce and communicate meanings that are typically resisted intensely by the promoters of mega-events. Indeed, mega-events are sites of struggle where powerful economic and political interests are often forced to defend what they would prefer to have taken for granted, an important point highlighted in analyses of World's Fairs in the United States.[34] Various groups of people, including residents and visitors, often use and interpret mega-events for ends rather different from those inscribed within them by their makers, suggesting that the consumption of mega-events and other tourism-oriented spectacles is always contextual and relational. People's interpretations of mega-events are filtered through prior experience, one's social location and identity (race, class, gender, and so on), and one's conversations and engagement with others. Understanding the cultural construction of mega-events and other spectacles requires addressing a range of processes from encoding the practices of institutions involved in the representation of spectacles to individual and collective responses to these dominant representations.

The above points provide a challenge to accounts that emphasize mega-events as instruments of hegemonic domination that serve the needs of capital or reinforce and perpetuate the status quo. While attention to issues of power and domination is necessary and important, it is also vital to understand which groups and interests oppose different aspects of mega-events, how mega-events can divide pro-growth coalitions and undermine capital accumulation for some class factions, and which contending groups use mega-events to advance their own resistant agendas. In many accounts of mega-events, there is insufficient attention given to issues of opposition and contestation, and the extent to which domination and resistance may presuppose each other and thus represent two sides of the coin of mega-event planning and redevelopment. Analyzing the different dimensions of mega-events also means exploring what social identities are connected with different mega-events, and how people use and consume mega-events to reinforce or challenge identity categories. In this sense, while particular mega-events are produced by a combination of local power interests and multinational corporations, and regulated by various governmental frameworks, it is also necessary to explore the lived consumer experience and the role of human agents in shaping meanings and representations of different mega-events for oppositional and resistant purposes.

Disruption and organized resistance

As forces of creative destruction, mega-events are highly turbulent and provide a venue for articulating political dissent, furthering agendas for social justice, and directing global media attention on social problems. Over the years, people in relatively powerless positions have attempted to appropriate spectacular imagery including major promotional themes of mega-events to challenge dominant stereotypes and relations of domination and subordination. In their discussion of the 1986 World's Fair in Vancouver, Olds and Ley noted, although the exposition was organized by a political and economic elite, that evidence from a survey of 2,200 visitors pointed "to a fractured and negotiated power that was never absolute."[35] In this interpretation, expositions and other mega-events can be sources of social unrest as well as sources of social control. For example, the 1984 Louisiana Exposition, the last World's Fair staged in the United States, was a major spectacle that was bound up with the promotion of an African American identity that fed into local mobilizations to undermine the stigma of blackness and claim new bases of cultural authenticity in New Orleans.[36] The unsuccessful Toronto 2000 Olympic bid generated considerable opposition based on a "bread not circuses" theme that exposed and aggravated social tensions and led to major modifications to the bid.[37] Far from being a smokescreen to hide social problems, spectacles can become platforms for people to articulate discontent and launch mobilizations.

Today, in cities around the world, mega-events have become conspicuously associated with disruption and organized resistance, with widespread protest and antagonism being the norm rather than exception. In many places, the planning and staging of mega-events has generated intense tensions among different groups and organizations over who benefits and who suffers from pre-event preparations and post-event patterns of investment and disinvestment. Gold and Gold have described the disruption of the speech by the mayor of Athens in November 2004 by protesters demonstrating against the staging of the 2004 Olympics in Greece.[38] In April 2008, thousands of demonstrators forced the cancellation of the last leg of the Olympic torch ceremony in Paris with repeated disruptions of the procession, escalating international protests over China's human rights record ahead of the 2008 Games in Beijing. Further disruptions of the torch relay in London, San Francisco, and other cities were unprecedented in their scope and organization and displayed the antagonism people feel toward government efforts to forge trade ties with China. Others raised concerns that China's lack of political freedom was incompatible with the values enshrined in the Olympic charter. Four years later, in July 2012, up to four hundred people marched in Tower Hamlets in east London to protest against what they claimed was the "Corporate Olympics." On the eve of the Olympic Games in Sochi, in February 2014, gay rights activists across the world organized protests in 19 cities calling for Olympic sponsors to speak out over Russia's controversial laws on homosexuality. These examples reveal how the Olympic Games serve as a stage or venue for articulating dissent and challenging inequalities and injustices worldwide.

The worldwide proliferation of anti-mega-event sentiment belies a notion of mega-events as instruments of hegemony or ideological mollifiers, or sources of collective placation. Unlike the past, where opposition to mega-events was often muted or exceptional, today we witness an explosion of unrest and protests led by opposition coalitions dedicated to drawing global attention to the inequities and anti-democratic nature of spectacles. Diverse forms of dissent are now spreading internationally to sports spectacles such as the Olympics, as opponents raise alarm on a host of problems including the negative effect of event preparations on indigenous people, huge cost overruns, post-event benefit shortfalls, endemic political corruption, undemocratic decision making, and escalating competition and bidding wars to host mega-event. Forms of financing that rely on huge public subsidies to private developers have become sources of community opposition in an era of neoliberal fiscal retrenchment and eroding federal and state aid to cities.[39] The organization and logic of the mega-event reflects and reinforces destructive inter-urban competition which promotes a "race to the bottom" in which governments engage in various neoliberal strategies—e.g., privatization, deregulation, and so on—to attract tourism investment activity in their jurisdictions, resulting in lower wages, deteriorating public investment, and increased post-event dependency of the local economy on tourism.

Activists around the world increasingly confront the exclusionary nature of mega-event planning and, through access to global communication and media networks, are able to circulate messages of local struggles and oppositional ideas through these media. Thus, a major reason for the eruption of conflict is the globalization of media in which communication and information technologies can now expose the disconnection between constructed images and urban reality and thereby call into question claims made by mega-event promoters. Whereas mainstream media typically present positive images of mega-event preparations and activities, other media channels in an increasingly digital world can provide critical imagery, eyewitness accounts, and reports of the negative aspects of mega-events, as well as a diversity of critical perspectives. More significantly, activists can use the technologies of globalized media to foster new alliances, solidarities, and mobilizations to place issues of global justice and the destructiveness of mega-events squarely in the center of the important socio-economic, ecological, and political issues and concerns of our time.

Mega-events as crisis-prone

In recent years, a plethora of global ecological, geopolitical, and financial crises have had severe negative impacts on the tourism and convention business in both developed and less developed nations. At the end of 2004, the South and South East Asian regions, whose sectors had already been battered by the stultifying SARS virus, experienced the catastrophic effects of the tsunami disaster. Perhaps most damaging for countries such as Thailand was that the disaster affected some of their prime international tourist locales. The global financial crisis of 2008, propagated from the consequences of the deregulation of the US housing market to the banking sector in the developed world, ultimately affected availability of credit globally and negatively impacted retail consumption, entertainment and travel for pleasure and business in both developed and less developed regions. The oil price spike of 2007 and the food price crisis of 2008 are other examples of globally coupled crises that affected the travel and entertainment sectors. More recently, the massive earthquake and tsunami that battered Japan in 2011 killed over 19,000 people and unleashed the world's worst nuclear crisis in a quarter-century. These crises, as well as the crises of the September 11, 2001 terrorist strike in New York City and Hurricane Katrina in New Orleans and the US Gulf Coast have exposed a new insecurity about the future of investments in entertainment and tourist development and have revealed how urban crises can spread havoc across the globe.

Unprecedented global ecological, political, and economic crises have affected the scope, origins, and destinations of investments in entertainment, patterns of consumption, tourist flows, the motives and styles of migration and travel, the organization of cross-scale interactions pertaining to travel, and the relationship between tourism and mega-events. The proliferation of global political and economic crises, together with turbulent and widespread protests surrounding mega-events, have raised the specter of tourist disinvestment and posed new challenges to the mega-event strategy. As Eric Cohen has noted, "the most significant emergent counter-trend to globalization, with far reaching implications for tourism, is the threat of a profound structural crisis in the global economic system, brought about by the socioeconomic consequences of dominant neoliberal economic policies."[40] Mega-events and other urban spectacles are becoming more, not less, vulnerable to systemic crisis as neoliberal policies and regulatory strategies become the transmission belts for rapidly diffusing international crises of over-accumulation, deflation, and under-consumption (lack of consumer/tourist demand and buying power). Indeed, the eruption of a host of interconnected economic, ecological, and political crises raises questions surrounding the credibility, effectiveness, and legitimacy of mega-events as vehicles of growth and prosperity.

New forms of political mobilization and cross-border solidarities are being established among the marginalized and excluded as they increasingly confront the deleterious consequences of neoliberal tourism policies and regulatory strategies. Cottrell and Nelson point out that Olympic political contention has grown substantially over the decades in terms of the particular actors engaged in contention, the tactics they use, and the resistance they face.[41] Yet political contention has also been growing through other mega-events, including the World Cup and International Expositions as different transnational advocacy networks, international institutions, and national governments increasingly struggle over power, sovereignty, and economic resources. Today, we witness the spread of mega-events to Eastern and Southern nations as cities in these regions increasingly embrace the logic of spectacle and entertainment to trumpet their uniqueness and distinctiveness, and thereby promote a favorable urban image in the global marketplace.[42] The globalization of the mega-event strategy has therefore been associated with the globalization of networks of resistance and opposition. Today, activists around the world are using mega-events as stages or forums to challenge the ideology of unfettered pro-growth development and advocate for a more inclusive and democratic decision making process. New forms of strategically targeted resistance may therefore represent both obstacles to the globalization of mega-events and spurs to the continuing global spread and transformation of the mega-event strategy.

Conclusion

In this chapter, I have presented the concept of creative destruction as a heuristic device to understand and explain the contradictory and conflicted dynamics of mega-event production. A related contribution has been to show how the explosion of opposition to mega-events reflects the geographically uneven and politically volatile trajectories of tourism development that have occurred over the last several decades. My argument has been that the *creation* of consumption oriented mega-events has been associated with the *destruction* of prior institutional frameworks, power relationships, settlement spaces, and attachments to place. This process of creative destruction has occurred in a context of fiscal austerity, adoption of cost-cutting measures by cities, privatization, and industrial deregulation. The production of urban space for mega-events has also been assisted by creative-destructive transformations in the nature of urban governance: in particular, what scholars have referred to as the growth of the "neoliberal city," the "competition state," and the "entrepreneurial city."[43] Central to this process of urban neoliberalization has been the intensification of inter-urban competition and bidding wars among cities to attract footloose capital. As Horne has pointed out:

> Urban and regional governments in many advanced capitalist economies compete with one another to offer incentives to private developers of sports and entertainment complexes, and even downtown entertainment districts, in the belief that this is the best (or only) way to bring investment, shopping, and vitality back to decaying downtowns.[44]

This inter-urban competition has taken place not simply in terms of attracting and retaining industrial production and residents but also in marketing cities as tourist and entertainment destinations, a process that is spreading globally as non-Western cities compete with Western cities to host mega-events especially the Olympics.[45]

As I have pointed out, the process of mega-event development has been bitterly resisted. Indeed, the positive and promotional rhetoric of mega-event sponsors belies the undemocratic, authoritarian nature of the planning process and the severe negative socio-economic impacts of mega-events on local people and communities. Today, the planning and staging of mega-events reveal competing versions of urban reality, troubling racial and ethnic politics, and resultant social protest. The tremendous investment of human, financial, and physical resources into mega-events like World's Fairs and the Olympic Games means that issues of transparency, accountability, and oversight will be critically scrutinized. In addition, because mega-events construct and mediate fundamental social controversies, they have contradictory effects, partly legitimating the system, and partly delegitimizing it. Importantly, tourism and related spectacles and mega-events unleash conflicts between inclusion and exclusion, democracy and capitalism, domination and resistance, and, in doing so, create new openings for struggle, resistance, and transformation.[46]

Currently, we are at a crossroads where the forces of neoliberalized urban redevelopment confront the forces of democratic and inclusive planning and social justice. On the one hand, it remains to be seen whether the powerful contractions and crisis tendencies inherent in the mega-event strategy will provide openings for more progressive and democratic appropriations of urban space and governance. On the other hand, the mega-event strategy has revealed itself to be highly tenacious, resilient, and capable of adapting to different societal arrangements and diverse political-institutional conditions. Graeme Hayes and John Horne have suggested that despite increased attention to environmental stewardship in mega-event discourse, the development model "remains one of a hollowed-out form of sustainable development . . . predicated on the satisfaction of transnational investment flows."[47] One ominous trend is that as cities embrace the mega-event strategy, they engage aggressively in destructive place-making policies that enhance the power of transnational capital to influence government affairs at the expense of local residents. Eviction pressures for mega-events are being ratcheted up in non-Western cities undergoing rapid urbanization since valuable land is in short supply. A lasting legacy of mega-event redevelopment in less-developed countries will likely include escalation in land and housing prices and greater dependency of the local economy on tourism. As we contemplate these rather grim scenarios, it becomes urgently relevant to current struggles to work toward alternative urban futures grounded on the principles and priorities of democracy and social justice. A critical perspective on mega-events is vitally necessary to reveal the negative impacts of spectacles, but also to illuminate the potentiality for progressive urban transformation.

Notes

1 Harvey, *The Condition of Postmodernity*; Brenner, *New State Spaces;* Smith, *Uneven Development.*
2 For overviews, see Rydell, *All the World's a Fair*; Broudehoux, "Spectacular Beijing."
3 Harvey, "Voodoo cities"; Harvey, *The Condition of Postmodernity*; Kearns and Philo, *Selling Places.*
4 Eisinger, "The politics of bread and circuses."
5 Marx and Engels, *The Communist Manifesto.*
6 Schumpeter, *Capitalism, Socialism and Democracy*, 3.
7 Harvey, *Urbanization of Capital*, 3
8 Harvey, *Limits to Capital*; Harvey, "Urban process under capitalism"; Harvey, *Condition of Postmodernity.*
9 Harvey, "Geography of capitalist accumulation," 246.
10 Gammon et al., "Examining the Olympics"; for a critical overview, see Roche, *Mega-events and Cosmopolitanism*; Roche, *Mega-events and Modernity.*
11 Hayes and Karamichas, *Olympic Games, Mega-events, and Civil Societies*; Watson and Kopachevsky, "Interpretations of tourism as commodity."
12 Britton, "Tourism, capital, and place"; Gold and Gold, *Olympic Cities*, 1–2; McLaren, *Rethinking Tourism and Ecotravel*; Samuel and Stubbs, "Green Olympics, green legacies?".
13 For an overview, see Brenner and Theodore, *Spaces of Neoliberalism.*
14 Bristow, *Critical Reflections on Regional Competitiveness*; Malecki, "Jockeying for Position."
15 Gotham, "Resisting urban spectacle"; Horne and Manzenreiter, "Sports mega-events"; Hiller, "Mega-events, urban boosterism and growth strategies"; Surborg et al., "Mapping the Olympic growth machine"; Gold and Gold, "Olympic cities"; Shoval, "A new phase in the competition for the Olympic Gold."
16 Roche, "Part 1 sports mega-events, modernity and capitalist economies"; Gruneau and Neubauer, "A gold medal for the market"; Getz, "Event tourism."
17 Harvey, *The Condition of Postmodernity*, 92.
18 Hall, "Urban entrepreneurship, corporate interests and sports mega-events," 60.
19 Lenskyj, *Inside the Olympic Industry*; Lenskyj, *The Best Olympics Ever?*; Lenskyj, "The Olympic Industry and Civil Liberties"; Lenskyj, *Olympic Industry Resistance*; Sánchez and Broudehoux, "Mega-events and urban regeneration"; Shin and Li, "Whose games?"
20 Gustafson, "Displacement and the racial state"; Greene, "Staged cities": Olds, "Urban mega-events, evictions, and housing rights"; Broudehoux, "Spectacular Beijing."
21 Cox et al., *The Olympics and Housing.*
22 Davis, "International events and mass evictions," 582.
23 Shin, "Life in the shadow of mega-events"; Shin, "Unequal cities of spectacle"; Shin and Li, "Whose games?"
24 Figures reported in Gold and Gold, *Olympic Cities*, 309.
25 Centre on Housing Rights and Evictions (COHRE). *Fair Play for Housing Rights*, 9.
26 Harvey, *The New Imperialism.*
27 Pillay and Bass, "Mega-events as a response to poverty reduction."
28 Vanwynsberghe et al. "When the games come to town," 2074.
29 Raco, "Delivering flagship projects in an era of regulatory capitalism," 195.
30 Lenskyj, *Inside the Olympic Industry*; Lenskyj, *The Best Olympics Ever?*; Lenskyj, "The Olympic industry and civil liberties"; Lenskyj, *Olympic Industry Resistance.*

31 Horne, "The four 'knowns' of sports mega-events."
32 Hiller, "Mega-events, urban boosterism, and growth strategies," 251–2.
33 Broudehoux, "Spectacular Beijing," 383.
34 Gotham, "Resisting urban spectacle"; Shlay and Giloth, "The social organization of a land-based elite."
35 Olds and Ley, "Landscape as spectacle," 191.
36 Gotham, *Authentic New Orleans*; Gotham, "Reconstructing the Big Easy"; Gotham, "Resisting urban spectacle."
37 Lenskyj, *Inside the Olympic Industry;* Kidd, "The culture wars of the Montreal Olympics."
38 Gold and Gold, *Olympic Cities*, 1–2.
39 Baade and Matheson, "Bidding for the Olympics: fool's gold?"; Coakley and Donnelly, *Sports in Society;* Crompton, *Measuring the Economic Impact of Visitors to Sports Tournaments and Special Events.*
40 Cohen, "Globalization, global crises, and tourism," 106.
41 Cottrell and Nelson, "Not just the games?".
42 For an overview, see Shipway and Fyall, *International Sports Events.*
43 Hackworth, *The Neoliberal City*; Jessop, *The Future of the Capitalist State*; Harvey, *The Condition of Postmodernity.*
44 Horne, "The four 'knowns' of sports mega-events," 84.
45 Hall, "Urban entrepreneurship, corporate interests and sports mega-events."
46 Gotham, "Reconstructing the Big Easy"; Gotham, "Resisting urban spectacle"; Gotham, "Theorizing carnival"; Gotham and Krier, "From culture industry to the society of the spectacle"; Gotham, *Authentic New Orleans*; Gotham, "Fast spectacle"; Gotham, "Critical theory and Katrina."
47 Hayes and Horne, "Sustainable development," 749.

Bibliography

Baade, R. and Matheson, V. "Bidding for the Olympics: fool's gold?" In C. Barros, M. Ibrahimo and S. Szymanski (eds.). *Transatlantic Sport*, pp. 127–51 London: Edward Elgar, 2002.

Brenner, N. *New State Spaces: Urban Restructuring and State Rescaling in Western Europe.* Oxford: Oxford University Press, 2004.

——— and Theodore, N. (eds.). *Spaces of Neoliberalism: Urban restructuring in North America and Western Europe.* London: Blackwell Publishing, 2002.

Bristow, G. *Critical Reflections on Regional Competitiveness: Theory, policy, practice.* London: Routledge, 2010.

Britton, S. "Tourism, capital, and place: towards a critical geography of tourism." *Environment and planning D: society and space*, 9(4) (2010): 451–78.

Broudehoux, A. "Spectacular Beijing: the conspicuous construction of an Olympic metropolis." *Journal of Urban Affairs* 29(4) (2007): 383–99.

Centre on Housing Rights and Evictions (COHRE). *Fair Play For Housing Rights: Mega-Events, Olympic Games and Housing Rights.* Geneva: COHRE, 2007.

Coakley, J. and Donnelly, P. *Sports in Society.* Toronto: McGraw-Hill Ryerson, 2004.

Cohen, E. "Globalization, global crises and tourism." *Tourism Recreation Research*, 37(2), (2012): 103–11.

Cottrell, M.P., and Nelson, T. "Not just the games? Power, protest, and politics at the Olympics." *European Journal of International Relations* (2010): doi: 10.1177/1354066110380965

Cox, G., M. Darcy, and M. Bounds. *The Olympics and Housing: A Study Of Six International Events And Analysis Of Potential Impacts Of The Sydney 2000 Olympics.* Housing and Urban Studies Research Group, University of Western Sydney, 1994.

Crompton, J. (n.d.) *Measuring the Economic Impact of Visitors to Sports Tournaments and Special Events*: http://www.rpts.tamu.edu/faculty/EconomicImpact.pdf.

Davis, L.K. "International events and mass evictions: A longer view." *International Journal of Urban and Regional Research*, 35(3) (2011): 582–99.

Eisinger, P. "The politics of bread and circuses: building the city for the visitor class." *Urban Affairs Review*, 35(3) (January 2000): 316–33.

Gammon, S., Ramshaw, G., and Waterton, E. "Examining the Olympics: heritage, identity and performance." *International Journal of Heritage Studies*, 19(2) (2013): 119–24.

Getz, D. "Event tourism: definition, evolution, and research." *Tourism Management*, 29(3) (2008): 403–28.

Gold, J.R., and Gold, M.M. (eds.). *Olympic Cities: City agendas, planning and the world's games, 1896–2012.* London: Routledge, 2007.

———. "Olympic cities: regeneration, city rebranding and changing urban agendas." *Geography Compass* 2(1) (2008): 281–99.

Gotham, Kevin Fox. *Authentic New Orleans: Race, Culture, and Tourism in the Big Easy.* New York: New York University (NYU) Press, 2007.

———. "Critical theory and Katrina: disaster, spectacle, and immanent critique." *City: Analysis of Urban Trends, Culture, Theory, Policy, Action.* 11(1) (2007): 81–99.

———. "Fast spectacle: reflections on Hurricane Katrina and the contradictions of spectacle." *Fast Capitalism.* 2(2) (2007): 126–67.

———. "Reconstructing the Big Easy: racial heritage tourism in New Orleans." *Journal of Policy Research in Tourism, Leisure and Events.* 3(2) (2011): 109–20.

———. "Resisting urban spectacle: The 1984 Louisiana Exposition and the contradictions of mega events." *Urban Studies.* 48(1) (2011): 197–214.

———. "Theorizing carnival: Mardi Gras as perceived, conceived, and lived space." In *Alienation and the Carnivalization of Society*, Jerome Braun and Lauren Langman (eds.), pp. 93–118. New York and London: Routledge, 2001.

———, and Krier, Dan. "From culture industry to the society of the spectacle: critical theory and the Situationist International." In *No Social Science Without Critical Theory*, Harry Dahms (ed.). *Current Perspectives in Social Theory.* 25 (2008): 155–92.

Greene, S. J. "Staged cities: mega-events, slum clearance, and global capital." *Yale Human Rights and Development Journal*, 6(1), 6 (2014).

Gruneau, R., and Neubauer, R. "A gold medal for the market: the 1984 Los Angeles Olympics, the Reagan era, and the politics of neoliberalism." In *The Palgrave Handbook of Olympic Studies*, Helen Lenskyj and Stephen Wagg (eds.). London: Palgrave Macmillan, 2011.

Gustafson, S. "Displacement and the racial state in Olympic Atlanta 1990–1996." *Southeastern Geographer*, 53(2) (2013): 198–213.

Hackworth, J. *The Neoliberal City: Governance, ideology, and development in American urbanism.* Ithaca, NY: Cornell University Press, 2007.

Hall, C.M. "Urban entrepreneurship, corporate interests and sports mega-events: the thin policies of competitiveness within the hard outcomes of neoliberalism." *The Sociological Review*, 54(s2) (2006): 59–70.

Harvey, David. *The Condition of Postmodernity: An Enquiry into the Origins of Cultural Change.* New York: Blackwell, 1989.

———. "The geography of capitalist accumulation: a reconstruction of Marxian theory." In *Spaces of Capital: Towards a Critical Geography* , David Harvey (ed.), pp. 237–66. New York: Routledge, 1975 [2001].

———. *The Limits to Capital*, new edn. Oxford: Blackwell, 1999.

———. *The New Imperialism*. Oxford: Oxford University Press, 2003.

———. "The urban process under capitalism: a framework for analysis." *International Journal of Urban and Regional Research*. 2 (1978): 101–31.

———. *The Urbanization of Capital: Studies in the History and Theory of Capitalist Urbanization*. Baltimore, MD: Johns Hopkins University Press, 1985.

———. "Voodoo cities." *New Statesman and Society*. September 30, Vol. 1 (1988): 33–5.

Hayes, Graeme, and Horne, John. "Sustainable development, shock and awe? London 2012 and civil society." *Sociology*, 45(5) (2011): 749–64.

———, and Karamichas, J. *Olympic Games, Mega-events, and Civil Societies: Globalisation, environment, resistance*. London: Palgrave Macmillan, 2011.

Hiller, H.H. "Mega-events, urban boosterism and growth strategies: an analysis of the objectives and legitimations of the Cape Town 2004 Olympic bid." *International Journal of Urban and Regional Research*, 24(2), (2000): 449–58.

Horne, John. "The four 'knowns' of sports mega-events." *Leisure Studies*, 26(1) (2007): 81–96, doi: 10.1080/02614360500504628.

———, and Manzenreiter, W. "Sports mega-events: social scientific analyses of a global phenomenon." *Sociological Review*, 54(Suppl. 2) (2006): 1–187.

Jessop, B. *The Future of the Capitalist State*. Cambridge: Polity, 2002.

Kearns, Gerry, and Chris Philo, *Selling Places: The City as Cultural Capital, Past and Present.* Oxford: Pergamon Press, 1993.

Kidd, B. "The culture wars of the Montreal Olympics." *International Review for the Sociology of Sport* 27(2) (1992): 151–61.

Lenskyj, H. *The Best Olympics Ever? Social Impacts of Sydney 2000*. Albany, NY: SUNY Press, 2002.

———. *Inside the Olympic Industry: Power Politics and Activism*. Albany, NY: SUNY Press, 2000.

———. "The Olympic industry and civil liberties: the threat to free speech and freedom of assembly." *Sport in Society* 7(3) (2004): 370–84.

———. *Olympic Industry Resistance: Challenging Olympic power and propaganda*. Albany, NY: SUNY Press, 2008.

Malecki E.J. "Jockeying for position: what it means and why it matters to regional development policy when places compete". *Regional* Studies, 38 (2004): 1093–112.

Marx, Karl, and Friedrich Engels. *The Communist Manifesto*. London: Penguin, 2002.

McLaren, D. *Rethinking Tourism and Ecotravel*. Bloomfield, CT: Kumarian Press, 2003.

Olds, K. "Urban mega-events, evictions and housing rights: the Canadian case." *Current Issues in Tourism*, 1(1) (1998), 2–46.

———, and Ley, D. "Landscape as spectacle: world's fairs and the culture of heroic consumption." *Environment and planning D: society and space*, 6 (1988): 191–212.

Pillay, U., and Bass, O. "Mega-events as a response to poverty reduction: The 2010 FIFA World Cup and its urban development implications." *Urban Forum*, 19(3) (2008): 329–46.

Raco, M. "Delivering flagship projects in an era of regulatory capitalism: state-led privatization and the London Olympics 2012." *International Journal of Urban and Regional Research*, 38(1) (2014): 176–97.

Roche, M. "Mega-Events and cosmopolitanism: observations on Expos and European culture in modernity." In *The Ashgate Research Companion to Cosmopolitanism*, M. Nowicka and M. Rovisco (eds.). Farnham: Ashgate, 2011.

———. *Mega-Events and modernity: Olympics and expos in the growth of global culture.* London: Routledge, 2000.

———. "Mega-events and modernity revisited: globalization and the case of the Olympics." *Sociological Review*, 54(s2) (2006): 25–40.

Rydell, Robert W. *All the World's a Fair: Visions of Empire at American International Expositions, 1876–1916.* Chicago, IL: University of Chicago Press, 1984.

Samuel, S., and Stubbs, W. "Green Olympics, green legacies? An exploration of the environmental legacies of the Olympic Games." *International Review for the Sociology of Sport*, 48 (2012): 485–504.

Sánchez, F., and Broudehoux, A.M. "Mega-events and urban regeneration in Rio de Janeiro: planning in a state of emergency." *International Journal of Urban Sustainable Development*, 5(2) (2013): 132–53.

Schumpeter, Joseph A. *Capitalism, Socialism and Democracy*. New York: Harper, 1950.

Shin, H.B. "Life in the shadow of mega-events: Beijing Summer Olympiad and its impact on housing." *Journal of Asian Public Policy*, 2(2) (2009): 122–41.

———. "Unequal cities of spectacle and mega-events in China." *City: analysis of urban trends, culture, theory, policy, action*, 16(6) (2012): 728–44, doi: 0.1080/13604813.2012.734076.

———, and Li, B. "Whose games? The costs of being 'Olympic citizens.'" *Beijing. Environment and Urbanization*, 25(2) (2013):559–76.

Shipway, R., and Fyall, A. (eds.). *International sports events: Impacts, experiences and identities.* London: Routledge, 2013.

Shlay, A.B., and Giloth, R.P. "The social organization of a land-based elite: The case of the failed Chicago 1992 World's Fair." *Journal of Urban Affairs*, 9(4) (1987): 305–24.

Shoval, N. "A new phase in the competition for the Olympic gold: the London and New York bids for the 2012 Games." *Journal of Urban Affairs* 24(5) (2002): 583–99.

Smith, N. *Uneven development: Nature, capital, and the production of space.* Athens: University of Georgia Press, 2008.

Surborg, B., R. Vanwynsberghe and E. Wyly. "Mapping the Olympic growth machine: transnational urbanism and the growth machine diaspora." *City — Analysis of Urban Trends, Culture, Theory, Policy, Action* 12(3) (2008): 341–55.

Vanwynsberghe, Rob, Björn Surborg and Elvin Wyly. "When the Games come to town: neoliberalism, mega-events and social inclusion in the Vancouver 2010 Winter Olympic Games." *International Journal of Urban and Regional Research*, 37(6) (2013): 2074–93.

Watson, G.L. and Kopachevsky, J.P. "Interpretations of tourism as commodity." *Annals of Tourism Research*, 21 (1994): 643–60.

3 Mega-events, media, and the integrated world of global spectacle

James Compton

Late in the second half of Italy and Uruguay's 2014 group-round World Cup match, Italian defender Giorgio Chiellini fell to the turf clutching his shoulder. He was quickly followed by Uruguay's star-striker Luis Suárez who sat on the pitch clenching his front teeth in both hands as if they might fall out at any moment. This sort of theatrical display is a familiar soccer trope in which players feign injury in the hope of drawing a foul. Not much new here. Except, upon examination via instant replay, it was shown that Suárez appeared to have deliberately bitten Chiellini. The altercation marked the third time in Suárez's career that he faced allegations of biting opposing players. Pictures of the event immediately started to circulate via mainstream newswires, broadcasters, websites, and social media. But the real fun was on Twitter, where movie mashups of the bite proliferated. Suárez was depicted as the Great White shark in the movie, *Jaws*; he was a muzzled Hannibal Lecter; while another mashup inserted his image into a promotional poster for the *Twilight* vampire saga.

Major brands also got into the act. According to *Adweek*, "Bud Light and Listerine quickly bought Promoted Tweets around the #Suarez hashtag, with the beer brand playfully utilizing a picture of a bitten-into bottle. Listerine set-up a social newsroom before the Cup began for these types of marketing opportunities."[1] McDonald's in Uruguay attracted an enormous amount of news media attention with a tweet in Spanish that read: "Hola @luis16suarez, sitequedaste con hambrevení a darle un mordisco a una BigMac ;)"—"Hi @luis16suarez, if you get hungry come and take a bite from a BigMac ;)." Adidas, smarting from the unwanted association, decided to pull poster advertisements featuring Suárez from Rio's famous Copacabana Beach—the site of FIFA's official FanFest events. Tourists were taking photos of themselves being bitten by Suárez, who is depicted in the ad—part of the global sports outfitters "All in or Nothing" campaign—with his jaws agape. A short six-second video circulated on Vine, Twitter's micro video-sharing app, showing a loop of all three of Suárez's biting incidents.

At first blush, the Suárez biting episode appears to map nicely onto what Henry Jenkins and colleagues call "spreadable media," a term used to describe an emerging networked participatory culture in which people use, mix, reuse, and spread online content. This new "convergence culture" is said to be open, participatory, and democratizing as it breaks up old top-down models of mass production.[2]

In contrast to Jenkin's celebratory view, I argue in this chapter that the biting scandal is a particular example of how sports mega-events are implicated in the general acceleration of media in global sporting cultures.[3] The study of mega-events has paid insufficient attention to the political economy of global media, the construction of global audience commodities, and the politics of cultural performance. This chapter addresses these issues with specific reference to the proliferation and growing importance of mega-events in global capitalism. In particular, the chapter explains the increasingly significant role played by global sporting spectacles in capitalism's need to accelerate the processes of production, circulation, and consumption. Using the concept of the "integrated spectacle," outlined over fifty years ago by the French social critic, Guy Debord, the chapter also examines contradictions that emerge between "concentrated" and "diffuse" forms of spectacularized sports mega-events.

Sport and the integrated spectacle

In a critical commentary on Debord, Alan Tomlinson warns against the superficial use of the concept of spectacle in relation to large-scale sporting events.[4] Indeed, scholars often misuse Debord's concept of the "society of the spectacle." For example, in an otherwise useful correction to the claims made by Jenkins and others, Jodi Dean suggests Debord's "account of the spectacle is embedded in a model of broadcast media," and, therefore, suffers from the assumption that power is exercised as "a matter of top-down control, of actors and spectators."[5] However, the integrated spectacle—the core concept applied in what follows—does not focus attention solely on image producing media. As Debord notes, the "mass media" can be only understood as the spectacle in a "limited sense." They are, he says, "its most stultifying manifestation."[6] The media represent, in a partial way, the workings of the entire society, a society in which social relations are mediated by the production, distribution, and consumption of commodities. As Sut Jhally argues: "While the sports spectacle is an objectified vision of the world, it cannot be contrasted to actual social activity because it *invades* material reality which takes up within it the spectacular order."[7] The integrated spectacle compels us to address a broad range of questions concerning how and why contemporary power relations have become aestheticized in the context of high-volume production systems involving flexible forms of management, labor performance, and an acceleration of production-consumption turnover time.[8]

The concept of the integrated spectacle utilizes Debord's analysis of reification within consumer culture; that is, how popular culture is increasingly subjected to objectification, rational organization, and control by impersonal market forces. From this perspective, sports mega-events are component parts of an integrated spectacular system of abstraction, commodity production, distribution, and exchange.

Particular attention is paid to action taken by various agents—advertisers, activists, broadcasters, journalists, and political professionals—to rationally organize and control popular forms of news and, crucially, to the promotional logic they deploy. Spectacular media events—such as the Olympics and the World Cup—constitute revealing moments along the circuit of production, distribution, and consumption.

Global sporting spectacle and accelerated culture

The production of mega-sporting spectacles is constitutive of capital's need to accelerate the time of production, distribution, and consumption in order to remain competitive and increase profits. As David Harvey and Bob Jessop argue, the uneven spatio-temporal dynamics of capitalist globalization require spatio-temporal fixes to overcome tensions and crises in the flow of capital.[9] The overproduction crisis of the 1970s, for example, was overcome, in part, through the introduction of information and communication technologies that allowed for newly networked global supply chains. The elimination of space through the acceleration of time continues today with investments in Internet and social media technologies—tools used to integrate world markets and accelerate the flow of commodities and financial capital: "Critically, the more integrated the world market, the greater the acceleration of this competition and its pressures on capital accumulation, with the result that they become the decisive features of capital accumulation."[10] This cycle of acceleration is witnessed, not only in new technologies, but also the rate of social change and a general acceleration of the pace of life where the widespread adoption of mobile networked media, and the demands of value circulation penetrate everyday life 24/7.[11] "At present," argues Jonathan Crary, "the particular operation and effects of specific new machines or networks are less important than how the rhythms, speeds, and formats of accelerated and intensified consumption are reshaping experience and perception."[12]

The cultural turn in the acceleration of global capitalism is exemplified in the expanding "media-sport cultural complex" and its integration with digitally networked media sport.[13] Mega-sporting spectacles are "inextricably tied to the rhythms and regimes of an expanding media-industrial complex"[14] and in this sense, are linked to the accelerated flow of capital and the reduction of turnover time. As David Harvey points out, the latest round of global financialization and the pressure for short-term profits can be viewed both as a cause and effect of mega-spectacles: "Those trading in information and all the accoutrements of the economy of spectacle and the manufacturing of images and fetish desires are also part of the deal, as well as all those who trade in futures, no matter how, fictitious these turn out to be."[15] Moreover, argues Harvey, the "sales and advertising industry is now one of the largest sectors of the economy in the United States and much of its work is dedicated to the acceleration of the turnover time of consumption."[16] Mega spectacles, such as Olympic opening ceremonies, act as key promotional fulcrum points for the circulation and consumption of other promotional commodities.[17] A wide array of global consumer brands are involved, but so too is the state, where nation branding figures prominently. In the Olympics in 2008, Beijing asserted itself as a modern economic giant with a venerable ancient tradition; the London 2012 Opening ceremonies served as a backdrop to re-boot the image of "Cool Britannia," while Russian President Vladimir Putin declared the Sochi 2014 Games an international validation of post-Soviet Russia.

Debord's concept of the integrated spectacle captures the dialectical contradiction between the diffuse (market logic) and concentrated (state-bureaucratic and corporate control) forms of spectacle. According to David L. Andrews:

> Spectator sport, like the Disney Corporation itself, evokes Debord's conceptualizing in both the monumental (the proliferation of sport media mega-events) and vernacular (the social relations and experiences mediated by ancillary commercial texts, products, and services) understandings of the integrated spectacle.[18]

On the one hand, post-Fordist networked capitalism is *concentrated*, in that a small group of corporate media behemoths remain dominant players. On the other hand, capitalism promotes forces that push to *disaggregate and de-emphasize* convergence strategies.[19] This tension is evident within the media-sport cultural complex where capital's ongoing process of creative destruction plays out. For example, the digitally networked distribution of sporting events is disrupting established televisual broadcast and cable models of spectacular production. Yet, the introduction of multiple screens through the use of Internet and mobile devices (smartphones and tablets) has created both challenges and new opportunities for capital and nation states. Broadcast television remains dominant, but fans are increasingly reaching for their "second screen" for scores and digital video in a "360-degree mega sporting event experience."[20]

In an effort to understand the new environment, broadcasters have launched their own research into how sports fans consume media across platforms. NBC began these efforts during the 2008 Beijing Olympics. But, it was in Vancouver during the 2010 Winter Games that the broadcaster ramped up its tracking efforts, collecting data on "TV ratings video-on-demand usage, viewing through personal video recorders, and traffic to its digital coverage on computers and mobile phones."[21] One of the new data sources during the Vancouver games came from TiVo. The digital video recording company submitted data on its customers' time-shifting behavior. The data are crucial for NBC because of the premium placed on live coverage by advertisers. The name given to the project was TAMI, or Total Audience Measurement Index.[22] NBC apparently liked what it found. In May 2014, the American broadcaster inked a US$7.5 billion deal with the IOC for exclusive multi-platform rights to the games from 2021 through to 2032. The network also agreed to a US$100 million signing bonus for promotion of the games from 2015 to 2020.[23]

As Hutchins and Rowe note: "The intensity of competition for rights to media sport is matched by commercial anxieties about the exercise of tight control over content distributed via the Internet."[24] This contradiction between "usufructory rights" (rights that pertain to active use) and private property rights has created challenges for the corporate sponsors and broadcasters who pay such exorbitant fees to the IOC to secure exclusivity.[25] It is within this uncertain context that the economic importance of sports mega-events is manifest. Olympic and World Cup spectacles attract live worldwide audiences of unsurpassed scale. The powerful allure and "value of media sport resides in the attractive unscripted drama of live competition, and the demand for up-to-the-moment match and event results by fans."[26] It is spectacular sporting events that offer a particularly effective mode of resolving the contradiction between an overabundance of media content (a result, in part, of accelerated production) and the finite time available to consume it in a 24-hour day: "This mismatch between an excess of content and the time to attend to it means that the specific ways in which people can be induced to pay attention, and for how long, become the primary units of value for rights sellers and purchasers."[27] Sports mega-events provide that opportunity on a global scale, with the BRIC nations, and their expanding middle classes, viewed as enticing sites of future growth for networked digital capital.[28]

Promotional circulation and the digitally networked media sport complex

Sports mega-events are particularly well-suited promotional fulcrum points for the circulation of commodities because of the unscripted dramas that play out through athletic competition. Melodramatic storytelling is at the heart of media spectacles, and these spectacles allow for the efficient coordination of labor and other economic and cultural resources by media organizations.[29] It is this rationalization of resources into a handful of major events that allows networked media capital to sustain the scale and intensity of coverage—of everything from political scandals to the FIFA World Cup.

Sporting spectacles are particularly good examples of how "emotional labour"[30] involving both workers and consumers is used to foster a "complex network of branded commodity signs . . . from which the consumer is encouraged to derive a positive and consistent sensory experience."[31] As Debord wrote: "The spectacle manifests itself as an enormous positivity, out of reach and beyond dispute. All it says is: 'Everything that appears is good; whatever is good will appear.'"[32] Indeed, over the years that NBC Sports has televised the Olympics, it has poured enormous resources into developing a style that plays to the emotional attachment of audiences and emphasizes "positivity."[33] In my view, the self-conscious work to produce intensely felt sporting spectacles is homologous with recent experiments in the acceleration of promotional commodities using digital media networks.

Digital video has proven to be a key commodity in the development and promotion of digitally networked capital generally and the digitally networked media-sport complex, in particular. Digital video's "eureka moment" came in 2005 during the global broadcast of the Live 8 charity concerts to raise funds meant to ease poverty in Africa. The music spectacle demonstrated the successful integration of transnational broadcasting with large-scale online streaming of a live event.[34] Advertisers and broadcasters took note of how digital video could enhance their convergence strategies. Following this, in 2008, NBC Universal's combined properties broadcast 3,600 hours of live video coverage during the Beijing games, with streaming accounting for 2,200 hours. This tripled the company's live coverage during the 2004 games in Athens.[35] Broadband coverage of the 2008 Olympics also increased across Europe and in Latin America.[36] The trend continued for the London 2012 Games which became, at that time, the most watched TV event in the history of the United States, drawing 219.4 million viewers, when including both broadcast and online audiences. As Tang and Cooper note: "Compared to the 2008 Beijing Olympics, online viewing for the London Games grew 182% and mobile viewing jumped 279%."[37] Another US streaming record fell during the Sochi 2014 Games when 2.1 million people live-streamed Canada's win over the United States during the men's hockey semi-final.[38] More records toppled a few short months later in the important US market during the World Cup in Brazil. The early round match between Germany and Portugal broke streaming records for online digital video bandwidth use provided by Akamai Technologies, using, at its peak, 4.3 terabits per second of streaming video, erasing the previous record of 3.5 terabits per second established only five months earlier during the Canada–US men's hockey semi-final.[39] The World Cup match also saw ESPN and Spanish-language broadcaster Univision set viewership records that would be wiped out days later when 25 million combined cable, broadcast and online viewers would watch the United States tie Portugal 2–2, reaching more eyeballs than events like the NBA Finals and the World Series baseball.[40]

Univision's nearly half-million dollar technological investment directed at delivering World Cup games into homes faster than their English-language competitors paid off, with the broadcaster edging out ESPN and ABC "by a matter of seconds."[41] The premium placed on the accelerating speed of digital video circulation was breathtaking, and the sports media complex couldn't have been happier. FIFA's Director of Television Niclas Ericson declared the ratings success of the US-Portugal game "an important milestone in the audience history of soccer in the U.S."[42] American visitors to FIFA.com, the organization's official website, accounted for close to a quarter of its global traffic and downloads of the FIFA World Cup App.[43]

The 2014 World Cup demonstrated the ability of sporting mega-events to expand accumulation opportunities for digital capital while simultaneously reintegrating fragmented audiences. ESPN's Senior VP of Digital Product Management Ryan Spoon declared the success of digital streaming during the World Cup to be "an opportunity for us to, as our business cards say, serve sports fans anywhere in the world, on any device." Streaming was not displacing television, it was, said Spoon, being tied "into our core TV offering."[44] The live-streaming of all 64 World Cup Matches by ESPN, Univision and other sports broadcasters, was being used as a hub for the further distribution of promotional commodities through digital media networks, which now provided opportunities for cross-platform ad sales to the major sponsors of the World Cup. McDonald's, Coca-Cola and Anheuser-Busch all invested in multi-screen ad buys, giving them access to what they considered to be "a passionate, highly engaged fanbase."[45]

Television still dwarfs digital consumption, with one survey suggesting it occupies up to 4.5 hours per day for some viewers. However, consumer research indicates that the proliferation of mobile devices has been a key driver in spiking digital video use, accounting for "22 percent of overall digital video consumption."[46] The growth of digital video consumption during World Cup 2014 was part of a broader trend toward increased investment in its production and distribution by the digitally networked media-sport complex. Time Inc., the owner of *Sports Illustrated* (SI), teamed up with league equity partners, the NBA, MLB, NHL and Nascar to launch the new digital sports network 120 Sports in June 2014—during the World Cup. Billing itself as "the first multi-sport, league-built live streaming video network," 120 Sports was a direct play to integrate sporting content across multiple mobile platforms 24/7 while retaining league control over content reproduction. It also provided a digital distribution hub for SI's new video unit, developed to tap into the mounting ad market for digital video, which is more lucrative than regular online display advertising. Aimed at a mobile audience, 120 Sports video is produced, ideally, in short two-minutes-or-less bites for sports consumers, whose attention spans are assumed to be short.[47] Many of the clips are cuts from in-studio jock-talk discussion panels. Lacking a partnership with FIFA, Planet Fútbol, SI's online soccer site, had relatively limited offerings for World Cup fans during the tournament, although there were attempts to tap into the spectacle. For example, on June 25, SI posted a link to a Vine loop showing Argentine superstar Lionel Messi's goal against Nigeria.

Social media, spectacle, and the digitally networked media-sport complex

Mobile and social media are viewed as expansion opportunities by the digitally networked media-sport complex. They are tools to integrate fragmented audiences while simultaneously increasing promotional circulation. NBC partnered with Facebook and Instagram during both the 2012 London Olympics and the 2014 Sochi Games. NBC premiered some of its video content from Sochi on Facebook including a feature on the friendship between American rapper Macklemore and speed skater J.R. Celeski.[48] Univision's embrace of Twitter during the 2014 World Cup was particularly telling. The broadcaster struck a deal with Twitter to join its sponsored tweet campaign during the tournament. The Twitter Amplify program used Univision's @UnivisionSports Twitter handle to circulate "real-time highlights" to targeted users during the tournament, sponsored by State Farm Insurance and McDonald's. Univision's Hispanic target audience are heavy users of mobile technology, with 72 percent owning smartphones, "10 points higher than for the average U.S. consumer." Twitter Amplify's head of sports Laura Froelich touted the program using the language of social connectivity: "We know sports are a big part of the global conversation on Twitter, so beaming amazing content directly to mobile devices is a perfect way for anyone to feel like they're part of the event, especially one as massive as the World Cup."[49]

This kind of promotional language fits hand-in-glove with Henry Jenkins' notion of "affective economics," where, he argues, "the ideal consumer is active, emotionally engaged, and socially networked."[50] The deeply felt emotional experiences of sports fans allow marketers to strike a responsive chord with consumers in an overcrowded consumer market. As Mark Andrejevic notes, Jenkins assumes that control over this form of "emotional capital" lies with consumers, who can withdraw, or appropriate their "love" of consumer brands as they see fit.[51] The Suárez biting spectacle, viewed from this perspective, is one of a series of "information accidents" in which sports fans struggle to control the objects of their affection.

However, connectivity has a political economic context. Contra the "emotional capital" paradigm, José van Dijck argues that ideological values and logics are embedded in social media, working to construct a culture of connectivity: "Platform tactics such as the popularity principle and ranking mechanisms hardly involve contingent technological structures; instead, they are firmly rooted in an ideology that values hierarchy, competition, and winner-takes-all mind-set."[52] Governing protocols instruct users on how to use social media interfaces:

> For instance, because Facebook wants you to share information with as many people as possible, the platform scripts actions such as joining lists, groups, and fan pages. Facebook's protocols guide users through its preferred pathways; they impose a hegemonic logic onto a mediated social practice.[53]

There is user resistance, and the protocols are under constant negotiation, but the default settings on Twitter and Facebook, work to inscribe a preferred pattern of usage designed to maximize "data flows between platforms . . . vital to companies like DoubleClick (owned by Google) and Advertising.com (AOL) selling targeted personalized messages."[54]

Through the use of techniques such as "sentiment analysis," marketers do not simply monitor an independent conversation among passionate sports fans, or "brand communities;" they are aggregating massive amounts of data on consumer behavior in order to rationalize their business models. According to Andrejevic, sentiment analysis "creates ad hoc, astroturfed brand communities, built not by consumers with shared interests but by search algorithms that assemble conversations or posts about particular brands and topics."[55] Analyzed from this perspective, media response to the Suárez biting spectacle during the 2014 World Cup is not accidental; it is highly predictable. Corporations, such as McDonald's and Listerine have made sizable investments designed to tap into and amplify the multiple spectacles that erupt during the course of the World Cup. The #Suarez hashtag is one prominent example of "sentiment analysis" at work. Within it, we can see the integrated spectacle's core contradiction between the concentrated and the diffuse. An older model of mass-produced sporting event, based on a logic of integration, is giving way to a sporting spectacle where flexible online production and circulation strategies amplify and organize affective attachments to fleeting online commodities. "Underneath this user-centered rationale of connectedness," argues van Dijck, "is the owner-centered logic of connectivity."[56] In the process, following van Dijck, everyday cultural practices of rabid sports fans sharing their affections for their teams by swapping stories with friends "become algorithmically mediated interactions in the corporate sphere."[57]

More than 8 million Twitter posts were sent during the US–Portugal World Cup match, while more than 20 million people posted roughly 46 million Facebook interactions about the game.[58] The drama of Brazil's humiliating 7–1 hometown loss to Germany in the World Cup semi-final became the most tweeted sports event in history with over 35.6 million tweets.[59]

It should be noted that most people on the Internet are not using Twitter. According to the Pew Center, only 18 percent of Internet users in the United States are on Twitter, and the *Wall Street Journal* reports that only 44 percent of the 974 million existing Twitter accounts have ever sent a tweet.[60] But this is not to say that Twitter lacks a promotional punch. Not all Twitter users are created equal. Celebrities (including sports heroes) and politicians are far and away the most influential and prolific users of Twitter.[61] This emerging dynamic has not escaped the attention of marketers of all stripes, who, by utilizing Twitter's Amplify program, are investing in an "algorithmic push of intensity over quality in short periods of heavily circulated messages that may become trends."[62] Self-promotion is the dominant use of the social media site and the quantity of tweets is rapidly expanding as Twitter becomes integrated into the routines of television producers, sports leagues and franchises, politicians and everyday users, including sports fans: "The daily number of Twitter messages increased from 27 million in 2009 to 290 million in February 2012."[63]

Tapping into sports mega-event spectacles

In the digitally networked world of contemporary global capitalism, the concentrated and diffuse forms of sporting mega-event spectacles allow for a wide range of social actors to witness dramatic events and comment on them. In doing so, despite the diversity of individual reactions and commentaries, individual commentators, sometimes ironically, expand the scale and intensity of the spectacle. On this point, Brett Hutchins has documented the snowballing use of Twitter by elite athletes as a seemingly innocent tool for self-promotion.[64] The personal use of social media by athletes, whether it be blogs, Facebook, or Twitter, was initially viewed with trepidation by governing bodies such as the IOC and FIFA, which saw in these technologies a threat to control over their branding. But these organizations have come to embrace social media as a way to expand and accelerate the promotional flow of image commodities. FIFA went so far as to create a page on its official website devoted exclusively to the World Cup's top "social moments," which, according to FIFA, included a selfie tweet from German midfielder Lucas Podolski with German Chancellor Angela Merkel following the team's 1–0 victory over Argentina in the World Cup final. Chancellor Merkel wasn't the only politician to successfully tap into the World Cup spectacle. US President Barack Obama inserted himself into the promotional flow on a number of occasions, including June 14, 2014 prior to US's match with Ghana. A Vine video was tweeted of Obama saying "Go Team USA. Show the world what we're made of." The tweet was linked with the #GoTeamUSA, #WorldCup and #USMNT hashtags. The president's handlers would later release a photo of Obama aboard Air Force One watching the US vs. Germany match.

As noted above, the accelerated flow of promotional messages is enhanced through the mediation of algorithms and the use of sentiment analysis to monitor and organize audiences. One particularly high-profile example of this practice is found in the #OneNationOneTeam hashtag that was used by a plethora of American sports franchises and leagues during the World Cup. "This Sunday, we're fútbol fans," tweeted the NFL's Oakland Raiders, in the lead-up to US's much anticipated game with Portugal on June 22, 2014. They weren't alone. The Buffalo Bills official Twitter account posted: "@ussoccer we're with you all the way!" The Chicago Bears tweeted their support, as did the NBA's Utah Jazz: "Sunday is finally here! Support @usoccer vs. Portugal at 4pm MT." All these tweets were linked to #OneNationOneTeam hashtag. Broadcast media also got into the act. "They say no cheering in the press box? We're cheering!" tweeted NBC's *Today* show. Gatorade tweeted "United. In name and game." Alongside the Gatorade June 22nd tweet was this tweet from the United States embassy in the United Kingdom: "We've done it before, we can do it again. Team #USA #OneNationOneTeam." Once again, we see the integration of promotional messaging among state, sports and commercial actors made possible through the articulation of the emotional trope of national pride and unity.

It is important to note that digital media allow private individuals to tap into sports mega-events in increasingly creative ways. Alex Broad's @SochiProblems Twitter account is a case in point. Broad, a 20-year-old journalism major at Centennial College in Toronto, started @SochiProblems on February 4, 2014 on a lark. In three days, the account had 240,000 followers, including reporters from the *Washington Post*, ABC News and media outlets across Europe. In the lead-up to the Sochi Games, media organizations across North America and Europe were running a series of critical stories. Questions were being raised about whether the Olympic venues would be ready on time; and allegations of corruption were made about Russian oligarchs who were said to be skimming millions off construction contracts, which were reportedly costing a record US$55 billion. The media frame of generalized disorder and corruption had been set and @SochiProblems was able to ride the wave. "Having no luck in Sochi," tweeted CNN sports reporter Harry Reekie, who posted a picture of the broken curtain rod in his hotel room. Other contributors noted the pair of toilets in the athletes' center that lacked a privacy wall, while others pointed to the large number of stray dogs wandering the streets of Sochi. "Rebellious stray dogs must be stopped. #SochiProblems," tweeted Broad. And when only four of five Olympic rings opened during the opening ceremonies gala, Broad retweeted CNN reporter Ryan Sloane's post that t-shirts were now available with the image of the failed spectacle. True to the ephemeral nature of digitized promotional circulation, the account is now long dormant. But, at its peak, the *Washington Post* reports it was attracting 50 tweets per minute.[65]

Political contradictions and the integrated spectacle

As we've seen, the promotional circulation of digital commodities is not necessarily always flattering to sports mega-events and their partners. In Sochi, for example, diffuse forms of the spectacle found themselves in contradiction with the concentrated spectacle endorsed by the IOC and the Putin government. One particularly embarrassing retweet on @SochiProblems came from the *Washington Post*. The newspaper was running a story claiming that one of the torch bearers in Sochi was romantically linked to Russian President Vladimir Putin. It wouldn't be the only uncomplimentary story. LGBT and human rights activists, outraged by a Russian "anti-gay propaganda" law, pressured advertisers to denounce the law, organizing 19 rallies in major metropolitan centers. Some Olympic sponsors, such as McDonald's, announced their support for human rights without explicitly mentioning the anti-gay measures.[66]

A more interesting impact was in the promotional branding adopted by a wide range of media and corporate entities. While President Vladimir Putin suggested gays should be "relaxed and calm" in Sochi, but should "please leave the children alone," numerous media outlets from around the world displayed their support for LGBT rights by modifying their brand logos with rainbow colors. These included Google, Britain's Channel 4, the *Guardian* newspaper, and the *New Statesman* magazine. The *Guardian* noted the "happy accident" that NBC's iconic peacock logo is already multi-colored. A group calling itself Sponsors for Olympic Equality encouraged others to advertise LGBT Olympic ads; some did. Corporate sponsors of the American Olympic team, AT&T, yogurt maker Chobani, and DeVry University all spoke out directly against the Russian legislation. Those corporations which had paid US$100 million for global marketing rights, such as Coca-Cola and McDonald's, delivered general statements opposing discrimination.[67] The United Nations tweeted a photo of Secretary General Ban Ki-moon sporting rainbow-colored gloves while holding one of the Olympic torches. Canadian bobsledder Justin Kripps tweeted on #SochiProblems that his personal website appeared to have been censored. Kripps reported that he could no longer access his website from Russia after a selfie he took of his bearded four-man team wearing nothing but briefs appeared on several gay and lesbian websites. The Citizen Lab blog, operated by the University of Toronto's Munk School of Global Affairs suggested the site was probably a victim of "collateral filtering" and not directly targeted.[68] But many tweeters and bloggers reported apparent interference with their transmissions.

On the opening day of the Sochi Olympics, February 7, police arrested a group of LGBT protesters who had unfurled rainbow flags in Moscow's Red Square. The event attracted some media scrutiny. But the most attention would eventually fall on an all-woman punk band whose situationist antics were aimed at exposing the political contradictions at the heart of the Sochi Olympics. The Russian punk band Pussy Riot garnered global notoriety for its opposition to Putin's policies when, in 2012, three members of the band were jailed for two years on charges of hooliganism, after they sang a song critical of President Putin inside Moscow's

Christ Savior Cathedral. The band's "Punk Prayer" and the trio's subsequent imprisonment, made them instant pop icons following widespread news coverage, fueled, in part, by celebrity appeals from Pete Townsend of The Who, former Beatle Paul McCartney, and pop megastar Madonna. The singer used her August 7, 2012 concert in Moscow to give a short speech supporting the jailed protesters before delivering a song with the band's name painted on her back while donning one of the band's trademark balaclavas.[69]

The jailed band members were subsequently released December 23, 2013 as part of a general amnesty that many commentators, including Pussy Riot, dismissed as a transparent attempt to appease critics in the lead-up to the games. Upon release, band members continued to speak out and use their new-found status as anti-authoritarian pop celebrities to insert themselves into the spectacular flow of image commodities. February 4, three days before the Sochi opening ceremonies, two members of Pussy Riot were interviewed by American comedian Stephen Colbert, who satirizes conservative political pundits. Nadya Tolokonnikova and Masha Alyokhina criticized the Putin government's treatment of the LGBT community and offered the following bon mot: "We have different ideas about a bright future, and we don't want a shirtless man on a horse leading us into that bright future," referring to a famous PR photo taken of the Russian president. The next morning the pair visited the *New York Times* editorial board before taking the stage later that night at the Barclay's Center in Brooklyn, during Amnesty International's human rights concert. They were introduced by Madonna, who was among the many celebrities who now wanted to be associated with the punk activists' brand of anti-authoritarian feminism. "Anybody can be Pussy Riot," Ms. Alyokhina said. "You just have to put on a mask and stage an act of protest."[70]

Thirteen days later on February 18, images of Pussy Riot members being whipped by Russian Cossak militiamen in Sochi were circulating on cable and network TV news and online. The band had been attempting to film a video for their new song "Putin will teach you how to love the motherland," when they were attacked. Members of the band had been detained a few days before and had tweeted photos of their detention. Video of the assault was quickly inserted into the music video that, one day later, went viral. Pussy Riot were performing the contradiction of the concentrated and diffuse spectacle.

Conclusion

One of the key arguments in any critical political economic analysis is that history often unfolds "behind people's backs," requiring us to consider significantly unintended consequences of human action. In this chapter, I have noted how digital media have worked hand-in-glove with sports mega-events to create new commodities and to increase the acceleration of capitalist production, circulation and consumption on a global scale. Debord wrote about contradictions between the diffuse and integrated nature of the spectacle in modern capitalism well before the advent of the digital age. However, in the age of Google, Facebook, Twitter, and other forms of social media, it is sometimes suggested that the sheer diversity of communication, and the new capacity to follow events and to comment on them across multiple and mixed-media platforms, has ushered in a new world of human agency and participatory culture. The digitally networked world, where sports mega-events provide a combination of action, drama, and celebrity rarely available in other areas of life, is a sports fan's delight.

But it is also a world where the rules of the participatory media game are shaped by a relentless push for image promotion, branding, and capital accumulation on a global scale. That push has brought sports mega-events, transnational BINGOs (business-oriented international non-governmental organizations) such as FIFA and the IOC, mega-corporations, and ambitious political regimes, into relationships of mutual interest. These interests underlie forces of spectacular integration that are so powerful that often *criticism itself has become part and parcel of the spectacle.* Guy Debord imagined that critical political responses, to a world that reduced a vast majority of its citizens to be passive spectators to society and history, were limited to an attempt to create "situations" meant to turn the spectacle against itself. Today, as the example of Pussy Riot in Sochi suggests, situationist attempts to use mega-events as opportunities to subvert the society of the spectacle have themselves become part of the promotional machinery of the global marketing of events and experiences. But this in itself means that mega-events and the corporate and media machinery that sustain them, can never be completely seamless forms of domination or oppression. More than ever, contradiction has become an omnipresent feature of a world of globalized spectacle.

Notes

1   Johnson, "Big Brands React."
2   Jenkins et al., *Spreadable Media.*
3   Hutchins, "Acceleration of Media," 237–57.
4   Tomlinson, "Theorizing Spectacle: Beyond Debord," 44–60.
5   Dean, *Blog Theory,* 109.
6   Debord, *Society of the Spectacle,* 19.
7   Jhally, "Spectacle of Accumulation," 53.
8   Harvey, *Condition of Postmodernity.*
9   Harvey, *Condition of Postmodernity*; Jessop, "Spatiotemporal Dynamics," 135–58.
10 Jessop, "Spatiotemporal Dynamics," 142.
11 Rosa, "Social Acceleration," 77–112.
12 Crary, *24/7,* 39.
13 Rowe, *Sport, Culture Media*; Hutchins and Rowe, *Sport Beyond Television.*
14 Andrews, "Disneyization, Debord," 91.
15 Harvey, *Seventeen Contradictions,* 178–9.
16 Ibid., 236.
17 Compton, *Integrated News Spectacle.*
18 Andrews, "Disneyization, Debord," 95.
19 Yong Jin, "New Wave," 761–72.
20 Tang and Cooper, "Olympics Everywhere," 866.

21 Krashinsky, "Watching the Watchers."
22 Ibid.
23 McCarthy, "NBC secures $7.5bn Deal."
24 Hutchins and Rowe, *Sport Beyond Television*, 21.
25 Harvey, *Seventeen Contradictions*, 39.
26 Hutchins and Rowe, *Sport Beyond Television*, 21.
27 Ibid., 27.
28 Anderson, "News Companies Make Play,"; Barboza, "Olympics Ratings Bonanza."
29 Compton, *Integrated News Spectacle*.
30 Bryman, "Disneyization of Society," cited in Andrews, "Disneyization, Debord."
31 Andrews, "Disneyization, Debord," 99–100.
32 Debord, *Society of the Spectacle*, 15.
33 Andrews, "Disneyization, Debord," 98.
34 Compton and Comor, "Integrated News Spectacle, Live 8," 29–53.
35 Hutchins and Mikosza, "Web 2.0 Olympics,";Weprin, "NBC Planning."
36 Hutchins and Mikosza, "Web 2.0 Olympics."
37 Tang and Cooper, "Olympics Everywhere," 851.
38 Sandomir, "Streaming Hockey Continues."
39 Spangler, "World Cup Streaming Records."
40 Carter, "TV Numbers in U.S."
41 Mahler, "Biggest Scorer."
42 Associated Press, "FIFA Hails Milestone."
43 Tabuchi, "American Soccer Fans Dominate."
44 Spangler, "World Cup to Kick."
45 Ibid.
46 Bilton, "5 Charts."
47 Moses, "Time Inc. Announces Launch;" Steel, "Leagues Join Time Inc."
48 Chariton, "Facebook and Instagram."
49 Spangler, "State Farm, McDonald's;" Spangler, "World Cup to Kick."
50 Jenkins, *Convergence Culture*, 20.
51 Andrejevic, "Work Affective Economics Does," 607.
52 vanDijck, *Culture of Connectivity*, 21.
53 Ibid., 31.
54 Ibid., 57.
55 Andrejevic, "Work Affective Economics Does," 611.
56 vanDijck, *Culture of Connectivity*, 50.
57 Ibid., 65.
58 Carter, "TV Numbers in U.S."; Spangler, "World Cup Streaming Records."
59 Khan, "Brazil v Germany."
60 Koh, "44% of Twitter Accounts,"; Smith et al., "Mapping Twitter Topic Networks."
61 vanDijck, *Culture of Connectivity*.
62 Ibid., 77.
63 Ibid., 77.
64 Hutchins, "Acceleration of Media."
65 Dewey, "Viral Twitter Account."
66 Associated Press, "Gay-Rights Advocates."
67 Davison, "Big Olympic Sponsors."
68 Canadian Press, "Canadian Bobsledder Justin Kripps."

69 Herszenhorn, "In Russia, Maddona Defends."
70 Kassel, "Anybody can Pussy Riot."

Bibliography

Anderson, Monica. "News Companies Make Play for India's Growing Digital Market." August 22, 2014: http://www.pewresearch.org/fact-tank/2014/08/22/news-companies-make-play-for-indias-growing-digital-market/.

Andrejevic, Mark. "The Work that Affective Economics Does." *Cultural Studies* 25, no. 4–5 (2011): 604–20.

Andrews, David L. "Disneyization, Debord, and the Integrated NBA Spectacle." *Social Semiotics* 16, no. 1 (2006): 89–102.

Associated Press. "FIFA Hails 'Milestone' ESPN Rating for US-Portugal," June 24, 2014: http://sports.yahoo.com/news/fifa-hails-milestone-espn-rating-160407084--sow.html.

———. "Gay-Rights Advocates Target Sponsors Over Law," *The New York Times*, February 6, 2014, B16.

Barboza, David. "Olympics are Ratings Bonanza for Chinese TV." *New York Times*, August 22, 2008, C1.

Bilton, Ricardo. "5 Charts: The Shifting Landscape of Digital Video Consumption, " September 9, 2014: http://digiday.com/publishers/shifting-state-digital-video-consumption-5-charts/

Bryman, Alan. "The Disneyization of Society." *Sociological Review* 47, no. 1 (1999): 25–47.

Canadian Press. "Canadian Bobsledder Justin Kripps Says His Website 'Censored' in Russia," February 7, 2014: http://www.winnipegfreepress.com/canada/canadian-bobsledder-justin-kripps-says-his-website-censored-in-russia-244238581.html

Carter, Bill. "TV Numbers in U.S. Tie Show Draw of the Cup." *New York Times*, June 24, 2014, B13.

Chariton, Jordan. 2014. "Facebook and InstagramTeaming up with NBC for Sochi Olympics." January 16, 2014: http://lostremote.com/facebook-and-instagram-teaming-up-with-nbc-for-sochi-olympics_b40542.

Compton, James R. *The Integrated News Spectacle: A Political Economy of Cultural Performance*. New York: Peter Lang, 2004.

——— and Edward Comor. "The Integrated News Spectacle, Live 8 and the Annihilation of Time." *Canadian Journal of Communication* 32, no. 1, (2007): 29–53.

Crary, Jonathan. *24/7: Late Capitalism and the Ends of Sleep*. London: Verso, 2013.

Davison, Janet. "Big Olympic Sponsors Tread Softly Around Russia's Anti-gay Law." February 7, 2014: http://www.cbc.ca/news/big-olympic-sponsors-tread-softly-around-russia-s-anti-gay-law-1.2526092.

Dean, Jodi. *Blog Theory: Feedback and Capture in the Circuits of Drive*. Cambridge: Polity, 2010.

Debord, Guy. *The Society of the Spectacle*, translation by Donald Nicholson-Smith. New York: Zone Books, 1995 [1967].

Dewey, Caitlin. 2014. "Viral Twitter Account Rounds Up All of Sochi's Problems." *Washington Post*, February 6, 2014: http://www.washingtonpost.com/blogs/worldviews/wp/2014/02/06/viral-twitter-account-rounds-up-all-of-sochis-problems/.

Harvey, David. *The Condition of Postmodernity: An Enquiry into the Origins of Cultural Change*. Cambridge, MA: Blackwell, 1989.

Harvey, David. *Seventeen Contradictions and the End of Capitalism*. Oxford: Oxford University Press, 2014.

Herszenhorn, David M. "In Russia, Madonna Defends a Band's Anti-Putin Stunt," *New York Times*, August 8, 2012, A3.

Hutchins, Brett. "The Acceleration of Media and Sport Culture: Twitter, telepresence and online messaging," *Information, Communication & Technology* 14, no. 2 (2011): 237–57.

——— and Janine Mikosza. "The Web 2.0 Olympics: Athlete Blogging, Social Networking and Policy Contradictions at the 2008 Beijing Games," *Convergence* 16, no. 3 (2010): 279–97.

——— and David Rowe. "From Broadcast Scarcity to Digital Plenitude: The Changing Dynamics of the Media Sport Content Economy," *Television & New Media* 10, no. 4 (2009): 354–70.

——— and David Rowe. *Sport Beyond Television: The Internet, Digital Media and the Rise of Networked Media Sport*. New York: Routledge, 2012.

Jenkins, Henry. *Convergence Culture*. New York: NYU Press, 2008.

———, Sam Ford, and Joshua Green. *Spreadable Media: Creating Value and Meaning in Networked Culture*. New York: NYU Press, 2013.

Jessop, Bob. "The Spatiotemporal Dynamics of Globalizing Capital and Their Impact on State Power and Democracy," in *High Speed Society: Social acceleration, power, and modernity*, edited by Harmut Rosa and William E. Scheuerman, 135–58. University Park, PA: Penn State Press, 2009.

Jhally, Sut. "The Spectacle of Accumulation: Material and Cultural Factors in the Sports/ Media Complex," *Insurgent Sociologist* 12, no. 3 (1984): 41–57.

Johnson, Lauren. "Big Brands React to Luis Suarez's World Cup Biting Incident," *ADWEEK*, June 24, 2014: http://fuelthefuture.adweek.com/news/technology/big-bra nds-react-luis-suarez-s-world-cup-biting-incident-158549.

Kassel, Mathew. "Anybody can be Pussy Riot." *New York Observer*, February 6, 2014. http://observer.com/2014/02/anybody-can-be-pussy-riot/#ixzz3ImNYOvA5.

Khan, Mehreen. "Brazil v Germany the Most Tweeted About Sporting Event in History." *The Telegraph*, July 9, 2014: http://www.telegraph.co.uk/sport/football/world-cup/ 10955671/World-Cup-2014-Brazil-v-Germany-the-most-tweeted-about-sporting-event-in-history.html.

Koh, Yoree. "44% of Twitter Accounts Have Never Sent a Tweet," *wsj.com*, April 11, 2014: http:// blogs.wsj.com/digits/2014/04/11/new-data-quantifies-dearth-of-tweeters-on-twitter/.

Krashinsky, Susan. "Watching the Watchers: New Viewing Habits have Broadcasters Scrambling to Keep Pace." *Globe and Mail*, February 12, 2010, B1.

Mahler, Jonathan. 2014. "Biggest Scorer in World Cup? Maybe Univision." *The New York Times*, July 13, 2014, A1: http://www.nytimes.com/2014/07/13/business/media/ biggest-scorer-in-world-cup-maybe-univision.html?_r=0.

McCarthy, Tom. "NBC secures $7.5bn Deal to Broadcast Olympics Through 2032." *Guardian*, May 7. http://www.theguardian.com/media/2014/may/07/nbc-olympics-7billion-deal-television-rights.

Moses, Lucia. "Time Inc. Announces Launch of New Sports Network." February 20, 2014. http://www.adweek.com/news/press/sports-illustrated-announces-launch-new-sports-network-155838.

Rosa, Harmut. "Social Acceleration: Ethical and political consequences of a desynchronized high-speed society," in *High Speed Society: Social acceleration, power, and modernity*, edited by Harmut Rosa and William E. Scheuerman, 77–112. University Park, PA: Penn State Press, 2009.

Rowe, David. *Sport, Culture and the Media: The Unruly Trinity*, 2nd edition. Berkshire: Open University Press, 2004.

Sandomir, Richard. "Streaming of Hockey Continues to Expand." *New York Times*, February 22, 2014, D3.

Smith, Marc A., Lee Rainie, Ben Shneiderman and Itai Himelboim. "Mapping Twitter Topic Networks: From Polarized Crowds to Community Clusters." February 20, 2014: http://www.pewinternet.org/2014/02/20/mapping-twitter-topic-networks-from-polarized-crowds-to-community-clusters/#summary-of-findings.

Spangler, Todd. "State Farm, McDonald's are Spanish Broadcaster's First Twitter Amplify Sponsors for World Cup." *Variety*, June 18, 2014: http://variety.com/2014/digital/news/univision-pacts-with-twitter-for-2014-world-cup-sponsored-video-tweets-1201223263/.

———. "World Cup Sets New Internet-Video Streaming Records for ESPN, Univision and Akamai," *Variety*, June 17, 2014: http://variety.com/2014/digital/news/world-cup-sets-new-internet-video-streaming-record-1201221997/.

———. "World Cup to Kick U.S. Device Use Into High Gear," *Variety*, June 12, 2014: http://variety.com/2014/digital/news/world-cup-to-kick-u-s-devices-into-high-gear-1201217566/.

Steel, Emily. "Leagues Join Time Inc. in Digital Sports Network." *New York Times*, June 25, 2014, B3.

Tabuchi, Hiroko. "American Soccer Fans Dominate FIFA's Online Audience," July 1, 2014: http://bits.blogs.nytimes.com/2014/07/01/american-soccer-fans-dominate-fifas-online-audience/.

Tang, Tang and Roger Cooper. "Olympics Everywhere: Predictors of Multiplatform Media Uses During the 2012 London Olympics," *Mass Communication and Society* 16, no. 4 (2013): 850–68.

Tomlinson, Alan. "Theorizing Spectacle: Beyond Debord," in *Power Games: A Critical Sociology of Sport*, edited by John Sugden and Al Tomlinson, 44–60. London: Routledge, 2002.

vanDijck, José. *The Culture of Connectivity: A Critical History of Social Media*. New York: Oxford University Press, 2013.

Weprin, Alex. "NBC Planning Over 3,600 Hours of Olympics Coverage," *Broadcasting & Cable*, July 7, 2007: http://www.broadcastingcable.com/article/CA6466416.html.

Yong Jin, Dal. "The New Wave of De-convergence: A New Business Model of the Communication Industry in the 21st Century." *Media, Culture & Society* 34, no. 6, (2012): 761–72.

4 Modernization, neoliberalism, and sports mega-events

Evolving discourses in Latin America

Simon Darnell and Rob Millington

Recent years have seen an increasingly institutionalized relationship between sport and development on an international scale: the International Olympic Committee (IOC) now enjoys permanent observer status at the United Nations (UN), the UN itself operates its own Office on Sport for Development and Peace (UNOSDP), and April 6 is formally recognized as the "International Day of Sport for Development and Peace." A whole host of organizations also work towards mobilizing sport in the service of meeting international development goals such as education, health, economic growth, and even inclusion and equality. These organizations include national governments and state-funded agencies, non-governmental organizations, sport governing bodies, federations and clubs, private corporations, and sport celebrities.[1]

Yet, the recent institutionalization of Sport for Development and Peace (SDP) is but the latest incarnation of sport as a presumed catalyst for development. As scholars like Kidd have noted, social entrepreneurs have mobilized sport in support of development (broadly defined) for decades.[2] In this chapter, we examine a particular dimension of the relationship between sport and development—the hosting of sports mega-events (SMEs). We offer a comparative analysis of two significant SMEs in Latin America in the last half century: the 1968 Summer Olympics in Mexico City and the soon to be held 2016 Summer games in Rio de Janeiro, Brazil. We synthesize scholarly analyses of Mexico '68 and Rio '16 alongside media reports in order to assess the evolution of discourses of development ascribed to SMEs. Recognizing the different historical conjunctures from the 1960s to today, we argue that supporters of SMEs have consistently traded on development rhetoric in order to justify the expenses of hosting such events and the benefits to be accrued. Thus, despite some important differences between Mexico '68 and Rio '16, particularly in the context of political economy, there are also consistencies in the *kind* of development promises attached to these SMEs. Namely, SMEs continue to signify and support traditionally dominant ideas of development attached to the promises of modernization. We argue that rather than a shift away from modernization in parallel with development thinking more broadly, hosting of SMEs has moved towards a more fully integrated relationship between sport, development, corporatization and "celebration capitalism."[3] In turn, the advent of neoliberal globalization and the corporatization of the Olympic spectacle have only heightened the development stakes of hosting, and increased the seductive promises of modernity ascribed to SMEs.

Development as modernization

When linked to sport, the term "development" holds multiple meanings. On the one hand, "sport development" describes the organization of and investment in sport systems at local, regional, national, and international levels.[4] On the other hand, development is often used in reference to individuals, particularly young people, and is concerned with the ways in which sport participation may or may not foster positive development.[5] We deploy the term differently; we use development in reference to the social, political and theoretical understandings of, and debates over, improvement at the macro or global level of human affairs. In this way, we follow Nederveen Pieterse in defining development as "the organized intervention in collective affairs according to a standard of improvement."[6]

This definition holds several social and political implications. First, development is often underpinned by the premise (and promise) of enhancing, upgrading, and expanding social capacities and resources for more people and communities within a global political and economic system. Achieving these goals is far from a straightforward process, and calls into question historical, political, economic, and social relations of power. Second, and following from this, the dominant understanding of development is *not* a synonym for social change. As Rist has argued in his radical history of international development, social change has been a feature of all human societies, but the idea of *development* through rational human intervention (such as science, technology, and economics) is a decidedly modern phenomenon:

> Development consists of a set of practices, sometimes appearing to conflict with one another, which require—for the reproduction of society—the general transformation and destruction of the natural environment and of social relations. Its aim is to increase the production of commodities (goods and services) geared, by way of exchange, to effective demand.[7]

At the same time, and third, the conflicting nature of development means that its dominant forms have been regularly challenged, especially in response to broader shifts in geopolitics and political economy.[8]

While the concept of development can be traced to the nineteenth century[9] and even to antiquity,[10] many scholars recognize US President Harry Truman's inauguration speech of 1949 as the birth of the idea of development through modernization. In Point 4 of his address, Truman stated that humanity possessed for the first time the skills and resources necessary to overcome poverty and suffering in "underdeveloped areas" of the world and he called on nations to participate in a "worldwide effort for the achievement of peace, plenty and freedom." Whereas the relationship between the global North and South had to that point been primarily organized through structures of imperialism and colonization, Truman proposed that the goals of development could form new links between the world's rich and poor.[11] In so doing, Truman introduced "underdevelopment" in an ahistorical and nearly natural sense, a vision of those who had achieved development and those still to catch up, with little assessment of how these groups had come to be in such conditions.[12]

Truman's speech was situated within Cold War politics, influenced by nationalist surges and fears of growing communism. Thus the discursive shift from "the old imperialism" to a new "program of development" reframed the nations of the global South from colonial appendages to "underdeveloped" areas that now required the aid of the global North to spur economic growth,[13] a process to be pursued within a capitalist framework and in line with the goals of US foreign policy.

The 1950s and 1960s witnessed a strong belief in the promises and necessity of international development along such lines. The new geopolitical realities of decolonialization had increased the importance of a global development program, and the 1960s came to be a "Decade of Development," dominated in particular by development as modernization.[14] Led by researchers and policy makers in the US, modernization theory argued that the state should bring people and societies in line with modern, universal values of liberal democracy.[15] Industrialization and technology were central to this vision, as were Keynesian economic policies that would pursue growth under state control.

Through such initiatives, policy makers in the West hoped that economic growth and political reform would lead to stability and independence for traditionally peripheral nations. Thus, for the global North, modernization theory justified existing policies of economic growth and countering communism.[16] For Southern polities, modernization theory paved the way for new ruling classes to lead and benefit from development while ostensibly leading their nations into the modern world.

Mexico's Olympics and the dream of modernization

It is in this context that Mexico City bid for the 1968 Olympics. Sport held a prominent role in the cultural reforms of post-revolutionary Mexico. In the 1920s and 1930s, politicians saw sport as a panacea for the political, religious, social, and ethnic relations that had divided the nation in the pre-revolution era. Mass sport was introduced with the dual aims of fostering a sense of national unity while eliminating what were seen as undesirable traits within Mexican society.[17] The allure of the transformative nature of sport would come to inform Mexico's Olympic bid; sport could not only offer a training ground for discipline and responsibility among the younger generation, but also project the nation's vitality and potential to a global audience.

Further, Mexico's successful bid came amidst significant expansion of manufacturing that fuelled growth in the country's GDP. From the 1940s through the 1960s, Mexico enjoyed an economic boom from industrialization that saw growth in the Mexican oil industry and foreign investment from the United States.[18] Although this industrialization contributed to social stratification within the nation, Mexico seemed on the brink of achieving "First World" status. At least some of this economic growth was influenced by the Cold War politics of the 1960s that saw both the United States and the Soviet Union seek the allegiances of formerly colonized states. Concomitantly, nations of the global South or "Third World" increasingly sought to cash in on the development paradigm of the decade and challenge the First–Third World divide.[19] For Mexico, the symbolic value of the Olympics offered an opportunity to capitalize on these trends; thus the successful Mexico bid suggested that it, and Latin America more generally, were ready and able to assume a more prominent position within the international community.

Economic growth thus buoyed claims of development, making modernization theory particularly salient for Mexico City in 1968. It was a commonly held belief within Mexico and the international community that the Games would offer positive proof of modernization theory whereby nations in the global South could and would progress along the path from colonialism, through development, to democratic capitalism and a position of political economic prominence on the world stage. For supporters, the Games were to provide a final push towards modernization; growth in tourism, foreign investment, elevated nationalist spirit, and international recognition brought about by hosting the Games would mark Mexico's successful transition from a "developing" to a "developed" state.[20]

Beyond these structural and economic advancements, Mexico's claims to modernity were also discursively constructed. Indeed, given the trepidation that met the announcement of Mexico City as the host of the '68 games, there was a sense that Mexico would have to *prove* itself worthy of the Games and its status as a modern nation. Showcasing a modern Mexico that had broken away from its pre-modern past was of great importance to the Mexican Organizing Committee. The desire to portray a structurally modern, economically developed, and civilized Mexico was encapsulated within the "Mexico '68" logo itself, intended to be a "visual portrayal of the country's successful integration of its ethnic past to the modern world."[21] The logo was also designed to promote a cosmopolitan "Mexico of tomorrow" by using folklore to break from the past and projecting the liberated modern Mexican woman and bright colors as symbols of a modern Mexico.[22]

For these reasons, it is reasonable to situate Mexico '68 in the modernist framework of its time. However, the modernization approach to development was to reach its apogee in this era of Western economic expansion, associated with the successes of broad-scale industrialization and the growth of a Keynesian post-war emphasis on state-supported planning initiatives. Dependency theorists in Latin America began to argue that modernist development served mainly to facilitate capital accumulation but exacerbated the dependence of the periphery on the world's core economies.[23] Eventually, economic slowdowns and spiraling government debt led to economic reforms in the United States and United Kingdom in the 1980s, ushering in an era of neoliberal development policy whereby inefficiencies and regulations, particularly at the state level, were to be removed to allow markets to flourish.[24] By the time the 1984 Summer Olympics were held in Los Angeles, neoliberal policy discourse had effectively replaced modernization. Whereas investment in the Olympics in the 1960s and 1970s, including Mexico '68, had sought long-term social and economic stability, LA '84 saw Olympic hosting shift to servicing entrepreneurialism and wealth creation, as well as the promotion of cities as competitively world-class.[25]

Brazil's neoliberalism: the 2016 Olympics in Rio de Janeiro

It is within this conjuncture of global neoliberalism that in 2009 Rio de Janeiro was awarded the 2016 Summer Olympics. Politically, hosting the Games was a key part of then-President Lula de Silva's strategy to re-brand Brazil on a global stage, and offered a form of soft power to advance Brazil's political weight regionally and within the international community.[26] For the state, hosting the Games was understood as an opportunity to showcase Brazilian modernity through displays of initiative, civility, organization, and urban growth. These sentiments have quickly become part of the dominant understanding of the Games, reflected in both official policy and popular thought. An article in the French newspaper *Agence France Presse*, effectively summarizes these beliefs:

> This Brazilian city's historic win to host the 2016 Olympics follows a long, impassioned and at times frustrating campaign by Latin America's largest nation to reposition itself on the world stage. The effort by Brazil's most spectacular city is seen as part of a broader effort in which [the national government in] Brasilia is also aiming to become a permanent member of the UN Security Council and take a lead role in global efforts to slow climate change.[27]

Despite the neoliberal proclivities of the twenty-first century, there are notable residues of earlier theories of modernization in the discourses surrounding Rio '16. The state has positioned the Games in support of economic and social development, urbanization and industrialization, environmentalism, improved security, and tourism, all of which are understood to create a secure and modern Brazil, albeit in terms commensurate with the current dominant political economy.[28] As Gaffney summarizes:

> These points highlight the role that government officials intend for the Olympics to play in accelerating infrastructure modernization projects in Rio de Janeiro. Cryptic phrases such as promotion of Brazil and create a deeper, global understanding of modern Brazil are code for marketing the city and nation to highly mobile global capital.[29]

It is important to remember that Brazil's bid for the 2016 Olympics was not without precedent; the history of sport mega-events in Brazil maps onto broader political shifts tying sport mega-events to the teleology of modernity. For example, many of the developmental sensibilities that informed Mexico's 1968 bid had been operationalized somewhat similarly in Brazil's successful bids for the 1919 and 1922 South America Football Championships, as well as the 1950 FIFA World Cup. These events spurred a re-imaging of Rio's urban landscape as a modern space for continental and international audiences. The construction of the *Estadio das Laranjerias* for the 1919 event was to display "recently adopted European social practices in Brazil, [that] functioned as both sites and symbols of modernity carrying explicit messages about leisure, bodily discipline and social inclusion."[30] The 1950 World Cup in particular was seen as an opportunity to validate the promises of modernization theory where the construction of urban stadiums would project an image of industrialized modernity and reflect "a populist Keynesianism, [in] providing ample theatres for the production and consumption of Brazil's national pastime."[31]

Indeed, within the climate of Brazil's 1958, 1962 and 1970 World Cup victories, sport and sporting infrastructure continued to be a primary avenue through which the state invested in social and economic development. Yet a series of economic crises and high inflation rates, combined with volatile domestic politics in the mid-1980s, led to severely reduced investment in public infrastructure and to public debts common to the neoliberal "shocks" imposed through the Washington Consensus.[32] The repercussions of these shocks were visible in Brazil's sporting landscape; the stadiums of the modernist era were deemed dilapidated and antiquated, particularly within the contemporary Olympic era.

Rio's successful bid for the 2016 Olympics is thus best understood within the neoliberal conjuncture. While modernization theory continues to undergird many of the development rationalities of the event, Rio '16 is not simply a repackaging of earlier modernist tropes. In the vein of Boykoff's phrase, "celebration capitalism," Brazil has incurred massive spending in order to attract transnational capitalist investment and to promote a consumerism marketable to a globalized audience.[33] The 2008 bid outlined a public-private partnership in which corporate sponsors would bear a majority of the bill.[34] Yet experts expect the cost of the Games to run 50 percent over budget amidst accusations of corruption, delays in addressing the city's structural development—subway and bus lines, hotels, facilities—and fears over crime rates and pollution levels, expenses the government will have to reconcile.[35]

Contested visions: from Mexico to Brazil, and back again

Of course, the state has not been the only stakeholder that has worked to establish links between sports mega-events and modernist development. In Mexico '68, the International Olympic Committee's justification for awarding the Games to a nation in the global South was based on a mixture of altruism and paternalism amongst a mainly white, aristocratic IOC membership that never fully trusted the ability of a developing country to successfully host the event.[36] In Rio, the IOC has embraced globalization much more directly, making explicit the links between the economic benefits ostensibly awaiting Brazil (both domestically and internationally) and its position within the global capitalist marketplace.[37]

Indeed, the current neoliberal context, marked by globalization, flexible accumulation, and largely deregulated international media flows, has increased the extent to which the development promises of the Olympics are constructed through the opportunity they ostensibly provide host nations to shape and promote their image globally. For emerging or semi-peripheral states, accessing a global audience through hosting SMEs enables the promotion of alternative narratives and representations of the global South that can combat global presumptions of underdevelopment. Yet, these events may also re-deploy metonyms for underdevelopment—backwardness, incivility, poverty, crime—that risk further compromising political economic and social stability.

Such concerns were in fact apparent in Mexico, as the nation's "under-development'" was a discursive component of perceptions of the country abroad.[38] Thus, while Mexico was afforded an opportunity to present itself as a modern, developed nation, this representation was largely for a global North audience. The desire amongst Mexico's elite to project an image of modernity was fuelled by a fear that the Games might reveal their First World aspirations to be fraudulent to global North audiences and visitors.[39] As Eric Zolov contends, a shared sentiment amongst the Games stakeholders was one of "this is what *we are*; but there was much more of *they are, they're coming*."[40] North American media outlets were quick to point to Mexico's shortcomings, and drew upon discourses of underdevelopment couched in xenophobia and ethnocentrism. For instance, as Zolov notes, an editorial appearing in the *Detroit News* in 1965 criticized Mexico's "failure to hustle and bustle over the blessed event," drawing on racialized stereotypes of the lazy Mexican attitude.[41] Other reports highlighted Mexico's poor air quality, poverty, and high rates of crime, or questioned the speed at which the nation could "catch-up" to First World standards.[42] To combat such narratives, the Mexican Organizing Committee, at the behest of International Olympic Committee President Avery Brundage, commissioned scientific studies to demonstrate that levels of pollution were in line with other developed, modern cities, including London, Tokyo, and Los Angeles, all of which had successfully hosted the Games.[43] Further, to combat notions of a backward and idle nation, the Organizing Committee urged the populace to demonstrate the progressive and productive Mexico of the future. Mexico City authorities distributed 200,000 leaflets in the build-up to the Games, offering advice on various aspects of being a good host, all of which were underpinned by modernist notions of rationality and civility.[44] These sentiments were articulated most clearly by the Organizing Committee's public relations director, Roberto Casellas, who stated:

> Mexico wishes to show its true image to the world. We want to do away with the picture of the Indian sleeping his eternal 'siesta', and with the dramatic representation of a country plagued by revolutions. While both of these images may have been representative of Mexico's past, they are no longer true in the present. We want to make known our progress in the fields of science and technology. We want to show the inspired works of our artists, the charm of our cities, the great natural beauty or our countryside and our achievements in modern architectures.[45]

The Rio '16 Games are similarly imagined to broadcast Brazil's transformation into a developed, modern and globally recognized state. Still, despite efforts of the Brazilian Olympic Committee and the IOC to tout the improved infrastructure, increased economic activity, and social development that the Games will ostensibly provide, significant media coverage has still drawn on stereotypes of a country of revelry, violence, and poverty.[46] Violence in particular has been a dominant theme in media representations, especially in the immediate aftermath of Rio's successful bid. For example, the Canadian Broadcasting Corporation reported, "Streets are regularly closed because of shootouts and gunfights on subways are not uncommon. The IOC was more kind in its evaluation when it noted Rio's 'public safety challenges'."[47] *Time* magazine called attention to Rio's homicide rate, which at 47 per 100,000 residents was triple that of its bid competitor Chicago, and up 10 percent from the previous year.[48] Other media narratives have focused on stereotypical understandings of the Brazilian character—descriptions of the population that "danced into the evening in flip-flops and green-and-yellow bikinis to celebrate their city's selection"—rather than the image of a new, modern Brazil that the nation would hope to promote.[49]

Such perspectives echoed presumptions of the Mexican *mañana* several decades prior and, as with Mexico, likely present discursive barriers to the development vision that many within Brazil have attached to hosting SMEs. As Cornelissen notes, social and political elites in Brazil blend myths about their nation with visions of a realignment of the international development order.[50] In this way, the Rio Games are as much about projecting an image of modernity to the global North as they are about domestic development, similar to the notion in Mexico '68 that the world was coming. Such sentiments are captured in former Brazilian President Lula da Silva's comments:

> For the US, an Olympics is just one more Olympic Games. For Europe an Olympics is just one more Olympic Games. But for us it is something that really will be the reassurance of a continent, a country and its people. Because, here in Latin America, we always feel we have to prove how to do things.[51]

Thus, on the one hand, SMEs are still regarded as an *opportunity* for hosts (particularly in emerging countries) to promote a global image internationally. However, this is an opportunity only, with no guarantees as to how such ideas will be taken up in a global media marketplace. This is because discourses of underdevelopment attached to Latin American or South American countries such as Mexico and Brazil tend to endure, but also because of internal resistance that often meets SMEs as modernity projects further complicate image promotion. In Mexico, the bid for the '68 Games was viewed as "a top-down elite project in which members of the Mexican Organizing Committee had a firm idea of the image of Mexico they wanted to present to the world".[52] As a result, much of the Mexican public came to see the event as an exclusive project.

This view, combined with the social and economic cost of the Games, reopened political divisions over national development priorities,[53] divisions that rose to the fore during student protests in the build-up to the Games. Ten days before the opening ceremonies, thousands of protestors gathered in Mexico City to protest the Games. United under the banner of "We don't want Olympics, we want revolution!" protestors called for improvements to housing, education, and other social issues, before government forces—referred to as the "Olympic Battalion"— opened fire on the crowd, killing an estimated 300 in what has come to be known as the Tlatelolco Massacre.[54] Although the Games went on, the deleterious effects of the event outweighed any ostensible gains; ultimately, the 1968 Olympics failed to make good on the promise of "development" for Mexico.[55] Even though IOC President Avery Brundage declared the Mexico City Games the "best ever," the Games ultimately did little to disrupt the nation's image within the international community. Media accounts continued to suggest that Mexico "was not properly geared up to staging this modern unwieldy extravaganza of sport" and pointed to the Tlatelolco Massacre as evidence that the nation had yet to shed its violent, pre-modern history.[56] "The lasting reputation of Mexico 1968," Chris Bolsmann writes, "will be marred by . . . the massacre of protesting students days before the Opening ceremony. Despite its modernist desires, Mexico '68 did little to challenge the stereotype of Latin American military repression and human rights abuses."[57]

Resistance to the social and political maneuvering of the Olympics has also been a dominant theme in the lead-up to Rio '16. The Olympics, and the 2014 FIFA World Cup, have served as the foci of civic discontent, one significant node of which began in response to rising bus fares. Protestors have often cited the US$12.7 billion budget for the World Cup, and the US$14.4 billion bid the Brazilian Olympic Committee placed for the Olympics, a budget more than the combined bids of the three other finalists and one that is unlikely to be kept.[58] Such protests came to a head in June 2013, when as many as a million people took to the streets across 80 Brazilian cities to protest the events in light of poor public services, particularly in education and health care, and amidst accusations of government corruption.[59]

It is important to recognize that while the demonstrations in Brazil hold some similarities to Mexico '68, they have been more of a response to domestic policy issues more broadly. For instance, activists from the Free Fare Movement (the group originally protesting the rise in transit fares) have been joined by the Landless Workers movement that fights for access to land for poor workers, and by civil servants drawing attention to the misallocation of funds from public to private interests.[60] Teachers have been particularly prominent in the protests calling attention to the nation's poor education standards. "Thousands were in the streets and you saw posters saying teachers are worth more than Neymar," noted Wiria Alcantara, a member of the board of the teachers' union, referring to the Brazilian player who in May 2013 joined Barcelona for more than $75 million.[61]

The movement has found some success. Under mounting pressure, Brazilian President Dilma Rousseff announced that her government would spend $23 billion on political reforms and improvements to government services, including public transportation. Of the reforms, Rousseff said: "I mainly want to repeat that my government is listening to democratic voices. We must learn to hear the voices of the street."[62] Similarly, Brazilian Olympic Committee President Carlos Nuzman faced criticism from the IOC regarding the protests, and the BOC was instructed to communicate better, keep the public informed about spending, and coordinate with local governing bodies.[63] The protests have also reached the attention of the International Olympic Committee; in response to the mounting unrest in the country, the IOC has formed special task forces to hasten preparations for the event and ease the fears of the populace, which IOC Vice-president John Coates has called "the worst I have experienced."[64]

Conclusion

Through comparative analysis, we have attempted to read some of the dominant development narratives ascribed to SMEs and to analyze how these changed and/ or stayed the same from the Mexico City Olympics in 1968 to the games in Rio de Janeiro in 2016. In turn, we have tried to understand development politics in relation to the proposed benefits of SMEs. We find that despite the fact that development orthodoxy has shifted from modernization in the 1960s to largely neoliberal initiatives today, the development discourses of Mexico '68 and Rio '16 hold important similarities: they continue to signify and support the pursuit of social and economic stability, recognition on a global scale, and improved participation in global capitalism. That said, while these promises were pursued in Mexico '68 through the Keynesian-inspired statist policies of the time, in Rio '16, the pursuit of modernity is more strongly connected to the neoliberal logic largely begun in 1984 at the Los Angeles Olympics. Namely, the Rio games are seen as a way to open up Brazil to foreign investment and the pursuit of private, and corporate wealth creation.[65] However, the fact that the Brazilian government has poured such vast amounts of money into these events suggests a quasi-statist approach to government-led neoliberal development.

Several implications follow from this. First, the specific seductions of development as modernization—that it justified policies of economic growth for the global North and put new ruling classes in charge of development in the South—maintain some purchase for explaining SMEs today. For example, awarding the Olympic Games to emerging powers such as China and Brazil, and combining this with its activities at the UN and participation in the SDP sector, allows the IOC to project an internationalist image as it ostensibly shares the benefits of elite sport across the globe. At the same time, local elites are the primary beneficiaries of hosting SMEs in semi-peripheral states, due in large part to the ways in which SMEs open up public money for private enterprise, a point which connects to our second implication.

Boykoff argues that the processes and politics of hosting SMEs are a manifestation of a globalized "celebration capitalism," whereby public resources are made available to private interests and for private benefits.[66] There are important points of continuity between neoliberalism and celebration capitalism, although Boykoff views the latter as a more expansive and useful concept. Nonetheless, in our view, the notion of celebration capitalism helps to explain the successful re-inscription of neoliberal development philosophy in the new millennium. If the logic and policies of neoliberalism have retained their hegemonic status despite events such as the 2008 financial crisis,[67] this is likely due to a reinvention of neoliberal logic in ways that have built consent within the current context. The case of Rio '16 suggests that SMEs have successfully maintained or even renewed the promises of modernity and global recognition, and done so in ways that support deregulation, privatization, accumulation and the opening of new markets. Celebration capitalism through SMEs may therefore signal less of a break from neoliberalism, and more the latest, "improved" version of neoliberal policy.

The neoliberal turn in development since the 1980s, and the influence of globalization and corporatization on the Olympic spectacle, seems only to have increased support for the development promises of the Olympics. Despite regular evidence that SMEs fail to meet development expectations, they are still regularly looked to as evidence of the promises of a neoliberal conception of modernity. For that reason it seems pertinent to ask what kinds of development politics are being solidified or rendered hegemonic in the case of SMEs in the global South? By our analysis, these developments suggest a measure of discursive continuity from the 1960s to today. While it is largely true that development is no longer a process done to the global South by the North in the manner proscribed by Truman, the concepts of development ascribed to SMEs are still revelatory of the hegemony of modernist and economistic development. Like the institutionalization of sport itself, this process of hegemony is still too often viewed as a simple result of human interaction or various benign shifts in the social and political context rather than the actions of differently resourced actors.[68] Clearly in the case of hosting SMEs, not all countries and institutional stakeholders are on equal footing and so some enjoy the ability to set the development agenda and solidify notions of what development is, and what it is not. The hegemony of modernist and capitalist development via SMEs and amidst the resilience of neoliberal globalization is evident in that such logic does not need to be wholly implemented by external agents—some countries in the global South will take it on themselves.

At the same time, it is important to consider ongoing resistance. As discussed above, the Olympics have long drawn attention to, and been a lightning rod for, social and political unrest. The banishment of Apartheid South Africa at the 1964 Games, the student protests and Black Power salute at Mexico '68, and the boycott of the 1980 Soviet Union Games by 62 nations are examples, as are more recent protests surrounding environmental degradation and economic costs at the 2010 Vancouver and 2012 London Games. Even in Tokyo, protestors have already begun to organize around the rising cost of the 2020 Olympics.[69] With most of these protests, leaders (like Brazil's Rousseff) claim they are listening to dissenting voices, but such resistance is generally incorporated into a hegemonic system that continues to recycle the development justifications of hosting SMEs.

Yet, critiques and protests of the neoliberal policies and celebration capitalism inherent in hosting the Olympics (i.e., privatization, using public moneys for private means, accumulation by dispossession, environmental degradation, etc.) may be disrupting dominant discourses regarding the socio-economic good brought about by the Games. Recent accounts suggests that National Olympic

Committees are increasingly withdrawing their bids due to lack of public support;[70] the bidding for the 2022 Olympic Winter Games has seen Sweden, Poland, Ukraine, and Germany withdraw after public polls demonstrated a lack of support. More recently, Oslo withdrew its bid citing a "lack of popular support for the high cost and the hopeless pampering requirements of IOC," leaving only Beijing, China, and Almaty, Kazakhstan firmly in the running.[71] Indeed, the backlash to the $50 billion price tag of the Sochi 2013 Olympics, recent protests over civil rights abuses in Russia (see Boykoff's chapter in this volume), and cuts to social systems in Brazil, has forced the IOC to re-evaluate the requirements of hosting the Games.[72] These changes, outlined in the IOC's "Agenda 2020," have been directed at making the Olympics more marketable to host cities by lowering the cost and size of the Games, and allowing the Games to be held in more than one country, a notion potentially attractive to Gulf nations such as Qatar and regional powers like India.[73] These shifts are significant in illustrating that while discourses of modernist development ascribed to SMEs remain hegemonic, they continue to be challenged, negotiated, and resisted, suggesting the need for ongoing critical analysis.

Notes

1 See Giulianotti and Darnell, "Sport for Development."
2 Kidd, "New Social Movement."
3 See Boykoff, *Celebration Capitalism.*
4 See Hylton, *Sport Development.*
5 See Coakley, "Youth Sports."
6 Nederbeen Pieterse, *Development Theory*, 3.
7 Rist, *History of Development*, 13.
8 See, for example, Nederveen Pieterse, *Development Theory*; Payne, *Global Politics*; Williams, *International Development.*
9 See Cowen and Shenton, *Doctrines of Development.*
10 Rist, *History of Development.*
11 Ibid., 73.
12 Ibid.
13 Sachs, *The Development Dictionary.*
14 Rist, *History of Development*, 90.
15 Gilman, *Mandarins of the Future.*
16 See Rist, *History of Development*; Gilman, *Mandarins of the Future.*
17 Brewster, "Patriotic Pastimes."
18 Brewster, "Changing Impressions of Mexico."
19 Bolsman and Brewster, "Mexico and South Africa."
20 Zolov, "Showcasing 'Land of Tomorrow'."
21 Brewster, "Changing Impressions of Mexico," 34.
22 Zolov, "Showcasing 'Land of Tomorrow'."
23 NederbeenPieterse, *Development Theory.*
24 Payne, *Global Politics.*
25 Gruneau and Neubauer, "Gold Medal for Market."
26 Schausteckde Almeida et al., "2016 Olympic Paralympic Games."

27 Cited in Darnell, "Olympism in Action," 70.
28 Darnell, "Olympism in Action"; Gaffney, "Mega-Events and Rio."
29 Gaffney, "Mega-Events and Rio," 23.
30 Ibid., 12.
31 Ibid., 15.
32 Gaffney, "Mega-Events and Rio"; Klein, *The Shock Doctrine.*
33 Boykoff, *Celebration Capitalism.*
34 Kiernan, "Brazil Olympic Raises Budget."
35 Kiernan, "Brazil Olympic Raises Budget"; Kiernan, "Brazil Official to Leave"; Zimbalist, "FIFA, IOC Monopolies Make Games Expensive."
36 Bolsmann, "Mexico and South Africa."
37 See Millington & Darnell, "Constructing and Contesting Olympics."
38 Zolov, "Showcasing 'Land of Tomorrow'," 161.
39 Brewster, "Teaching Mexicans How to Behave."
40 Zolov, "Showcasing 'Land of Tomorrow'," 160, original emphasis.
41 Ibid.,165.
42 Zolov, "Showcasing 'Land of Tomorrow'"; Brewster, "Teaching Mexicans How to Behave"; Brewster, "Reflections on Mexico '68"; Bolsmann and Brewster, "Mexico and South Africa."
43 Brewster, "Changing Impression of Mexico."
44 Brewster, "Teaching Mexicans to Behave."
45 Cited in Brewster, "Changing Impression of Mexico," 37.
46 Tomlinson et al. "Before and After Vuvuzela."
47 Drapack, "Rio de Janiero gets 2016 Olympics."
48 Padgett and Downie, "Rio's Olympic Win."
49 Tomlinson et al., "Before and After Vuvuzela," 45.
50 Cornelissen, "Geopolitics of Global Aspiration."
51 Ibid., 3022.
52 Brewster, "Changing Impression of Mexico," 23.
53 Zolov, "Showcasing 'Land of Tomorrow'."
54 Jaime, "Rights-Mexico."
55 Bolsmann and Brewster, "Mexico and South Africa"; Brewster, "Teaching Mexicans How to Behave."
56 Brewster, "Changing Impressions of Mexico," 43.
57 Bolsmann, "Mexico and South Africa," 105.
58 Lundy, "Brazilians have Reason to Protest."
59 Lundy, "Brazilians have Reason to Protest"; Mayer, "Brazil Protest Show Cost."
60 Lundy, "Brazilians have Reason to Protest"; Mayer, "Brazil Protest Show Cost"; Watts, "Brazil's World Cup Disaster."
61 Cited in Panja and Biller, "Brazil Riots Threaten Games."
62 Associated Press, "Brazil Raise Transit Funding"
63 Wade, "2014 World Cup, Olympics, High-risk."
64 Agence France Presse, "Olympic Officials Rio Preparation."
65 Darnell, "Olympism in Action."
66 Boykoff, *Celebration Capitalism.*
67 Crouch, "Strange Non-Death of Neo-Liberalism."
68 See Gruneau, "Modernization or Hegemony."
69 Associated Press, "Protestors Tokyo Olympic Stadium."
70 Manfred, "Bidding 2022 Olympics Disaster."

71 Crouch, "IOC Hits out as Norway Withdraws Olympic Bid"; Wilson, "Dream of Hosting Olympic Games."
72 Crouch, "Norway Withdraws Olympic Bid."
73 Futterman, "Olympics Tries Fix Itself"; Rumsby, "Doha Takes Steps Closer to Closer to Hosting."

Bibliography

Agence France Presse. "Olympic Official Calls Rio Preparation the 'Worst I have Ever Experienced'." *Business Insider* (Online), April 29, 2014.

Associated Press. "Brazil to Raise Transit Funding $23B After Protest: President Rousseff Says She Will Push Debate on Political Reforms." *Canadian Broadcasting Corporation*, June 24, 2013; www.cbc.ca/news/world/brazil-to-raise-transit-funding-23b-after-protests-1.1389307.

———. "Protestors March Against Tokyo Olympic Stadium." *USA Today*, July 5, 2014: www.usatoday.com/story/sports/olympics/2014/07/05/protesters-march-against-tokyo-olympic-stadium/12241799.

Bolsmann, Chris. "Mexico 1968 and South Africa 2010: Sombreros and Vuvuzelas and the Legitimisation of Global Sporting Events." *Bulletin of Latin American Research*, 29, no. 1 (2010): 93–106.

———, and Keith Brewster. "Mexico 1968 and South Africa 2010: Development, Leadership and Legacies." *Sport in Society*, 12, no. 10 (2009): 1284—98.

Boykoff, Jules. *Celebration Capitalism and the Olympic Games*. New York: Routledge, 2014.

Brewster, Claire. "Changing Impressions of Mexico for the 1968 Games." *Bulletin of Latin American Research*, 29, no. 1 (2010): 23–45.

Brewster, Keith. "Patriotic Pastimes: The Role of Sport in Post-Revolutionary Mexico." *International Journal of the History of Sport*, 22, no. 2 (2005): 139–57.

———. "Reflections on Mexico '68." *Journal of the Society for Latin American Studies*, 1, no. i (2010b): 68.

———. "Teaching Mexicans How to Behave: Public Education on the Eve of the Olympics." *Bulletin of Latin American Research*, 29, no. 1 (2010a): 46–62.

Coakley, Jay. "Youth Sports: What Counts as 'Positive Development'?" *Journal of Sport & Social Issues*, 35, no. 3 (2011): 306–24.

Cornelissen, Scarlett. "The Geopolitics of Global Aspiration: Sport Mega-Events and Emerging Powers." *International Journal of the History of Sport*, 27, nos. 16–18 (2010): 3008–25.

Cowen, M.P. and R.W. Shenton. *Doctrines of Development*. Abingdon: Taylor & Francis, 1996.

Crouch, David. "IOC Hits out as Norway Withdraws Winter Olympic Bid." *Financial Times*. October 2, 2014.

———. *The Strange Non-Death of Neo-Liberalism*. Malden, MA: Polity Press, 2011.

Darnell, Simon. "Olympism in Action, Olympic Hosting and the Politics of 'Sport for Development and Peace': Investigating the Development Discourses of Rio 2016." *Sport in Society*, 15, no. 6 (2012): 869–87.

Drapack, Michael. "Rio de Janeiro gets 2016 Olympics." *Canadian Broadcasting Corporation*. October 2, 2009: www.cbc.ca/m/touch/sports/story/1.805587.

Futterman, Matthew. "The Olympics Tries to Fix Itself: Faced with Dwindling Number of Cities Interested in Hosting the Games, IOC Enacts Radical Changes to Bidding Process." *Wall Street Journal*. December 8, 2014.

Gaffney, Christopher. "Mega-Events and Socio-Spatial Dynamics in Rio de Janeiro 1919-2016." *Journal of Latin American Geography*, 9, no. 1 (2010): 7–29.

Gilman, Nils. *Mandarins of the Future: Modernization Theory in Cold War America.* Baltimore, MD: Johns Hopkins University Press, 2003.

Giulianotti, Richard and Simon C. Darnell, S.C. (In press). "Sport for Development and Peace". In *Sport and Society,* edited by Barrie Houlihan and Dominic Malcolm. London: Sage.

Gruneau, Richard. "Modernization or Hegemony: Two Views on Sport and Social Development." In *Not Just a Game: Essays in Canadian Sport Sociology*, edited by Jean Harvey and Hart Cantelon, 9–32. Ottawa: University of Ottawa Press, 1988.

———, and Robert Neubauer. "A Gold Medal for the Market: The 1984 Los Angeles Olympics, the Reagan Era and the Politics of Neoliberalism." In *The Palgrave Handbook of Olympic Studies*, edited by Helen J. Lenskyj and Stephen Waggs, 134–62. Basingstoke: Palgrave Macmillan, 2012.

Hylton, Kevin. *Sport Development: Policy, Process, and Practice*. London: Routledge, 2013.

Jaime, Felipe. "Rights-Mexico: Call for prosecution of ex-President raises doubts." *Inter Press Service*. July 26, 2004.

Kidd, Bruce. "A New Social Movement: Sport for Development and Peace." *Sport in Society*, 11, no. 4 (2008): 370–80.

Kiernan, Paul. "Brazil Olympic Committee Raises Budget Estimate for 2016 Games." *Wall Street Journal*. January 23, 2014.

———. "Brazil Official to Leave 2016 Olympic Post." *Wall Street Journal*. April 2, 2014.

Klein, Naomi. *The Shock Doctrine: The Rise of Disaster Capitalism.* Toronto: Vintage Canada, 2008.

Lundy, Matt. "Brazilians Have Reason to Protest the Cost of Olympics and World Cup." *Globe and Mail*. June 24, 2013: www.theglobeandmail.com/globe-debate/brazilians-have-reason-to-protest-the-cost-of-olympics-and-world-cup/article12742114.

Manfred, Tony. "The Bidding for the 2022 Olympics is a Disaster Because Everyone Figured out that Hosting is a Total Waste." *Business Insider.* May 27, 2014: www. businessinsider.com/2022-olympics-host-cities-2014-5.

Mayer, Andre. "Brazil Protests Show Cost of Hosting Major Sports Events: Protests Continuing Amid Confederations Cup Tournament in Rio." *CBC News.* 29 June, 2013: www.cbc. ca/news/world/brazil-protests-show-cost-of-hosting-major-sports-events-1.1358504.

Millington, Rob, and Simon C. Darnell. "Constructing and Contesting the Olympics Online: The Internet, Rio 2016 and the Politics of Brazilian Development." *International Review for the Sociology of Sport*, 49, no. 2(2014): 190–210.

Nederveen Pieterse, Jan. *Development Theory*. London: Sage, 2010.

Padgett, Tim, and Andrew Downie. "Rio's Olympic Win." *Time Magazine*, 174, no. 15, October 19, 2009.

Panja, Tariq, and David Biller. "Brazil Riots Threaten World Cup as Nation Prepares for Games." *Bloomberg*, October 23, 2013: www.bloomberg.com/news/2013-10-23/brazil-world-cup-disruption-seen-outcome-of-rio-violent-protests.html.

Payne, Anthony. *The Global Politics of Unequal Development*. Basingstoke: Palgrave Macmillan, 2005.

Rist, Gilbert. *The History of Development: From Western Origins to Global Faith*. London: Zed Books, 2008.

Rumsby, Ben. "Doha Takes Steps Closer to Hosting 2024 Olympics." *Daily Telegraph*, November 19, 2014.

Sachs, Wolfgang. *The Development Dictionary: A Guide to Knowledge as Power*. London: Zed Books, 2009.

Schausteck de Almeida, Barbara, Wanderley Marchi Junior, and Elizabeth Pike. "The 2016 Olympic and Paralympic Games and Brazil's Soft Power." *Contemporary Social Science,* 19, no. 2 (2014): 271–83.

Tomlinson, Richard, Orli Bass, and Thomas Bassett. "Before and After the Vuvuzela: Identity, Image and Mega-Events in South Africa, China and Brazil." *South African Geographical Journal*, 93, no. 1 (2011): 38–48.

Wade, Stephen. "2014 World Cup, 2016 Rio de Janeiro Olympics High-risk, High-reward Events for Brazil." *National Post*, November 28, 2013: sports.nationalpost.com/2013/11/28/2014-world-cup-2016-rio-de-janeiro-olympics-high-risk-high-reward-events-for-brazil.

Watts, Jonathan. "Brazil's World Cup Courts Disaster as Delays, Protests and Deaths Mount: An Attack on the President's Office was Just the Latest Alarming Episode in the Run-up to June's Tournament." *Guardian*, February 16, 2014: www.theguardian.com/world/2014/feb/16/brazil-world-cup-disaster-delays-protests-deaths.

Williams, David. *International Development and Global Politics: History, Theory and Practice*. Abingdon: Routledge, 2012.

Wilson, Stephen. "Dream of Hosting Olympic Games sees Fewer Countries Bidding for the Honour, says IOC." *Courier Mail.* June 1, 2014: www.couriermail.com.au/sport/more-sports/drama-of-hosting-olympic-games-sees-fewer-countries-bidding-for-the-honour-says-the-ioc/story-fnii0hmo-1226938777202?nk=dfe3e9e3c0a64863cce4c6e5b1fe924a.

Zimbalist, Andrew. "FIFA, IOC monopolies make games expensive." *Boston Globe*, June 8, 2014.

Zolov, Eric. "Showcasing the 'Land of Tomorrow': Mexico and the 1968 Olympics." *The Americas*, 61, no. 2 (2004): 159–88.

5　Between Madiba Magic and spectacular capitalism

The FIFA World Cup in South Africa

Ashwin Desai

'Capitalism is both monstrous and magical'

David McNally[1]

The year is 2004. FIFA president, Joseph Sepp Blatter, announces to the world that South Africa will host the FIFA World Cup. Nelson Mandela is in the audience. Through tears of unrestrained elation, Mandela tells the audience and the watching world that he feels "like a boy of fifteen." The excitement in Zurich is matched in South Africa as thousands across racial and class divides erupt in spontaneous celebration.[2]

Mandela assures the world that "South Africa will deliver a tournament that will exceed your hopes."[3] The incumbent President of South Africa, Thabo Mbeki, is quick to promise that 2010 will be an African World Cup and, in millenarian terms, tells the world that it will be a catalyst for the resurgence of the continent:

> The successful hosting of the FIFA World Cup in Africa will provide a powerful, irresistible momentum to [the] African renaissance . . . We want to ensure that one day, historians will reflect upon the 2010 World Cup as a moment when Africa stood tall and resolutely turned the tide on centuries of poverty and conflict. We want to show that Africa's time has come.[4]

Madiba Magic, the World Cup, and the allure of modernity

The announcement in Zurich came exactly ten years after Mandela took office as the first democratically elected President of South Africa. From that day on, it seemed that the Mandela years were to be a series of spectacles. Nothing epitomized this more than the sporting fields of the country. The 1995 winning of the rugby World Cup, with Mandela resplendent in a Springbok jersey, was received with global acclaim. This was followed by the winning of soccer's African Cup of Nations. It was at this time that the idea of *Madiba* (Mandela) *Magic* caught the public imagination and we came to believe that something exceptional was being born in South Africa.[5] Mandela was seen as the "magnanimous sorcerer" and his actions and statements "acquired a providential hue."[6]

From sport to international visits and receiving of guests such as the Spice Girls at the Union Buildings, these were giddy times. In an age where leaders seemed to be photocopies of each other, our President was a rock star. Madiba shirts became a fashion statement. Hollywood came begging for autographs.[7] It signaled a time when those who suffered under the yoke of apartheid would take their place as fully-fledged citizens, under a new flag and national anthem, guided by a new constitution in a new South Africa. Mandela marked the closure of one long terrible worldwide history, defined by colonial dispossession and racial oppression. At the same time, he signaled an opening; of a time when all South Africans would be free from racial and economic exclusions, blessed to be living under the benevolent gaze of the Rainbow Nation of God.

Opening would be the operative word. Our economy, which for so long had operated behind protectionist barriers, was thrown open to a feeding frenzy by global competitors, as we lost one labor-intensive industry after another to East Asian sweatshops. We, who had been isolated from the world during apartheid, were now rushed at breakneck speed into the embrace of global competitiveness. People who bore the crushing weight of apartheid were now asked to bear the burden of shock capitalism.[8] Battles were lost. We were designated a "transitional" country, not a "developing" one, by the World Trade Organization (WTO), opening ourselves up to cheap imports and dumping, and we hastily agreed to lower our tariffs faster than even the WTO deemed necessary.

Exchange controls were relaxed in 1995 and then crucially, in 1999, Minister of Finance Trevor Manuel allowed big business to de-list from Johannesburg and re-list on the London Stock Exchange. Some of the country's biggest companies decamped with apartheid's plunder. The US$25 billion apartheid debt, odious in law, was to be honored. The final U-turn came without warning. The Reconstruction and Development Programme (RDP) was replaced by a series of neoliberal White Papers in sector after sector, culminating in the 1996 Growth, Employment and Redistribution (GEAR), a home-grown structural adjustment policy.[9]

From the jitters evoked by Mandela's 1990 call for nationalization and commitment to the Freedom Charter, the ANC had transmogrified into running a state which sought to fit snugly into serving the interests of global capital, especially financial, and legitimating the power of the IMF, the World Bank and the WTO.[10] These policies, codified in GEAR, were meant "to break current constraints and catapult the economy to higher levels of growth, development and employment needed to provide a better life for all South Africans."[11]

The race complexion of Parliament may have changed with the advent of democracy, but its economic policies largely stayed the same, albeit with a seeming commitment to a de-racialized redistributive bent. Big business was comforted by the reality that the commanding heights of the economy would remain the same as long as they ceded some value to politically connected blacks. A small black bourgeoisie emerged, hanging onto the coat-tails of white capital. A black middle class, mired in debt, displayed typical forms of conspicuous consumption. But, at other levels, results were meager. The expected growth rates did not materialize. Unemployment spiraled and poverty and inequality deepened.

Was it that, once more, "African economic sovereignty" was "to be sacrificed on the altar of corporate globalism"?[12] Not really. There was still a deep sense that Madiba Magic would conjure an audacious spell, propelling the country into the global economy while ensuring local levels of uplift and redistribution.

In this context, the 2004 announcement that South Africa would host the 2010 World Cup came at an opportune moment. The coming of the World Cup was seen as the spectacle which would bring spectacular results. W.W. Rostow's (1960) famous "take-off" to modernization seemed immanent in the time of the Cup's kick-off.

The world's greatest show—and a spectacular South African capitalism would be unleashed to stage it. World-class transport systems and gigantic stadiums would need to be built and they would show the world that South Africa was ready for large-scale investment. Tourists would flood the country. But, to attract such capital, it would be necessary to spend on an equally "world-class" scale, a point highlighted in President Kgalema Motlanthe's State of the Union Address in 2009:

> The true legacy of this spectacle will be our ability to showcase South African and African hospitality and humanity—to change once and for all perceptions of our country and our continent among peoples of the world. That depends on all of us; and to that we can attach no price![13]

Those who asked critical questions were quickly brushed aside as doomsayers and Afro-pessimists. The idea of "structural adjustment" pushed past dreams of "structural transformation," as South Africa embraced the idea of growth through spectacle. On this point, Gilman-Opalsky reminds us that "In the society of the spectacle, we tend to believe that we can achieve almost anything without structural transformation, thus revolution (which requires structural transformation) appears increasingly out of place."[14]

The World Cup would offer a dramatic shortcut into modernity. The North showed us a picture of our future. Preparing for the World Cup would bring infrastructure, fast transport systems and incredible stadiums that would be the new pyramids of Africa. President Thabo Mbeki had characterized South Africa as a country with two economies and the challenge was to support a high-tech first economy while in the process, uplifting the second.[15] The World Cup would be a game-changer in the quest to suture the disconnection between these two economies. South Africans began to see the World Cup like the cargo cults of old, bringing untold riches from afar. Beyond the immediate boost to the economy, the games would leave a legacy, showing South Africa as a can-do nation, throwing off the shackles of apartheid and now rightfully claiming our place in the first world.

Except that it was FIFA rather than South Africa that would largely determine the form and nature of the spectacle, as the government was forced to harmonize its vision of development with the need to obediently meet all of FIFA's requirements, while simultaneously funding the entire endeavor. More broadly, the model for gauging the success of the endeavor would be the West. Jabulani Moleketi, the deputy finance minister in Thabo Mbeki's cabinet, articulated this view clearly: "2010 will give us an opportunity to say there's this other Africa which can hold the biggest sporting competition in the world efficiently and like any other European country. We have an opportunity to change the attitude towards Africa and show what Africans can do."[16]

This imagined leap to modernity required stadiums that would be world class (like those in Europe) but would be given a stylistically African inflection:

> Mbombela Stadium in Nelspruit sports zebra-striped seats as well as six-teen orange pylons that supposedly recall giraffes, evoking the luxury game lodge aspect of African tourism. Soccer City in Johannesburg is a cavernous stadium modeled on an African calabash cooking pot, while Peter Mokaba Stadium in Polokwane boasts concrete and steel representations of the local, and unmistakable baobab tree.[17]

If ever there is an example of form being valued above content, the stadiums built for the 2010 World Cup are it. The symbols of Africa are displayed for a global audience, while the harsh content of the lives of local communities, untouched, if not made worse by such displays, are forgotten.

The Faustian side of spectacular capitalism

In his classic work, *Society of the Spectacle*, the French activist and theorist Guy Debord argues that

> The spectacle manifests itself in an enormous positivity beyond dispute, posi-tivity, out of reach. All it says is: "Everything that appears is good whatever is good will appear." The attitude it demands in principle is the same passive acceptance that it has already secured by means of its seeming incontrovert-ibility, and indeed by its monopolization of the realm of appearances.[18]

The Mandela years were a spectacle but were found wanting at the level of real change in the way capital was accumulated and redistributed. The result was what Ronnie Kasrils, former Cabinet minister in both the Mandela and Mbeki govern-ments, called a Faustian moment—that

> came when we took an IMF loan on the eve of our first democratic election. That loan, with strings attached that precluded a radical economic agenda, was considered a necessary evil, as were concessions to keep negotiations on track and take delivery of the promised land for our people. Doubt had come to reign supreme: we believed, wrongly, there was no other option; that we had to be cautious, since by 1991 our once powerful ally, the Soviet Union, bankrupted by the arms race, had collapsed. Inexcusably, we had lost faith in the ability of our own revolutionary masses to overcome all obstacles.[19]

During the Mandela years, when capitalism did not deliver, what was prescribed was more capitalism, in a more spectacular form. As Gilman-Opalsky states, South Africans became swept up in the "mythology about capitalism"

> that disguises its internal logic and denies the macroeconomic reality of the actually existing capitalist world . . . The stability and dynamism of capitalism promises indefinite intergenerational benefits, and a capacity for surviving all crises through innovation . . . The ideological and mythological strength of spectacular capitalism comes, *in the first place*, from the plaintive appeal of people, from mass deference, and the public inscription of authority.[20]

In South Africa, spectacular capitalism would be unleashed in the form of world-class transport systems and gigantic stadiums that would lift us from the dead-ends of the past and the cul-de-sacs of the present into the global mainstream of modern capital.

But, in many ways, there was nothing very new about this at all. After all the talk of Madiba Magic, we were back to the modernization theory of the 1950s and 1960s, back to the time of Rostow's handbook for modernization, his *Stages of Economic Growth: A Non-Communist Manifesto*. In the book, Rostow argued famously that it is possible to identify all societies, in their economic dimensions, as lying within one of five categories: the traditional society, the preconditions for take-off, take off, the drive to maturity, and the age of mass consumption.[21]

Even the ANC, a political party that initially embraced socialism, found itself subtly mouthing the platitudes of this early post-war and arguably colonial discourse. The World Cup would supposedly create the conditions for take-off, bringing in capital investment and an entrepreneurial culture.

The hollowness and ideological dimensions of this discourse were particularly felt in South African "host" cities. The World Cup dramatized graphically how "Urbanism is the mode of appropriation of the natural and human environment by capitalism, which, true to its logical development towards absolute domination, can (and now must) refashion the totality of space into *its own peculiar décor*."[22]

The city of Durban provides a particularly apt illustration. The city began to prepare for the World Cup in earnest. Almost immediately, street vendors came under the cosh, with about 1,200 people evicted from their trading stalls between 2006 and 2007. The mayor of Durban, Obed Mlaba, reflecting on the clean-up, said: "It is happening everywhere. We have cleaned many areas in the city and also the townships. This is a wonderful opportunity for us to clean up areas that have become unsavoury."[23]

The following month was the 2010 Preliminary Draw for the World Cup in the city. Street children were rounded up and given "free lodging and housing" at the overcrowded Westville Prison, thus exposing them to violent attacks, including rape and possible infection with HIV. The youths and some adults with small children were charged with loitering and punished with fines they could not afford to pay, thus facilitating the arrests.[24]

Security for the preliminary/qualifying draw was tight, with the national security departments telling Parliament that a 10-km "cordon" around the stadiums would be backed up with "air sweeps by fighter jets, joint border patrols with neighboring countries, police escorts for cruise ships and teams of security guards with 'diplomat' training" with the intention according to Safety and Security Minister Nathi Mthethwa, to "prevent domestic extremism, strike action and service delivery protests."[25]

But the biggest change to the city landscape was to be the building of a new stadium. One of the reasons for the upgrades and building of new stadiums are requirements set for international events by the organizations that grant countries the rights to hold them, such as the Olympics and FIFA World Cup™. Stadium design is also an important part of the process, with bigger, bolder and more dramatic structures built for each event. These come at a cost:

> "Starchitects" propose ever wilder arenas that everyone knows will come in at double or treble their estimates. They absorb labor, energy, materials, land and effort which are then not available for urban investment elsewhere. The global scale of such evanescent spending over the decades must be staggering.[26]

Even the location of stadiums is set by FIFA. The Cape Town stadium was initially proposed to be built in Athlone, north of the city, in a distinctly working-class district and in a part of the Cape peninsula that did not offer particularly good views of Table Mountain. This did not sit well with those in FIFA, considering the sweeping camera angles they might have used in the run-up to a game. FIFA thus insisted that the venue be in the city-bowl itself, in Greenpoint, within five kilometers of an already existing "world-class" stadium at Newlands.[27] Also, the particular demands imposed by FIFA meant that any possible hope of local economic benefit was kept to a bare minimum, with the exclusion, for example, of retail and food outlets that didn't abide by the association's stringent criteria. In South Africa, this meant that many informal vendors were excluded from the event, not only depriving tourists of possible local flavor, but preventing local entrepreneurs from gaining any financial benefit from the event.

In South Africa, large stadiums are particularly difficult to reconcile with longer-term needs, given that most teams draw paltry support. The national soccer team, appropriately named Bafana Bafana ("boys, boys"), is among the worst on the continent, ranked 80th in the world in November 2008. The official FIFA ranking as of September 2014, lists Bafana Bafana as 67th. Investing in facilities accessible to the poorest South Africans may well have had a greater developmental impact.[28] Trevor Phillips, former director of the South African Premier Soccer League, asked:

> What the hell are we going to do with a 70,000-seater football stadium in Durban once the World Cup is over? Durban has two football teams which attract crowds of only a few thousand. It would have been more sensible to have built smaller stadiums nearer the football-loving heartlands and used the surplus funds to have constructed training facilities in the townships.[29]

Phillips' point has merit. Standard operating costs, excluding renovations and repairs, for Moses Mabhida Stadium are R88.5m a year. Only R9m income is secured per year from rental of "non-bowl" space, such as restaurants, shops and a gym.[30] This leaves R79.5m income to be secured from the use of the stadium itself, just to meet operating costs. To meet this, the stadium must make a profit from ticket sales, in other words after artists or teams take their own cut of gate takings, of over R1.5m per week for every week of the year. As anyone can attest who regularly passes by the great, empty hulk of a building down Durban's Ruth First Freeway, this level of use is nowhere near being attained.

Kate Manzo argues that the idea of investing in the FIFA World Cup™ and the

> notions of "football now, development later" rely on two visible icons of hope, namely *spectacle* (football tournaments and festivals) and *infrastructure* (mainly football stadiums but also public transport to a lesser extent). These are the visual aspects of an outward-oriented development model aiming to boost foreign investment and tourism by attracting media attention, showcasing modernity, and circulating positive images of Africa to the world.[31]

Similarly, Alegi argues:

> Stadiums are seen as architectural expressions of a modern, technologically sophisticated, self-confident, proud African nation eager to score an Eiffel Tower-like branding effect on the world stage . . . World Cup stadiums have ideological implications as well. These arenas help to challenge pervasive negative views and stereotypes about Africa as backward, unchanging, "tribal", and hopeless continent.[32]

The 66,000 jobs created in construction for the 2010 World Cup were mainly temporary, and "in light of the more than R11.7 billion spent on stadiums, these mostly temporary jobs could be viewed as an incredibly expensive job creation programme."[33] One is reminded here of Jules Boykoff's conception of global mega-events as part of "celebration capitalism:"

> celebration capitalism manipulates state actors as partners, pushing us toward economics rooted in so-called public-private partnerships. All too often these partnerships are lopsided: the public pays and the private profits. In a smiley-faced bait and switch, the public takes the risks and private groups scoop up the rewards.[34]

In November 2012, the *Washington Times* confirmed South Africa had spent in excess of US$3 billion renovating the country to get ready for the finals, with US$1.1 billion alone spent on upgrading and building new stadiums around the country. US$1.3 billion was allocated to improving transport links across the country, and just shy of US$400 million was spent improving the ports of entry into the country.[35]

In the building of Moses Mabhida Stadium, one saw the neat coming together of old white capital and new Black Economic Empowerment money.[36] Yet, at the same time, ordinary South Africans were forced to make immediate personal sacrifices. For example, the provincial government of Mpumalanga threatened to reverse a R63 million land claim settlement unless the Matsafeni community surrendered a prime portion of its ancestral land for R1 to build Mpumalanga's flagship R1 billion stadium. In August 2008, the Pretoria High Court ordered that trustees of the Matsafeni Trust be replaced.[37] Jimmy Mohlala, speaker of the Mpumalanga municipality of Mbombela, was murdered in January 2009, allegedly for exposing these tender irregularities.[38]

The mayor was later found to be guilty of ordering the assassination. A report in the *Mail* and *Guardian* under the banner headline: "Pupils burn tyres in protest at World Cup Stadium" stated that over a thousand pupils demonstrated angrily at the stadium site in Nelspruit when the only two schools in the area were earmarked for demolition to make way for a parking lot.[39] Whenever the local community in Mbombela, which has enormous unemployment and no basic services, looks up at the stadium, they are reminded of the fact that "it was not worth spending on them even a fraction of the money spent on that."[40]

So what will happen to the "white elephants" of South Africa's World Cup legacy? In Durban's case, the stadium sits uneasily opposite an existing rugby stadium, which regularly fills its stands over and above any match at the Moses Mabhida. A feasibility study done before the stadium's construction suggested that athletics and rugby be accommodated in order to provide additional income streams and therefore make it self-sustaining. The study wasn't heeded.[41] As any supporter will tell you, staring at empty seats is a disheartening experience.

Icons of hope, icons of despair

On July 17, 2013, at the tribunal of the Competition Commission of South Africa, it was conservatively estimated that some R4.7 billion (US$1 billion) of "unfair profits" were made by construction companies for the 2010 FIFA World Cup and other projects. They were consequently fined a total of R1.5-billion (US$338 million). Seven construction companies that did not agree to the settlement, such as Group 5, Construction ID and Power, Construction now face possible prosecution.[42]

Stadiums talk, and in South Africa they reveal a broader narrative about the modernization project, the need to catch up with the West and the human costs involved: "Politicians seem determined to constantly seek political prestige through tourism ventures aimed at the rest of the world . . . attempting to hide the disenfranchised and dispossessed from view."[43]

The Moses Mabhida Stadium is *connected* to the broader political economy of Durban. The resources that go into its upkeep, millions every month, grab much-needed resources from those who are in dire need. It is *disconnected* in that its location means it is inaccessible to people in the townships. The Durban stadium suffered a R34.6 million loss in 2013 and currently costs R78 million to run.[44] World Cup grant funding, which contributed R15 million to the stadium, has now ended and the deficit stands at R151 million.[45] With rising municipal costs and a lack of tenancy uptake, the outlook is bleak. The eThek-wini municipality has now taken over the operational management of the stadium and recently sunk another R5 million into a new plan to attract popular artists to perform at the stadium.[46] However, at least thirty big events are needed for the stadium to break even.[47]

Durban plays host to three major football teams; Amazulu, Thanda Royal Zulu and Golden Arrows. Their fixtures attract between three to four thousand people.[48] But, the relegation of Golden Arrows Football Club to the first division saw losses of between R800,000 and R1.1 million in 2014, and "there was also the risk of the city losing stadium suite holders – who contribute R6.5m annually to the coffers." In a statement made by the stadium's general manager, Vusi Mazibuko, he said that those suite holders would probably not be renewing their leases.[49]

For over 300 days of the year, the Moses Mabhida Stadium lies empty. When it is used for soccer games, the stadium has few spectators. The spectacle is based on speculative capital. It soon moves on, like the World Cup itself, to hunt in new areas. But, for a South Africa faced with empty stadiums, the game becomes how to fill them.

We all know the fraud of the World Cup. The expected largesse from foreign investment never came, the stadiums lie empty, requiring millions for their upkeep. As British journalist Andrew Jennings put it: "South Africa bent over and let Fifa have their way. Officials and the government have sold South Africa down the river: 'Bye Africa, bye suckers!'"[50] For a while, the bread and circuses work. The case of South Africa demonstrates clearly how, contrary to what Max Weber expected, modernity can coexist with forms of charismatic leadership and magical thinking. In fact, modern state bureaucracies often feed off, use and encourage traditional forms of leadership, identity and mystical thinking to pacify dissatisfied social groups. But it is difficult in the long run to make a case for reliance on mega-events, secured by the Father of the Nation, and purported to somehow enrich all with the dividends of patriotism and act as the driver of sustained economic development.

Moses Mabhida stadium is a living example of how we were duped into believing that the World Cup would turn the country around and fire up the economy. One is reminded of George Steiner's memorable phrase: "maximum impact and instant obsolescence." Once you are on the treadmill, however, it's hard to get off. And so Durban bids for the Commonwealth Games as a springboard for the Olympics.

"A slow sort of country!" said the Queen. "Now, here, you see, it takes all the running you can do, to keep in the same place. If you want to get somewhere else, you must run at least twice as fast as that":[51] Lewis Carroll's Queen of Hearts gives us the metaphor for the impossible treadmill of joining the global economy and using it as a springboard for national development. If you do not get on, you face losing out on the investment that could boost the economy. When you do get on, it is on terms that leave you hostage to the bidding of global capital.

South Africa's mega-event "habit" is now deeply entrenched, to the extent that one might speculate on a kind of addiction rooted in the need to sustain the feel-good "high" of such events to mask the continuing realities of socio-cultural and class cleavages in the post-apartheid era.[52] As Jean-Marie Brohm points out when writing about the Olympic Games:

> Persepolis every four years; circuses and Games for other peoples of the world, oppressed, exploited and enslaved by capital . . . so the Olympics stage the leisure activities of the capitalist world; a spectacle of built-in waste, and planned obsolescence; a physical and mental extravaganza put on by one world getting rich at the expense of another.[53]

Driving past the Moses Mabhida Stadium these days, one cannot but be struck by the salience of Brohm's analysis. Not only does FIFA accumulate capital but their demands mean that massive infrastructure development is geared to capital's needs. Global finance capital in particular thrives in a world of large-scale investment in mega-projects, mega-events, and the legacies of short-term investment, long-term debt, and creative financing associated with them. The model also imposes a worldview in which the West becomes the unit of global measurement.

The World Cup, like the global flows of capital and commodities, has moved on. One is reminded of Manuel Castells' argument that "the flows of power generate the power of flows, whose material reality imposes itself as a natural phenomenon that cannot be controlled or predicted . . . People live in places, power rules through flows."[54]

The World Cup moved on, to Brazil. Stadiums have become a kind of battlefield. Workers die. People march. Slums get bulldozed. FIFA demands, governments meekly comply. Construction companies reap the profits. It has all happened before.

As Dave Zirin writes in his excellent book, *Brazil's Dance with the Devil*:

> When all you have is a hammer, everything looks like a nail. When you are the IOC and FIFA, every country, no matter how unique, is subject to the same sets of expectations. These organizations have proven, particularly in recent years, their relentless intention to hammer any peg, no matter how square, into the round holes they require—which means infrastructure, displacement, security, corporate branding on anything that stands still, and of course billions upon billions of dollars in state spending. This is particularly the case in the post-9/11 period where terrorism fears—both real and imagined—have provided a pretext for security details that resemble occupying armies. Any look at sporting mega-events over the previous ten years confirms this. It is difficult to imagine countries more different than Greece, Canada, South Africa, Russia, China, and the United Kingdom. Yet the demands—and the dangers—are eerily similar.[55]

Conclusion

I began this essay with a quote from David McNally about the monstrous and magical character of capitalism. In conclusion, I want to come back to this reference to magic: "Late capitalism is a conjurer's realm of wild money. So demonically out of control is financial wealth that, like an apparition, it appears able to materialize in monstrous concentrations only to melt away just as quickly."[56]

But still we expect some windfall. Now we are told that the Commonwealth Games and the Olympics will bring untold riches to this neck of the woods in terms reminiscent of Italo Calvino's *The Tribe with its Eye on the Sky*, who see a bewildering range of jet planes, flying saucers and guided missiles. The tribal witch-doctors tell them that this is a sign; their lives of degradation and drudgery will soon be over and the "barren savannah will bring forth millet and maize." That it is hardly worth us racking our brains over new ways of emerging from our present situation; we should trust in the Great Prophecy, rally round its only rightful interpreters, without asking to know more.[57]

Both the agents who buy the coconuts that the villagers pick and the witch-doctors hold that "it is in the power of the shooting stars that our entire destiny lies." But the narrator of the story senses the reality: "that a tribe that relies entirely on the will of shooting stars, whatever fortune they may bring, will always be selling off its coconuts cheap."

Once more, we are asked to believe that this occult capitalism filled with zombies and monsters will arrive in spectacular form to resurrect the economy and give us absolution.

Mandela is dead. Long live the Olympics! Long live!

Notes

1 McNally, *Monsters of the Market*, 114.
2 Alegi, "A Nation," 397.
3 In McKinley, "FIFA and the Sports Accumulation Complex," 24.
4 In Black, "The Symbolic Politics of Sport Mega Events," 268.
5 Lodge, *Politics in South Africa*.
6 Cabrujas in Coronil, *The Magical State*, 1.
7 Lukhele, "Post-prison Nelson Mandela."
8 Klein, *The Shock Doctrine*.
9 Terreblanche, *Lost in Transformation*.
10 Alexander, *An Ordinary Country*.
11 Department of Finance, "GEAR," 2.
12 Lukhele, "Post-prison Nelson Mandela," 293.
13 Motlanthe, State of the Nation address, February 6, 2009.
14 Gilman-Opalsky, *Spectacular Capitalism*, 98.
15 Desai, "Taylorism and Mbekism."
16 In Bolsmann, "Representation in the First African World Cup," 161.
17 Manzo, "Visualizing Modernity," 177.
18 Debord, *The Society of the Spectacle*, 15.
19 Kasrils, "How the ANC's Faustian pact sold out South Africa's poorest."
20 Gilman-Opalsky, *Spectacular Capitalism*, 17–22, original emphasis.
21 Rostow, *The Stages of Economic Growth*, 4.
22 Debord in Gilman-Opalsky, *Spectacular Capitalism*, 76, original emphasis.
23 *Daily News*, "Evicted Former Traders Seek Legal Redress," October 8, 2007, cited in Ngonyama, "The 2010 FIFA World Cup," 173.

24 *Daily News*, "Where are Durban's Street Children?," November 22, 2007, cited in Ngonyama, "The 2010 FIFA World Cup," 174.
25 News 24, May 7, 2010. http://www.news24.com/SouthAfrica/News/Police-unveil-SWC-security-plan-20100507.
26 Jenkins, "The World Cup and Olympics threaten to overwhelm Rio."
27 Alegi, "A Nation to be Reckoned With," 409.
28 Desai andVahed, "World Cup 2010. Africa's Turn or the Turn on Africa?".
29 Rice, "Ready or not."
30 Fourbie and Dardagan, "Moses Mabhida down but not out."
31 Manzo, "Vizualising Modernity," 173, original emphasis.
32 Alegi, "A Nation to be Reckoned With," 414–15.
33 Idasa, "What's Left After the World Cup?", 8.
34 Boykoff, *Celebration Capitalism and the Olympic Games*, 3.
35 In Tighe, "The Tangible Legacy of FIFA and the 2010 World Cup."
36 Bahadur, "Tall Tales: Dissecting the Urban Legend of the Developmental Legacy of Durban's Moses Mabhida Stadium."
37 Ntsaluba, "Stadium Show Must Go On."
38 Eberl, "South Africa: Murder Enters the Field of Play."
39 *Mail and Guardian*, "Student anger at Cup Stadium in Nespruit."
40 Johnson, "Diary," 36.
41 *Anon.*, "Moses Mabhida turning corner?".
42 Cottle et al., "A Lesson for South Africa," 3.
43 Bahadur, "Tall Tales," 273.
44 Anon., "Moses Mabhida Turning Corner?".
45 Fourbie and Dardagan, "Moses Mabhida down but not out."
46 Ibid.
47 *Anon.*, "Moses Mabhida turning corner?"
48 For a fascinating article on football fandom in South Africa, see Fletcher, "You Must Support Chiefs: Pirates Already Have Two White Fans!"
49 Nondumiso, "Durban bankrolls a legend."
50 Evans, "Underbelly of World Football."
51 Carroll, *Through the Looking-Glass*, 152.
52 Black, "The Symbolic Politics of Sport Mega-events," 267.
53 Brohm, *Sport: A Prison of Measured Time*, 120.
54 Castells, *The Informational City*, 349.
55 Zirin, *Brazil's Dance with the Devil*, 147–8.
56 McNally, *Monsters of the Market*, 156.
57 In Bauman, *44 Letters from the Liquid Modern World*, 40.

Bibliography

Alegi, Peter. "A Nation to be Reckoned With: The Politics of World Cup Stadium Construction in Cape Town and Durban, South Africa." *African Studies* 67, no. 3 (2008): 397–422.

Alexander, Neville. An Ordinary Country: Issues in the Transition from Apartheid to Democracy in South Africa. Pietermaritzburg: University of Natal Press, 2002.

Anon. "Moses Mabhida Turning Corner?" *Sunday Tribune*, 21 September, 2014.

Anon. '"Student anger at Cup Stadium in Nelspruit." *Mail & Guardian Online*, September 29, 2008: http://www.mg.co.za/article/2008-09-29-student-anger-at-cup-stadium-in- nelspruit.

Bahadur, Aisha. "Tall tales: Dissecting the Urban Legend of the Developmental Legacy of Durban's Moses Mabhida Stadium." In S*outh Africa's World Cup. A Legacy for Whom?*, edited by Eddie Cottle, 255–80. Pietermaritzburg: University of KwaZulu-Natal Press, 2011.

Bauman, Zygmunt. *44 Letters from the Liquid Modern World*. Cambridge: Polity Press, 2013.

Black, David. "The Symbolic Politics of Sport Mega-Events: 2010 in Comparative Perspective." *Politikon: South African Journal of Political Studies* 34, no. 3 (2007): 261–76.

Bolsmann, Chris. "Representation in the First African World Cup: 'World-class', Pan-Africanism, and Exclusion." *Soccer & Society* 13, no. 2 (2012): 156–72.

Boykoff, Jules. Celebration Capitalism and the Olympic Games. London: Routledge, 2013.

Brohm, Jean-Marie. *Sport: A Prison of Measured Time*. Translated by Ian Fraser. London: Ink Links, 1978.

Carroll, Lewis. *Through the Looking Glass and What Alice Found There*. Hertfordshire: Wordsworth Editions, 1996.

Castells, Manuel. *The Informational City: Information, Technology, Economic Restructuring and the Urban-Regional Process.* London: Blackwell, 1989.

Coronil, Fernando. *The Magical State: Nature, Money and Modernity in Venezuela*. Chicago, IL: University of Chicago Press, 1997.

Cottle, Eddie, Paulo Capela, and André Furlan Meirinho. "A Lesson from South Africa. Are Construction Cartels Dramatically Increasing Brazil 2014 FIFA World Cup Infrastructure Costs?" Briefing Paper, Instituto de Estudos Latino-Americanos, Brazil, 2013.

Debord, Guy. *The Society of the Spectacle.*Translated by Donald Nicholson-Smith. New York: Zone Books, 1995 [1967].

Department of Finance. *Growth, Employment and Redistribution: A Macroeconomic Strategy*. Pretoria: Department of Finance, 1996: http://www.treasury.gov.za/publications/other/gear/chapters.pdf.

Desai, Ashwin. "Taylorism and Mbekism." *Africanus: Journal of Development Studies* 37, no. 2 (2007): 272–87.

———— and Goolam Vahed. "World Cup 2010: Africa's Turn or the Turn on Africa?" *Soccer and Society* 11, no. 1 (2010): 154–67.

Eberl, Nikolaus, "South Africa: Murder Enters the Field of Play." *Business Day*, January 8, 2009: http://allafrica.com/stories/200901080080.html.

Evans, Sally. "The Underbelly of World Football." *Times Live*, May 29, 2010: http://www.timeslive.co.za/opinion/article461110.ece/The-underbelly-of-world-football.

Fletcher, Marc. "You Must Support Chiefs: Pirates Already Have Two White Fans!" In *South Africa and the Global Game: Football, Apartheid and Beyond*, edited by Peter Alegi and Chris Bolsmann, 79–94, London: Routledge, 2010.

Fourie, B. and C. Dardagan. "Moses Mabhida down but not out, says city." *Independent Online News*, February 3, 2014: http://www.iol.co.za/news/south-africa/kwazulu-natal/moses-mabhida-down-but-not-out-says-city-1.1641053#.VYfk0KaKs3g.

Gilman-Olpasky, Richard. *Spectacular Capitalism: Guy Debord & the Practice of Radical Philosophy*. London: Minor Compositions, 2011.

Idasa. "What's left after the World Cup?" Pretoria: *Idasa*, 2010: http://www.idasa.org/media/uploads/outputs/files/epolitics1.pdf.

Jenkins, S. "The World Cup and Olympics threaten to overwhelm Rio – yet there is time to create a sensation out of disaster". *Guardian*, April 23, 2014: http://www.theguardian.com/cities/2014/apr/23/world-cup-olympics-rio-de-janeiro-brazil-sensation-disaster.

Johnson, R.W. "Diary." *London Review of Books* 31, no. 24 (2009): 36–7.

Kasrils, R. "How the ANC's Faustian pact sold out South Africa's poorest." *Guardian*, 24 June 24, 2013: http://www.theguardian.com/commentisfree/2013/jun/24/anc-faustian-pact-mandela-fatal-error.

Klein, Naomi. *The Shock Doctrine: The Rise of Disaster Capitalism*. New York: Picador, 2008.

Lodge, T. *Politics in South Africa: From Mandela to Mbeki*. Cape Town: David Philip/New Africa Books. 2002.

Lukhele, Francis. "Post-prison Nelson Mandela: 'A made-in-America hero'." *Canadian Journal of African Studies* 46, no. 2 (2012): 289–301.

Manzo, Kate. "Visualising Modernity: Development Hopes and the 2010 FIFA World Cup." *Soccer & Society* 13, no. 2 (2012): 173–87.

McKinley, Dale. "FIFA and the Sports Accumulation Complex." In *South Africa's World Cup. A Legacy for Whom?*, edited by Eddie Cottle, 281–312. Pietermaritzburg: University of KwaZulu-Natal Press, 2011.

McNally, David. Monsters of the Market: Zombies, Vampires and Global Capitalism. Leiden: Brill, 2011.

Motlanthe, Kgalema. South Africa's State of the Nation Address, Parliament, Cape Town, February 6, 2009: http://www.polity.org.za/article/south-africas-state-of-the-nation-address-february-6-2009-2009-02-06.

Ngonyama, P. "The 2010 FIFA World Cup: critical voices from below." *Soccer & Society*, 11 (1) (2010): 168–80.

Nondumiso, Mbuyazi. "Durban Bankrolls a Legend." *Mercury*, August 16, 2014: http://www.iol.co.za/news/south-africa/kwazulu-natal/durban-bankrolls-a-legend-1.1736468#.VY2hHVqr8yE.

Ntsaluba, Geina, "Stadium Show Must Go On." *Mail and Guardian*, June 25, 2008.

Rice, X. "Ready or not." *Observer*, June 3, 2007: http://www.theguardian.com/sport/2007/jun/03/newsstory.

Rostow, Walt Whitman. *The Stages of Economic Growth*. Cambridge: Cambridge University Press, 1960.

Schulz Herzenberg, Collette (Ed.), *Player and Referee: Conflicting Interests and the 2010 FIFA World Cup*. Monograph 169. Tshwane: Institute for Security Studies. 2010.

Terreblanche, Sampie. *Lost in Transformation: South Africa's Search for a New Future Since 1986*. Johannesburg: KMM Review Publishing Company, 2012.

Tighe, Sam. 2014. "The tangible legacy of FIFA and the 2014 World Cup: A Network to Nowhere." *Bleacher Report*, February 17, 2014: http://bleacherreport.com/articles/1962867-the-tangible-legacy-of-fifa-and-the-2014-world-cup-a-network-to-nowhere.

Zirin, Dave. *Brazil's Dance with the Devil: The World Cup, the Olympics, and the Fight for Democracy*. Chicago, IL: Haymarket Books, 2014.

Part II
States of exception

6 Mega-events and the city of exception

Theoretical explorations of the Brazilian experience

Carlos Vainer

The hosting of the 2016 Olympic Games by Rio de Janeiro is the outcome of a process during which a new concept of the city and of urban planning has set in. It also expresses the consolidation of a new coalition of local forces, which started to take shape under the auspices of Mayor Cesar Maia.[1] A symbolic moment of this development, if not the one that gave rise to it, was the drafting of the Strategic Plan for the City of Rio de Janeiro in 1993 and 1994:

> On November 22, 1993, Rio de Janeiro City Hall signed an agreement with the Trade Association of Rio de Janeiro (ACRJ) and the Federation of Industries of Rio de Janeiro (FIRJAN) for promoting the Strategic Plan for the City of Rio de Janeiro (PECRJ). On February 4, 1994, 46 companies and business associations founded the PECRJ Maintenance Consortium, securing resources for financing the activities and, particularly, to contract professionals from a Catalan consulting firm, who would act as Executive Directors of the Plan, and other private consultants. On October 31 of that same year, in a solemn ceremony, the City Council was installed—"the highest body of the Strategic Plan for the City of Rio de Janeiro," read the invitation signed by three parties, the Mayor and the Presidents of ACRJ and FIRJAN.[2]

In the following year, the plan was passed in a ceremony in which, after many other authorities, including the presidents of FIRJAN and ACRJ, Jordi Borja, from the Catalan consulting firm TUBSA, Tecnologias Urbanas Barcelona S.A., made his speech in erudite rhetoric interspersed with remarks on the potential of the city and the creative spirit of its people.[3]

This process resulted in the candidacy of the new mayor Luiz Paulo Conde and the city's first bid to host the Olympic Games, which was also advised by the Catalan consultants. The Catalans had already introduced sports mega-events into the agenda of the Strategic Plan for the City of Rio de Janeiro—"Rio Always Rio"—but which could also be called "Rio finally Barcelona": "The sporting tradition of Rio and its natural and human resources allow placing its bid to host the 2004 Olympics, with excellent possibilities. And, following the example of other cities, Rio may take advantage of the games for its transformation."[4]

No wonder, after Rio had been chosen to host the 2016 Olympics and the 2014 FIFA World Cup[5] that the same consultants returned to teach residents how to turn the Wonderful City into a "Barcelona." Rio de Janeiro's chapter of the Brazilian Institute of Architects organized an event with the suggestive name of "Olympics and the City—Rio-Barcelona Connection". In 2010, as 15 years before, the same characters, the same project, the same rhetoric . . . and the same business.[6]

What Rio residents are experiencing today is the result of a slow, complex, but continuous process of formation of a new hegemonic coalition able to propose, and impose on the "city in crisis" a new project and a new destiny. What concepts of the city underlie this process? What is the coalition that now overwhelms a city that went through an undeniable crisis of hegemony, so long deprived of any project—be it among those that dominate, or the ones who are dominated, at the heart of the right and the left? Obviously, the processes shaping the city of Rio de Janeiro cannot be understood only by analyzing local dynamics. In this chapter, I try to find the links and connections that lead to new concepts of the city and new forms of planning—concepts that support and strengthen the new dominant coalition and its city project.

From normative planning to flexibility: the new features of strategic power

To identify the nature and origin of the city and urban planning models that prevail in Rio today, the first step is to understand that the offensive of neoliberal thought has had profound influences on urban policies. It is well known that for a long period of approximately forty years after World War II, modern urban planning expressed concepts and rules reflecting a Keynesian consensus. Concisely, the projection of the Keynesian consensus onto the city can be expressed as follows:

1   The structure of the city inherited from pre-capitalism or early capitalism does not meet the new demands of production and mobility (of goods and people).
2   The rupture with the old city, through radical urban renewal processes, is expected to conjure up a new city; one which modernist planners dreamed of as rational and functional as well as healthy and capable of accommodating the housing and service needs of the working class.
3   State government intervention is essential to ensure both the implementation and evolution of the modern city, because the market tends to produce urban imbalances and, in some cases, even urban crises (housing crisis, particularly housing for the working class, mobility crisis, etc).
4   The state's rational and rationalizing intervention must be based on a view of the whole city (comprehensive) and of its structure and dynamics.
5   Like governmental intervention in the economy, urban intervention and planning may go against some interests of private parties, as well as certain economic and urban dynamics; this intervention is legitimate since it is intended to ensure the predominance of the collective interest—the public interest—which is also, almost always, the general interest of capital.

The most perfect and thorough form of the urban planning model accomplished under the auspices of the Keynesian consensus was expressed in the idea of the "master plan," with its comprehensive approach, its guidelines for growth and densities, zoning, functionalization and rationalization of land use, among other mechanisms of organization, disciplining and regulating the "chaotic movement" of capital in the city. The plan was meant to rid the city of "urban crisis" and "urban chaos," thereby ensuring healthy housing for workers and integrating them into urban life, in the fashion of Fordism, Taylorism and the welfare state, integrating them in a broader way into the post-war capitalist bourgeois society.

The crisis of Taylorism-Fordism and the Social Welfare State in the 1970s challenged this model and also exerted its effects on the city. It is true that the functionalist rationalism of modern planning had already been criticized as early as in the 1960s, most famously by Jane Jacobs.[7] Nevertheless, the crisis of the Keynesian consensus and its gradual replacement with a new neoliberal consensus—the guidelines of which were consolidated in the so-called "Washington Consensus"—would also have profound repercussions on the concepts of the city and the current models of urban planning. The crisis of the Welfare State and the Keynesian patterns of state intervention in the economy also announced the "crisis" of the modern city and modern standards of urban planning. What might be called "urban adjustment"[8] and the reconfiguration of the ways of planning the state's action in the urban space correspond to the structural adjustment and the economic reform of the state as a whole.

While the Washington Consensus, and the International Monetary Fund's (IMF) structural adjustment plans reconfigured national economies in both central and peripheral countries, a readjustment and new urban consensus was called for. Instead of modern and comprehensive planning strongly marked by the state's directive and normative action, expressed in zoning and master plans, a new model promoted the idea of *competitive* planning, intended to be flexible, market-friendly and market-oriented.

Much has already been said and written about this model, whose dominant mode is so-called "strategic planning."[9] My purpose is not to reproduce the findings of this research but to explore the concepts and practices of power that are at the base of this planning model. The reflections intended here about the relationships among strategic planning, mega-events and power in the city are based on the notion that the strategic approach adopted by the current dominant sectors implies, suggests and depends, first and foremost, on a strategy of power. Whenever possible, the recent and ongoing processes in the city of Rio de Janeiro will illustrate my theoretical argument.

The notion of "flexibility" is at the heart of the strategic thinking that dominates the new forms of competitive urban planning:[10]

> The flexibility, globalization and complexity of the new global economy requires the development of strategic planning, capable of introducing a coherent and adaptive methodology in the multiplicity of meanings and signs of the new production and management structure.[11]

"Flexibility" makes direct allusion, without mediation, to the notion of business efficiency and also to the idea of "windows of opportunity." Efficient management for competing cities requires the ability to seize opportunities more quickly than competing urban places. Once more, the Catalans proved to be the most qualified heralds of the *business-city* set of ideas: "The forms of management and contracting must ensure transparency and swiftness and respond to *criteria of economic efficiency and social effectiveness rather than to political or bureaucratic control.*"[12]

What matters most in this rich excerpt is the clear and uncompromising opposition established between economic efficiency and social effectiveness, on the one hand, and bureaucratic and political control, on the other hand. First, one might call attention to the synonymy established between political control and bureaucracy, in an evident reduction and disqualification of politics. Reduced and associated with bureaucracy, politics is impoverished and loses relevance, in a clear effort to "depoliticize" the city. Secondly, the assimilation of *economic efficiency* and *social effectiveness* with *swiftness* appears. The proposition comes from MBA courses and their handbooks, which state that the actual strategic agent, the good manager, is he or she who makes quick decisions, seizing opportunities.

A few years ago, in an attempt to characterize the urbanization that was imposed at the end of the twentieth century, François Ascher coined the rather fitting expression "ad hoc urbanism." It is important to highlight the terms in which this author sought to summarize the canons of modern urbanism, which were being replaced by those of postmodern urbanism:

> Modern urbanism was built upon substantial concepts of the *general interest or common interest*. That means that public decisions, the plans with their obligations and their prohibitions, public achievements, exceptions to the right to use one's property freely (subjection), expropriations and taxes were legitimized by collective interests regarded as more important than individual interests.[13]

In contrast to the certainties that supported concepts and propositions of modern urban planners, Ascher, following the path of many others, proposed that post-modernity—characterized by uncertainty and multiplication/fragmentation of social actors and interests—would erode the foundations of the previously unquestionable "common interest" and, a fortiori, the stand from where speeches were delivered by its alleged spokespersons or, if you prefer, its prophets: the rationalist planners.

Instead of "common interest," a recognition (of the legitimacy) of the multiplicity of interests would have been enthroned. Reason would have to yield to negotiation and the general rule would be substituted with case-by-case agreements. Asher made the case that a "New Urbanism" "privileges negotiation and compromise rather than the application of the majority rule, the contract rather than the law, the ad hoc solution rather than the norm."[14]

Speaking of the first steps of market-oriented planning, under the government of Margaret Thatcher, Ascher also says:

> Actually, the objective was not to abandon public intervention as a whole, but to subordinate it to the demands of private players. Then, the British government promoted the orientation of the urban planning as a means of following up the "spontaneous" urban development, so as to create conditions that would allow the intervention of private players as they wished and to act where the private rationale alone was unable to solve an infrastructure organization problem.[15]

Following up on "spontaneous urban development," i.e., *market* development, required flexibility: the "ad hoc urbanism" that resulted defined the promotion of business opportunities as the tenets of a new city and a new plan.

Under the market's seemingly spontaneous movement, the city must operate as a true company and be conducted as such. Therefore, it is logical to say that the city must be handed over without hesitation and without mediation to those who understand business: capitalist entrepreneurs. After countless events for the dissemination of its guidelines, the World Bank made the new message clear: "The private sector must take over the direction of local economic strategies."[16] From this perspective, the continuity of political or bureaucratic control and planning in city life would erode the city's ability to *seize business opportunities* and, therefore, prove itself to be economically efficient, socially effective and, above all, competitive. The company-city must be planned just as a company is. Strategic planning is required because it has proved to be the almost universal method of business planning.[17]

What are the consequences of the ideological/conceptual and methodological/implementation of the corporate/entrepreneurial city? As we argue below, it represents "In all respects, a radical negation of the city as a political space—as a polis. After all, as Marx said, on the threshold of the hidden abode of production is written 'No admittance except on business.'"[18]

In capitalist enterprise, there is neither time nor conditions for the workers to reflect on values, to discuss philosophy or to compare utopias. Here, pragmatism, realism and practicality reign. Productivity is the only law and profit is the only end and the only moral value. The corporate city, in line with its paradigm, expresses this banishment of politics.

From ad hoc urbanism to the exception as a rule: the city of exception

What Ascher called "ad hoc urbanism," with its emphasis on markets and *flexibility*, others have called "urban entrepreneurialism."[19] In such analyses, it is suggested that the "city-as-corporation," has become a continuous and systematic process of disqualification of politics. The Catalan consultants' criticism of "political and bureaucratic control" in Rio goes even further, proposing that political parties should not participate in municipal elections: "The citizen confrontation does not correspond to that between the national parties. Ideally, political parties should refrain from running in municipal elections."[20]

The assumption is that there would not be political and ideological divergences in the city, but only "local affairs," to which the townspeople would relate, because, after all, everyone in the city would be equals and equally interested in affirming the competitiveness of their city. The city would have no room for either ideologies or politics, only for interests. In fact, there would be only one true and legitimate interest: urban productivity and competitiveness, essential conditions for growth.

The charismatic, individualized leader, who is traditionally seen as a diversion or a threat to modern forms of democracy, appears in this strategic discourse rather as the most virtuous embodiment of the new managerial power and, more importantly, an essential requirement of the success of the corporate city. For Castells and Borja, "strong personality and dynamism" come to explain what they consider success stories: "Lisbon, with Sampaio, and Barcelona, with the emblematic figure of Maragall, are good examples" that "it is hard to find a positive response when there is no individualized leadership and, in many cases, the mayors are a crucial figure."[21]

The de-politicization, centralization and charismatic individualization of power are somehow a consequence and a condition of the corporate city, since they create the environment that promotes the flexibility on which good businesses depend.

In view of the challenge posed by a supposed market of cities, which has become increasingly competitive, the now market-friendly and market-oriented state must be freed of rigid rules to be able to take advantage of the windows of opportunity, to meet the demand of different segments of the urban capital. A new rule imposes itself in answer to the regulatory standards: the case-by-case ad hoc, flexible negotiation in the pursuit of flexible accumulation. Instead of the master plan, the master project; instead of the comprehensive plan, we increasingly experience pinpointed acupuncture-like urbanism.[22] The exception becomes the rule.

We have thus arrived at the *city of exception*, of measures that are always exceptional, which can be found "in the paradoxical situation of legal measures that cannot be understood in the plane of the law."[23] In Giorgio Agamben's work, we find the solid and rich reflection on the state of exception which, on establishing the exception as the rule, presents itself as "the legal form of that which cannot have a legal form . . . this no man's land, between public right and the political fact, and between legal order and life".[24] However, Agamben's research and reflection go even further when they point not only to the fact that the state of exception is the transformation of the exception into a rule, but also to the transformation of the state of exception itself into the rule of the contemporary state.

Throughout the twentieth century, the state of exception—or emergency—began to be declared in situations considered similar to a war, as in the case of economic and political crises. However, this extension could not be made without using the military metaphor and without proclaiming that economy was analogous to war.[25] This "permanent state of emergency," even if undeclared, lays the foundations for and authorizes the continued use of exceptional measures, transforming what was once "a temporary and exceptional measure into a government technique."[26]

The discussion about the state of exception is not limited only to the field of the philosophy, doctrine and history of law. For over 150 years, it has been the object of the Marxist debate about the nature and forms of the capitalist state. The classical terms to express different political systems of this type have been Caesarism, Bonapartism, Bismarckism and, in Latin America, also Caudillism. In classic Marxist analyses, from Marx to Poulantzas, all these forms of strongly individualized power, which would be joined by fascism and the military dictatorships that were typical of Latin America, would form what Poulantzas called the "state of exception."[27]

By this, Poulantzas meant the general crisis of hegemony that he believed would vary according to different approaches and historical processes. In Marxist approaches, among some nuances, there is a consensus that the state of exception is characterized as a type of regime in which the ruling classes cannot directly take over the reins of power and in a certain way choose a "Bonaparte" or a specific group—for example, the military—to run the state. In Marx's analysis of French Bonapartism, this occurs when there is a relative balance of power between the dominant and the dominated classes, or according to Poulantzas, because an inability to resolve, under the democratic republic, the contradictions between different dominant fractions.[28] In any case, a crisis of hegemony is at the origin of the exception state. Now, these rapid theoretical explorations allow us to resume the discussion about the characterization of the city of exception, understood as a new system of urban government.

Mega-events and the city: from flexible urbanism to the city of exception in Rio de Janeiro

While it is not possible to transpose the theoretical analyses briefly presented in the previous section to an examination of the exercise of power and the state's organization at the city level, it is possible to extract some interesting clues that would allow working with the hypothesis that postmodern, competitive and strategic planning on an increasingly global stage signals the emergence of what we called here as competition between *cities of exception*.

Let us focus, initially, on the crisis issue, both in Agamben's work and Marxism, which provides the (actual or fictitious) origin of the state of exception. The examination of the discursive construction of the advocates of strategic planning highlights the strategic role of the crisis. Indeed, the Catalan theoreticians see the existence of the crisis, or rather, the feeling that there is an urban crisis, as a requirement for the proposed model to be feasible and successful. Without the crisis, they affirm that it is impossible to unify the urban nation around a charismatic leader to whom all the urban classes would somehow delegate the power, so as to lead the city, in an agile and flexible way, to win over the competition with other cities.

This requirement is formulated as "a widespread sense of crisis of growth or loss of opportunities that would allow overcoming the confrontations between players related to the conflicts of everyday life."[29]

It is necessary to circumvent and overcome internal conflicts, as in the typical example of Bonapartism, and this movement is accomplished through a systematic disqualification of political parties, the reverse side of the charismatic leader's affirmation. The leader calls for civic union for overcoming the urban crisis, which is the economic and political crisis, and it is this urban crisis that establishes a new form of constitution, legitimization and exercise of power in/of the city as an urgent need.

The autonomy granted to the leader, like in all states of exception, is neither arbitrary nor unlimited, because it is exercised within the framework of the statement of the ruling classes' general interests, even if and when they are contrary to private interests of some of their class factions. The reconfiguration of hegemony finds in the relative autonomy of power the path, so to speak, to suspend political parties and the political dispute and the means to overcome resistance, wherever it may come from—from the dominated factions or from those dominant factions whose particular interests may have been affected.

In this way, the city of exception is established as a new form of urban regime. Notwithstanding the (formal) operation of the mechanisms and institutions that are typical of the representative democratic republic, the formal institutional apparatuses progressively relinquish a portion of their duties and powers. The law can now be ignored (suspended) and a growing portion of the state's public functions is transferred to agencies that are "free from bureaucracy and political control." Through centralization of decisions, personalization of power, charismatic leadership, ad hoc and flexible regulations, in the name of the crisis and wrapped up in the metaphor of war—to paraphrase Engels—the city of exception plays to the dreams of the urban bourgeoisie.[30]

In the case of Rio de Janeiro, which inspired this chapter, the forms of illegality and exception appear everywhere and multiply due to two new *emergencies*: the 2014 FIFA World Cup and the 2016 Olympics. Thus, for example, although the Statute of the City determines that all cities had to have a new Master Plan by July 2008, this happened only in December 2010. The City Hall and the City Council have partnered to produce new and generous (along with the big capitalistic investments) legislation of urban and tax favors and exemptions, turning the exception into the rule.[31] FIFA and the IOC have almost taken the power to regulate the forms for occupation of urban space, which occurs, for example, through the following means: entitlement to exclusive use of public sports facilities, the right to control trade and economic activities in urban areas of interest for megaevents, and the control of the advertising space of the city.

The Olympic Act (Law 12.035, 2009), approved by the Congress, transfers to private institutions the attributes of consulates, since it establishes that the Olympic ID card, delivered by IOC, will substitute for the visa delivered by consulates. Some critics have considered this exception a kind of national sovereignty resignation.[32] Despite the existence of legislation regulating the property rights on marks and symbols, this same law assures exceptional protection against profit or nonprofit uses of all "symbols related to the Games 2016"; that is, all labels and expressions such as "Olympic Games," "Paralympic Games," "Rio Olympics," "Rio 2016" and "any other variations or abbreviations, and those related or created in the future with the same goal, in any language, including those on internet web sites."[33] There is a popular joke that Rio's municipality and citizens will have to pay to use the name of the city in any kind of conversation or document.

To the amazement of jurists, the Brazilian state openly promotes the production of an extensive legal apparatus in clear violation of the existing constitution and legislation in force. As an example, the World Cup General Law (Law 12.633, 2012) authorizes an exception for the selling and consumption of alcoholic beverages in stadiums, which is forbidden by earlier Brazilian legislation (the Fan Statute).[34] Beyond this, there is a long chapter of fiscal exceptions: for example, exemptions of import taxes and of municipal services taxes in all cities hosting World Cup games. In Rio de Janeiro, international and national hotel chains will benefit from the exemption of territorial taxes till 2020. The FIFA and IOC "families" are also exempt from charges to get work permits approved. Federal law also creates a Special Tax System for building and reforming stadiums, exempting the contractors and FIFA from different obligations, including import taxes, and income taxes from all its personnel (Law 12.350, 2010, and others). According to the Brazilian Federal Income Tax Agency (*Receita Federal*), from 2011 to 2015, the amount of FIFA's fiscal exemptions will amount to US$230 million.

The commitment of public authorities and public resources to Brazil's mega-projects is unlimited. Another new law allows local and state governments to overcome the legal limit of debt to expenses related to public works and stadiums related to the game. At the same time, while public bids and contracts by the Federal Government must respect a general law (Law 8.666, 1963), a new law establishes special conditions to select and contract public works related to FIFA World Cup 2014 and the Olympic Games 2016.

FIFA and the IOC also have exclusive commercial rights in stadiums and their vicinity, as well in other urban areas they will designate. In Rio de Janeiro, a decree by the mayor (Decree 30.379, 2009) forbids any street commercial activity in areas of interest of the Olympic Games. Informal workers associations fear that the Beijing and South Africa's sad (best?) practices in banning street vendors will be reproduced, in a war against informal workers in general. This same decree commits the local government to clear all the municipal assets, even when occupied by third persons, and transfer them to the IOC when necessary. Besides an absurd transfer of public assets to a private organization, this rule violates the federal, state and municipal laws that assure priority uses of public land and buildings that must be for social housing.

In addition, human right activists and organizations are concerned with threats to civil and political rights. Despite the constitutional rule that public order and public security are a state responsibility, a federal decree creates an Extraordinary

Secretary for Security of Great Events, which are the Rio+20 Conference, the FIFA Confederations Cup 2013, the FIFA World Cup 2014 "and other events designated by the President of Republic" (Decree 7.538, 2011).

Taking recent strikes in stadium construction sites in many cities as a pretext, and probably learning from the South African experience, the Federal Senate has discussed a bill (PL 728/2011) with restrictions to the constitutional right to strike. Other threats to political rights come from the Rio de Janeiro mayor's decree, which Article 9 interdicts from July 29 to September 25, any mass gathering of more than 5,000 people. Moreover, there will "not be allowed events that could bring any inconvenience to the planning, operation, logistic, services or security of the 2016 Rio Games" (Decree 30379, 2009).

If the exception was progressively established as market-oriented flexibility, principles and concepts of the (competitive) strategic planning were adopted, it is not possible to ignore that the city of the mega-event transparently reveals, due to its extreme uniqueness, the true nature and meaning of neoliberal urban governance. In the Brazilian case, *all* cities hosting FIFA's World Cup, even though ruled by different political parties, adopted exactly the same perspective and acted in the same way. President Lula supported both proposals to host FIFA's World Cup and Olympic Games 2016. His government accepted all the claims by FIFA and IOC and committed to fulfill all their demands. Also, the federal Banco Nacional para o Desenvolvimento Econômico e Social (BNDES—the National Bank for Social and Economic Developpement) finances almost all investments related to sporting mega-events. Even if the IOC and FIFA, as well their local organizing committees, are private institutions, public funds are the main source of investments. As an aside, close connections between successive governments and large corporations engaged in public works are well known in Brazil, and some Brazilian transnational corporations are the main funders of electoral campaigns—including PT (Worker's Party) candidates, who are among the privileged beneficiaries of this suspected money.

Conclusion: the city of exception is the direct democracy of capital, but also of resistance

There is no doubt that the institutional forms of bourgeois representative democracy continue to operate, formally in Brazil and in Rio de Janeiro. The elected government governs; the municipal legislature legislates. However, in the current global conjuncture the *way* that they govern and legislate produces and reproduces situations and practices of exception, in which powers are transferred to groups that have corporate interests.

In this way, the state's autonomy excessively transforms and centralizes power. The banishment of politics from the increasingly corporate city turns civic power, including conceptions of what is in the "public" or "general" interest, into a tool that serves the private interests of different interest groups. As Ascher suggests, this is no longer a form of government in which the "general interest" gives way to new forms of negotiation.[35] Nor is it only about governing in favor of certain interest groups, the dominant groups. This is a new way in which relations between the state and private interests are completely reframed and instate new forms of hegemonic exercise. In this context, the *invisibility* of the decision processes becomes the rule, due to the disqualification of politics and the real decomposition of the "normal" forms of interest group representation. It is not possible to know who makes the decisions, and where, how and when the decisions are made—it is certain that it is not in formal venues where such decisions should be made in a democratic rule of law. So-called "public-private partnerships" and "urban operations" are a perfect example of this "expansion of power networks and crisscrossing parallel conveyor belts that link different branches and centers" away from the parties and the formal government, to which Jessop refers to describe the state of exception.[36]

These power networks and parallel conveyor belts provide the perfect foundations for public-private partnerships; in this way, *the city of exception is established as a direct democracy of capital.* This is what separates the contemporary form of the city of exception from Poulantzas' earlier theoretical-historical concept. For Poulantzas, the state of exception establishes and even takes the autonomous character of the capitalist state to its limit—vis-à-vis those of the social classes, even the ruling classes. The city of exception, on the contrary, despite the neoliberal rhetoric, reveals, in an almost transparent and immediate way, the equipping of the urban government by coalitions of economic interests that make the city, without mediation, the place where the power of capital and the capital of power interpenetrate and identify each other.

Of course resistance in the twelve cities that hosted FIFA's World Cup games—including Rio de Janeiro that also will host the 2016 Olympics—saw the creation of the World Cup People Committees of these cities united in a National Network of People Committees.[37] These organizations challenged politically and legally the exceptional measures implemented for these events as well as broader violations and threats to human rights. One result of this was an important publication of more than 70 pages which reported human rights violations, related to rights to housing, labor, information, democratic participation, environment, mobility and public security.[38]

In many neighborhoods and favelas facing forced evictions, people resisted. For example, in the Vila Autodromo in Rio de Janeiro, the local neighborhood association, with the technical support of students, experts and researchers from two public universities, prepared an alternative plan to eviction and presented it to the Mayor.[39] The struggle by the Vila Autodromo community gained interest from the international media in the large march organized by the People Summit during the Rio +2 Conference to denounce the evictions and support their resistance.

During the so-called "June and July Journeys," 2013, about 10 million people demonstrated in 500 Brazilian cities! The wave of protests began in some state capitals against increases in ticket prices for public buses. The violent action of police forces against the movement for free public transportation (Movimento Passe Livre) contributed to new and more massive rallies. On the eve of the FIFA

Confederations Cup, preparatory to the World Cup 2014, the government and FIFA would have liked to show a pacific people happy with sporting mega-events. Instead, the world witnessed police violence and huge demonstrations, with more than a million people in Rio de Janeiro protesting against the absurd expenditures for white elephant stadiums. "FIFA Go Home." "We do not want the World Cup," "Public Budget to Health and Education, not to Stadiums," "No more forced evictions," "Halt the corruption"—the message was clear.

In her address to the country on the Brazilian national television channel, in June 21, President Dilma Roussef recognized the legitimacy of the protests:

> Those who were in the streets yesterday gave a direct message to society and, moreover, to those who are in government at different scales. This message claims for more citizenship, for better schools, for better hospitals . . . for the right to participation. The direct message coming from the streets shows the claim for good public transportation at fair prices. The direct message coming up from the streets asks for the right to influence the decisions of governments, parliaments and judicial systems . . . Citizens instead of the economic vested interests must be heard first.

Even if this humble self-criticism had no consequences in government policies and decisions in the following months, there is no doubt that in 2013, the city was the issue.[40] Mega-events, public-private partnership, the neoliberal entrepreneurial city and the authoritarianism of the city of exception were judged . . . and condemned.

Notes

1 The reign of Cesar Maia spanned more than 15 years, as he took office as a mayor for the first time in January 1993. Elected through the PMDB party (a centrist party), he joined the PFL party (right-wing party) in 1995. He held the office of mayor three times (1993–96, 2001–04 and 2005–08). Luiz Paulo Conde (1997–2000) and Eduardo Paes (who took office in 2009) emerged in local politics under the tutelage of Cesar Maia, keeping essentially the same guidelines, practices and rhetoric.
2 Vainer, "Os liberais também fazem planejamento urbano?", 106.
3 Ibid.
4 Prefeitura da Cidade do Rio de Janeiro, *Plano estratégico da Cidade do Rio de Janeiro*, 52.
5 The 2014 FIFA World Cup matches took place in twelve Brazilian cities, including Rio de Janeiro (see Gaffney's discussion, this volume).
6 In March 2010, on the eve of the World Urban Forum, the event was promoted by the IAB-RJ, chaired by Sergio Magalhaes, who occupied a prominent position in the municipal administrations of Cesar Maria and Luiz Paulo Conde. The Sports Minister, the Governor of the State of Rio de Janeiro, Mayor Eduardo Paes, former Mayor Luis Paulo Conde and several international consultants participated, among others in the World Urban Forum. On the Catalan side, there were Pasqual Maragall, former mayor of Barcelona, now also hired as a consultant by Rio de Janeiro City Administration, and renowned Jordi Borja. It is worth mentioning that the event was supported by

the Official Spanish Chamber of Commerce, the Spanish Embassy, Telefônica, Gás Natural, Agbar Group (Catalan business, specialized in urban services, particularly water and sanitation), Abengoa (Seville Group specialized in energy, transport and telecommunications), Banco Santander, the consulting firm PricewaterhouseCoopers, ACC1Ó (Acción para la Inovación e Internacionalización de la Empresa Catalã, the agency set up by the Catalan Government for the internationalization of Catalan companies) and CB-CN (Catalan-Brazilian-Business Club).

7   Jacobs, *Death and Life of Great American Cities*.

8   Arantes, "O ajuste urbano: as políticas do Banco Mundial."

9   In this respect, see, among others, the works produced within ETTERN/IPPUR/UFRJ (State, Labor, Land and Nature Laboratory, of the Institute for Research and Urban and Regional Planning of the Federal University of Rio de Janeiro), especially: Vainer, "Os liberais também fazem planejamento urbano," and "Pátria, empresa e mercadoria," as well as Sánchez, "Cidade Espetáculo: Política," and *A reinvenção das cidade*; Oliveira, *Competitividade e pragmatismo no Rio de janeiro*, and Bienenstein, *Espaços Metropolitanos em Tempos de Globalização*.

10   What we have today in the field of urban planning is the domination of a set of methodologies that can be called competitive planning, which are identical in their assumptions and general conceptions, but differ in small details that actually have to do more with the need for product differentiation in the market for consulting firms than with background conceptual or methodological differences. Examples include Barcelona-style strategic planning; strategic planning of marketing; and situational strategic planning, among others. See, for example, Kotler, Haider and Rein, *Marketing público*; Ashworth and Voogd, *Selling the city*; Bouinot and Bermils, La gestion stratégique des villes; Castells, "The world has changed"; Borja and Castells, *Local y Global*; Castells and Borja, "As cidades como atores políticos"; Foxà, "Barcelona: estratégias"; Porter, "The competitive advantage of the inner city," and Matus, *Estrategia y plan*.

11   Castells, "The world has changed," 14.

12   Castells and Borja, "As cidades como atores politicos," 159, emphasis added.

13   Ascher, *Les nouveaux principes de l'urbanisme*, 83, emphasis added.

14   Ibid, 84.

15   Ibid., 86.

16   World Bank, "Urban Partnership."

17   Although it is almost a universal model, it is important to highlight that even in the field of corporate planning and in business schools, there are many controversies about the effectiveness and even viability of strategic planning. See, for example, Mintzberg, *The Rise and the Fall of Strategic Planning*.

18   Vainer, *Pátria, empresa e mercadoria*, 91.

19   Harvey, "Do gerenciamento ao empresariamento," 96.

20   Borja, *Barcelona*, 26.

21   Another important element of the Catalan recipe is the centralization of power, which is inseparable from charismatic and personalized power and from the depoliticization of the city administration. This explains why, in the context of European parliamentary systems, some advocate the replacement of the municipal parliamentary system with a municipal presidential system, as a way to weaken the political parties and the political control of such parties.

22   Ascher, *Les nouveaux principes de l'urbanisme*.

23   Agamben, *Estado de exceção*, 12.

24   Ibid.

25 Ibid., 13. On this point, Agemben cites a speech made by Roosevelt at the peak of the crisis in the 1930s: "I assume unhesitatingly the leadership of this great army of our people to command with discipline the attack upon our common problems . . . If Congress cannot adopt the necessary measures and if it is necessary to extend the national emergency, I shall not refrain from fulfilling the clear requirement of the duties incumbent upon me. I will ask the Congress for the only tool that I have left to deal with the crisis: broad executive powers to wage war against the emergency, powers as broad as those that I would be vested with if we had been invaded by a foreign enemy" (Roosevelt, 1938; quoted in Agamben, *Estado de exceção*, 37.

26 Agamben, *Estado de exceção*, 13.

27 Poulantzas, *Fascisme et dictature*; *Estado em crise*, and *Poder político e classes sociais*.

28 See Marx, "Lutta de classes" and "O Dezoito Brumário de Luís Bonaparte," and Poulantzas, *Poder et Politico*.

29 Borja and Castells, *Local y global*, 166. In this sense, the "success" of Barcelona's strategic planning is explained by the crisis—or sensation of crisis: "Several factors were responsible for the swiftness of the changes, such as: acute awareness of the urban crisis, which was shared by the major public and private players." See Borja, *Barcelona*, 8.

30 Engels considered Bonapartism as the "true religion of the bourgeoisie, because, like the other types of exception state (fascism, military dictatorship), it would increase the visibility of the common and universal trait, the 'theoretical trait that makes up the very capitalist type of state,' namely: the state's relative autonomy," Poulantzas, *Poder político e classes sociais*, 254.

31 It is worth noting that similar processes of urban and tax exception laws existed in several cities that hosted World Cup events in 2014. In this sense, Rio de Janeiro was a symbol and the most advanced city on the path to becoming a city of exception.

32 The federal World Cup General Law (Law 12.663, 2012) assures that all persons nominated by FIFA and those who bought a ticket to any World Cup game to automatically have a visa.

33 The same kind of rules are present in the World Cup General Law.

34 It is well known that this exception meets the requirements of FIFA, which has among its sponsors a large corporation from the beer-producing sector.

35 Ascher, *Les nouveaux principes de l'urbanisme*.

36 Jessop, "O Estado, o poder," 137.

37 *www.portalpopulardacopa.org.br/.*

38 Articulação Nacional dos Comitês Populares, *Mega-eventos e violações de direitos humanos no Brasil, 2012.*

39 Plano Popular da Vila Autódromo, *Plano de desenvolvimento.*

40 Vainer, "Quando a cidade vai às ruas," and Maricato, "É a Questão Urbana, Estúpido!".

Bibliography

Agamben, G. *Estado de exceção*. São Paulo: Boitempo, 2004.

Arantes, Pedro Fiori. "O ajuste urbano: as políticas do Banco Mundial e do BID para as cidades latino-americanas." Dissertação de mestrado, FAU-USP. São Paulo, 2004.

Articulação Nacional dos Comitês Populares da Copa. *Mega-eventos e violações de direitos humanos no Brasil*, 2012, 2ª edição: http://www.portalpopulardacopa.org.

br/index.php?option=com_k2&view=item&id=198:dossi%C3%AA-nacional-de-viola%C3%A7%C3%B5es-de-direitos-humanos.

Ascher, François. *Les nouveaux principes de l'urbanisme. La fin des villes n'est pasà l'ordre du jour*, Éditions de l'Aube, 2001.

Asworth, G.J. and Voogd, H. *Selling the city: marketing approaches in public sector urban planning*. London and New York: Belhaven Press, 1990.

Bienenstein, Glauco. *Espaços Metropolitanos em Tempos de Globalização: Um Estudo de Caso do Rio de Janeiro*. Rio de Janeiro, IPPUR/UFRJ, 2003.

Borja, Jordi (ed.). *Barcelona. Un modelo de transformación urbana*. Quito, Programa de Gestión Urbana/Oficina Regional para América Latina y Caribe, 1995.

——— and Castells, Manuel. *Local y Global. La gestión de la ciudades en la era de la información*. Madrid: Taurus, 1997.

Bouinot, Jean and Bermils, Bernard. *La gestion stratégique des villes. Entre compétition et coopération*. Paris, Armand Collin, 1995.

Castells, Manuel. "The world has changed: can planning change?". Austin, mimeo (Working Paper 030, City and Regional Planning, University of California at Berkeley), 1990.

———, and Borja, J. "As cidades como atores políticos." In *Novos Estudos CEBRAP*, n. 45, julho/1996: 152–66.

Foxà, Manuel de Forn i. "Barcelona: estrategias de transformación urbana y económica." S.l., mimeo, 1993.

Harvey, David. "Do gerenciamento ao empresariamento: a transformação da administração urbana no capitalismo tardio." *Espaço & Debates*, XVI, n. 39, 1996: 48–64.

Jacobs, Jane. *The Death and Life of Great American Cities*. New York: Vintage Books, 1961.

Jessop, Bob. "O Estado, o poder, o socialismo de Poulantzas como um clássico moderno." *Rev. Sociol. Polit.* [online], 17, n. 33, 2009: 131–44.

Kotler, P., Haider, D.H. and Rein, I. *Marketing público*. São Paulo: Makron Books, 1994.

Maricato, Erminia. "É a Questão Urbana, Estúpido!". In *Cidades Rebeldes: Passe livre e as manifestações que tomaram as ruas do Brasil*. São Paulo: Boitempo, 2013.

Marx, Karl. "Lutta de classes na França de 1848 a 1850." In Marx, Karl and Engels, Friedrich. *Textos*. São Paulo: Edições Sociais, 1977, vol. 3: 93–198.

———. "O Dezoito Brumário de Luís Bonaparte." In Marx, Karl and Engels, Friedrich. *Textos*. São Paulo: Edições Sociais, 1977, vol. 3: 199–285.

Mintzberg, Henri. *The Rise and the Fall of Strategic Planning*. Toronto: The Free Press, 1994.

Oliveira, Fabricio. *Competitividade e pragmatismo no Rio de janeiro: a difusão de novas práticas de planejamento e gestão das cidades na virada do século*. Rio de Janeiro: IPPUR/UFRJ, 2003.

Plano Popular da Vila Autódromo. *Plano de desenvolvimento econômico, sociale cultural, 2012*: http://www.portalpopulardacopa.org.br/vivaavila/index.php/ joomla-forums.

Porter, Michael E. "The competitive advantage of the inner city." *Harvard Business Review*, n. 3, May–June, 1995: 55–71.

Poulantzas, Nicos. *Estado em crise*. Rio de Janeiro, Graal, 1977.

———. *Fascisme et dictature: la IIIᵉ Internationale face au fascisme*. Paris, François Maspero, 1970.

———. *Poder político e classes sociais*. São Paulo: Martins Fontes, 1986.

Prefeitura da Cidade do Rio de Janeiro. *Plano estratégico da Cidade do Rio de Janeiro: Rio sempre Rio*. Rio de Janeiro, 1966.

Sanchez, Fernanda. *Cidade Espetáculo: Política, Planejamento e City Marketing*. Curitiba: Editora Palavra, 1997.

Vainer, Carlos. "Os liberais também fazem planejamento urbano: glosas ao "Plano Estratégico da Cidade do Rio de Janeiro." In Arantes, O., Maricato, E., and Vainer, C.B. *A Cidade do Pensamento Único. Desmanchando Consensos*. Petrópolis: Vozes, 5ª edição, 2009 [2000], pp. 105–19.

———. "Pátria, empresa e mercadoria: a estratégia discursiva do Planejamento Estratégico Urbano." In Arantes, O., Maricato, E., and Vainer, C.B. (eds.), *A Cidade do Pensamento Único. Desmanchando Consensos*. Petrópolis: Vozes, 5ª edição, 2009, pp. 75–103.

———. "Quando a cidade vai às ruas." In *Cidades Rebeldes: Passe livre e as manifestações que tomaram as ruas do Brasil*. São Paulo: Boitempo, 2013.

World Bank, "Urban partnership & the TWU Urban Division – 1998. The urban dialogues. Learning events summary notes." S.l., 1998.

7 Mega-events, urban image construction, and the politics of exclusion

Anne-Marie Broudehoux

In a context of global inter-urban competition, where the image of the city plays a crucial role in attracting investors, tourists, and taxpayers, holding mega-events has become a key instrument of city marketing. With their vast media coverage and strong branding power, world-class events, especially sporting mega-events such as the Olympics and the FIFA World Cup, are perceived as an unparalleled source of recognition and prestige for host cities, allowing them to make their mark on the world stage and to advertise their best assets. Once selected, future host cities go to great lengths to manipulate urban reality, using diverse imaging technique to project a flawless, idealized, postcard-perfect image that is visually appealing, but which can also be highly exclusive.

Mega-events are thus deeply entrenched in the politics of urban image construction. Not only do such events play a role in the spectacularization of the urban landscape, they also impose a particular worldview upon society, shaped by the interests, desires, and aspirations of local economic and political elites, international sporting federations and their global sponsors. Hosting mega-events exerts great pressure upon host cities to transform their urban environment to fit global expectations of modernity. Cities invest in spectacular urban projects that will attest to their economic performance, organizational efficiency, and cultural sophistication, while aspects of urban reality that suggest backwardness or decline are left out or often hidden, because they may tarnish the city's carefully constructed image.

This chapter investigates some of the concrete impacts of mega-events with specific reference to the policies that seek to exclude specific members of society from urban image construction. More specifically, the chapter examines mechanisms put in place by host cities to tackle the problem posed by the visibility of poverty, informality, and marginality in the urban landscape. It details diverse strategies devised by local authorities and event organizers to exclude, hide, beautify, and discipline the poor and their material manifestations. The chapter also investigates how population groups have mobilized against such exclusionary policies and it examines multiple forms of resistance that have emerged in reaction and investigates how they can stimulate the emergence of creative forms of resistance, incite social mobilization, and prompt the radicalization of hitherto apolitical population groups.

Observations made in this chapter result from nearly twenty years of research on the process of urban image construction in cities of the East and global South and more specifically from a long-term empirical study of two major BRICS cities: Beijing, host of the 2008 Summer Olympics, and Rio de Janeiro, host of the 2014 FIFA World Cup and 2016 Olympic Games. In both cities, spectacular urban events were driven by an image imperative, pursued as a way to improve their country's position on the global geopolitical stage, to further their integration into the league of "advanced" nations, and to strengthen their stature as rising economic powers. The following discussion is also based on a close study of other sporting mega-events located in BRICS countries, such as the 2010 Commonwealth Games in New Delhi and the 2010 South Africa World Cup.

Urban image construction as an exclusionary practice

In recent decades, the image of the city has taken center stage in urban public policy, as the economic survival of cities increasingly depends on their capacity to attract capital, high-paying visitors and wealthy residents.[1] In this context, visual control of the city's image has gained a strategic importance for policy makers who seek to enhance the attractiveness of their locality and increasingly base their decisions on aesthetic considerations.[2] Demands for a *competitive* urban image have turned urban redevelopment into a normative process, as civic leaders attempt to determine, control, and regulate their city's identity, often submitting it to what amounts to a dictatorship of the visual.

Urban image construction generally consists in the creative repackaging of local reality in order to create a unique and appealing urban image that can be put on display.[3] The urban spaces that are generated in the process consistently connote security, order, and economic success.[4] They must appear to be at once vibrant, exciting and reassuringly safe, while providing a complete package of assets linked to status, quality of life, and business opportunities. Based on an elitist conceptualization of what is deemed desirable, respectable or attractive, the resulting image embodies the desires and aspirations of those who have the power to shape the urban environment, and becomes the material concretization of their cultural imaginings and visual fantasies.[5]

For Rosalyn Deutsche, the construction of a unified, coherent, and cohesive urban image is a highly exclusive process that can only be achieved by expelling differences and conflicts within.[6] It entails the reduction of a rich, complex, heterogeneous urban reality into a simplified, homogenous whole. Similarly, Patsy Healy argues that urban image construction amounts to the creative projection of a fictional yet totalizing image of society, which undermines more plural, multidimensional, and progressive visions.[7] The process of urban image construction is thus deeply rooted in a politics of visibility and exclusion, as selective visualizations of place and space increasingly shape urban policy interventions.[8] Power is a determining factor deciding who and what is to be made visible.[9] Usually left out from representations are the ordinary landscapes of the poor, the black, the homeless, and the "unmodern," considered to be "out of place" in the city's public space by local political and economic leaders.[10] For Healy, the process of giving a city what elites believe is a "modern" face depends upon silencing the politically weak and making poverty—and the poor—purposely invisible.[11] Deutsche refers to this as a "politics of erasure," where undesirable groups are physically expelled from physical space, while their absence is discursively inscribed in representations of the city.[12]

Image construction in historical context

Historically, the practice of excluding certain aspects of urban reality, especially the poor and the indigent, has been linked to a desire, on the part of elites, to enjoy their wealth without remorse or culpability. In the nineteenth century, Engels described in detail the design of English mining towns, where shops and prominent buildings were located along major routes to conveniently hide the view of working-class neighborhoods, so that local bourgeois and mine owners could thus be spared the sight of the misery of those whose labor enriched them. Haussmann similarly gave nineteenth-century Paris a spectacular image of luxury and progress by hiding compact workers' housing behind prestigious façades. In *Paris Spleen*, Baudelaire highlights the discomfort felt by the Parisian elite at the sight of urban poverty.[13] His poem "The eyes of the poor" opposes the compassion-filled guilt of a young man, embarrassed by the opulence of the café where he sits, with the disgust and irritation of his fiancée, who cannot stand the stare of a poor "family of eyes," and begs the waiter to chase them out of sight. This poem illustrates the conflicted attitude of the French bourgeoisie towards poverty: a vexatious mix of shame and culpability, and an insufferable repulsion, tinged with resentment and hostility.

With the rise of modern liberal thought in the West, and the promise of a fair and equal society, the visibility of poverty raised uncomfortable questions about the egalitarian pretenses of capitalism. As a flagrant proof of the deceptive nature of free market orthodoxy, conspicuous poverty imperiled social stability by threatening to expose the fallacy of a system based on exploitation and inequity. Acknowledging its existence would destabilize the status quo and the state of denial elites had long sought comfort in. Furthermore, manifest poverty questioned the very promises of modernity, which had painted enlightenment as a path to universal betterment. Urban poverty was thus perceived as antithetical to urban modernity: it connoted a shameful lack of progress and a primitive state of backwardness.

Conspicuous poverty had ethical and religious implications as well, and stood as a shameful symptom of a morally faulty society. To give good conscience to those opposed to an equitable distribution of wealth, early twentieth-century social reformers devised strategies that helped displace the blame on the victim, often by associating poverty with disease and moral degeneracy. By exciting the fear of contamination and emphasizing the need to isolate the poor, reformers justified policies of socio-economic segregation mixed with attempts at symbolic extermination meant to render poverty invisible.[14]

In the course of the twentieth century, the rise of international tourism made nations more self-conscious about how they were perceived by the rest of the world. The weight of what John Urry would call the "tourist gaze" exacerbated the insecurities of local ruling elites who feared being perceived as underdeveloped or lagging, and justified the implementation of measures to hide—or at least displace—an overly visible poverty.[15] Over time, cities and nations developed sophisticated means to limit what was to be shown to the world, hiding what is deemed either irrelevant or detrimental to their image, and concealing those aspects that could cause reputational damage.

In the late twentieth and early twenty-first-century neoliberal era, especially in the context of the post-industrial urban crisis, strategies were developed to make invisible the growing precariousness that was born out of neoliberal policies. A revanchist urban discourse increasingly blamed those left behind by globalization and economic restructuring for the ongoing urban crisis.[16] Public space was made increasingly inhospitable for the poor and the marginal, using what Garnier calls a preventive "architecture of fear."[17] By focusing on public security and targeting troublemakers, urban policy helped divert attention from the real insecurities experienced in the city, in terms of access to labor, housing, or food. Events and festivals were used to re-appropriate public space for people of the "right sort" and intensive policing denied the homeless the simple "right to be seen."[18]

Mega-events, urban image construction, and the periphery

If image construction has become a standard urban practice in the contemporary city, the unique context created by the hosting of mega-events has exacerbated both the need and use of such practice. The need for economic survival, anxieties about one's position in the dominant world order, and a desire for recognition, status, and prestige are all factors that motivate city leaders to seek out mega-events. For nations in the East and global South, hosting mega-events is seen as a test of modernity, a performance indicator, and an occasion to establish themselves as models of organization and responsible management, which will help build their credibility as worthy players on the world stage. The tremendous symbolic weight placed upon these events endows local authorities with great leverage in the spectacular reorganization of urban space and the aesthetic control of the city's image. The sense of urgency generated by the tight deadlines typically associated with such events justifies the imposition of exceptional measures to counter urban disorder to reassure foreign visitors, such as tourists, journalists, television broadcasters, and even bloggers.

The extraordinary scope of media coverage of sporting mega-events, in particular, is another major factor motivating image-related initiatives. This global visibility explains the great pressure exerted by sports federations and event sponsors for the projection of a positive media image, however skewed, biased, and photoshopped. Being exposed to the scrutinizing eye of the global media also exerts added pressure on local hosts to do everything in their power to control every aspect of the event. Aware that no city is protected from the kinds of negative reporting that exposes inefficiencies and embarrassing episodes of mismanagement, civic officials and event promoters do not want to run the risk of making Olympic history as a symbol of poor planning, thereby inheriting the reputation of a barely averted disaster the city's most lasting Olympic legacy, as in the cases of Montreal and Athens. The pressure is even greater for events held in developing countries, often confronted with the prejudicial bias of a predominantly Western media, which seek to confirm long-held stereotypes about local inclinations for disorder, violence, and backward social practices. If event organizers wish to project a positive image of efficient planning and good management, journalists on the ground are often more inclined to confirm preconceptions or to expose the flaws and highlight the "competency deficit" of the host.[19]

This critical and assessing external gaze explains the defensive nature of many event-related image construction efforts. Such efforts focus on correcting negative perceptions of the city, addressing the main concerns of the international community, and proving that the city can perform in areas where its reputation is poor. In many cases, endemic problems that cannot be easily resolved are addressed by masking the issue, or diverting attention and putting emphasis elsewhere. As a result, the hosting of mega-events is often associated with a culture of covert deceit, as proponents deploy a vast range of persuasion techniques, both discursive and more concrete, to embellish reality, win over public opinion, and rally investors. Mega-event preparations are replete with unrealistic predictions and unproven assertions. They play a central role in the construction of host cities as highly controlled, make-believe dream worlds of unproblematic success, wealth, and prosperity, to the point where Solomon Greene talks of host cities as "staged cities."[20] If countless resources are used to build a picture-perfect image of spectacular progress and prosperity, with the construction of sparkling new buildings and stunning infrastructures, vast efforts are also deployed to actively conceal the landscapes of the poor, simply and often violently banished from sight.[21]

Countries on the margin, especially in emerging or developing countries face important hurdles in their efforts to project a positive image of the city. As emerging economies join in the race to host mega-events, they encounter important challenges related to their particular socio-economic realities and post-colonial condition.[22] Not only must they confront First-World bias in their bids to become potential host cities, but their stakes in hosting mega-events are also usually very high. When nations facing massive poverty and housing shortages spend their limited resources on hosting mega-events, it is not only in the hope of promoting economic development, but more importantly to escape marginalization, to overcome a precarious position in the symbolic ranking of nations, and to acquire global respect.[23] In October 2009, when Brazil won the bid to host the 2016 Olympics, then President Lula declared: "Brazil has left its second-class status behind and has joined the first class. Today we received respect."[24]

Mega-event strategies for making poverty invisible

The construction of an event-city thus condones several forms of exclusion in the spectacularization of the urban landscape: physical exclusion, with differential access to sites and events; legal exclusion, with new regulatory systems limiting behaviors and lifestyles, and visual exclusion, which mainly targets poor residents and their settlements. This last form of exclusion typically involves six strategies devised by host cities to unashamedly crop out unsavory aspects of urban reality, including the poor, the uncivilized, the unsightly, the dangerous, and the unmodern. They include:

1   *forced evictions*, with the bulldozing of material landscapes of poverty and the displacement of their population;
2   *concealment*, to hide the blight that cannot be displaced with the use of screens or walls;
3   *aestheticization*, to beautify poverty and make it more visually acceptable, thereby anesthetizing its political power;
4   *disciplining*, to reform the city's human landscape through civilizing campaigns and social beautification efforts;
5   *filtering*, with the adoption of extraordinary legal regimes and the creation of territories of exceptions limiting access to the event; and
6   *symbolic erasure*, the poor are rhetorically and effectively made invisible in media representations, tourism promotion, and event advertising.

Forced evictions

Among the most common responses to the excessive visibility of an embarrassing urban poverty is slum clearance, with the eviction and demolition of squatter settlements and the displacement of vulnerable residents. These practices, denounced when they occurred in Beijing, Seoul, New Delhi, Athens, and South Africa, have become a regular feature of mega-events, at least in emerging economies. In Beijing alone, 1.25 million people were evicted and had their quarters demolished to make way for large Olympic projects.[25] These displacements are generally justified by the construction of event-related infrastructure and venues, but many are obviously image-related. Mega-event franchise owners such as the IOC and FIFA often require the clearing of vast swathes of land around event venues, to create safety perimeters, to free up the views for global broadcast, and to protect visitors from a potentially dangerous and visually offensive urbanity. Unsightly slums are thus systematically removed from high-profile areas such as along the route of the Olympic torch.

Urban revitalization has long relied upon a rhetorical association between urban decay and crime to justify the violent dislocation of the poor. This association helps conceal the economic motivations of slum clearance, where the poor and their physical manifestations are seen as a liability in real-estate valuation. Slum clearance represents an opportunity for capital to expand into new territories, with the transfer of high-value urban land from the urban poor to middle- and upper-income groups. Speculators benefit from the potential rise in value of the land cleared of squatters, while municipalities benefit from new tax revenues.

Since access to basic housing is recognized as a human right (article 25 (1) of the Universal Declaration of Human Rights), it is becoming more politically difficult to justify forced evictions and massive demolitions. An alternate way to displace the poor without resorting to slum clearance is to combine several small-scale interventions that will effectively reduce the size of a settlement. For example, in Rio de Janeiro, as the city prepares to host the 2016 Olympics, the construction of cable cars, access roads, elevators, and sanitation systems are contributing to the gradual erosion of many favelas. Displaced residents are generally re-housed in the far periphery, away from job opportunities and basic services, or without fair compensation. The long commute, and added housing fees and transportation costs often result in a net impoverishment of these population groups. Massive displacements to the urban fringe also exacerbate socio-spatial segregation.

Concealment

A second means of hiding poverty in the preparation for sporting mega-events involves the erection of screen walls, built along the roadways linking event sites to the city center and the airport, in order to hide the most visible slums. These visual filters, which usually take the form of walls or hedges, can also consist of buildings or structures that block the view of poor neighborhoods. This is the case of the elevator to the favela of Cantagalo in Rio de Janeiro, built in 2010, where a disproportionately large tower located in the street's axis entirely conceals the view of the favela from Ipanema beach.

If the use of walls remains common, it is also highly controversial, because of its strong ideological charge and negative connotations, linked to notions of separation, isolation, and exclusion. Authorities will thus resort to clever rhetorical maneuvering and use more innocuous structures that are less symbolically charged to conceal poor neighborhoods from high-profile areas. One can think of the thick "bamboo curtain" planted in New Delhi in the months leading up to the Commonwealth Games of 2010, or the "ecolimits" or "accoustic barrier," along the road connecting the airport to downtown, erected in Rio de Janeiro, shortly after the announcement that the city would host the 2016 Olympics. However, local populations are rarely duped by such blatant attempts at denying their existence and such walls and barriers are quickly denounced, vandalized, and taken down by residents.

Aestheticization

A third approach to minimize the visibility of poverty combines several tactics of aestheticization and urban camouflage through visual discourses that are both neutralizing and pacifying. Here, poverty is neither hidden nor displaced, but embellished and controlled so as to become visually acceptable. This aestheticization often takes the form of façade projects that beautify the most visible portion of a neighborhood or landscaping interventions near the point of contact with the formal city that soften the interface between two separate worlds. Fresh coats of paint are applied on the street-facing sides of houses, broken windows are replaced, graffiti scrubbed away and new trees and flowerbeds are planted. Superficial "improvements" can soften the rough image of informal settlements, with the use of street names, house numbers, garbage collection, and other services that suggest the neighborhood's incorporation into the formal landscape but which may or may not survive the event.

In Rio de Janeiro, a common beautification initiative consists in painting the most visible part of favela houses in cheerful pastel colors, reducing the community to an assemblage of brightly colored blocks that could be the work of a clumsy child. Reminiscent of naive and idyllic representations of the favela first popularized in tourist art, this image is now imposing itself as the visual identity of the referent "favela" in the collective imagination. Despite being both reductive and a caricature, this approach was recently adopted by the state and imposed upon communities in various urban interventions, such as the accelerated growth program in Rocinha.

Given the popularity of "slum tourism" among foreign visitors, such beautification tactics clearly seek to reassure tourists of the inoffensive nature of these settlements. However, the patronizing nature of these interventions arguably contributes to the disqualification of the poor and perpetuates their subaltern position in contemporary society. It also masks the conditions of exclusion and exploitation from which these settlements were born and conceals traces of the discrimination and abandonment that its residents have long suffered and which are still inscribed on its walls.

Disciplining

A fourth strategy commonly used in host cities to hide or manage the poor is concerned with attempts to transform the city's human environment through social engineering programs. These initiatives seek to impose a new disciplinary landscape of order upon unruly residents and help produce a tame and obedient citizenry to fit global expectations of civility. City governments and NGOs promote campaigns that seek to turn unkempt masses into modern citizens by inculcating new values, altering behavior, and civilizing bodies. They also aim to purge the landscape of informal commerce upon which so many city dwellers depend for their survival.

It has become common practice for Olympic host cities to introduce restrictive legislation specifically directed at population groups considered undesirable to the city's image. In Beijing, countless migrant workers were expelled from the city for the duration of the event, while a vast state-led civilizing campaign banned all sorts of social behavior, such as spitting, and criminalized informal practices.[26] By conflating disorder and indiscipline with crime, public policies are marked by a growing intolerance to all forms of disorder and so-called "quality of life" crimes associated with poverty and informality. Measures range from anti-homeless and anti-mendicant laws, to repressive means of social control that criminalize the poor and their informal practices. They target specific classes of people who have themselves become markers of disorder, including vagrants, prostitutes, street children, panhandlers, drug users, the homeless, and certain classes of youth. In 2009, weeks after Rio was selected as host of the 2016 Olympics, Mayor Eduardo Paes initiated his "Shock of Order" initiative to crack down on urban disorder and petty crime. Modeled on the zero tolerance campaign perfected by Rudolf Giuliani in 1990s New York, the program is influenced by the "broken windows" theory, which rests upon the assumption that minor disorder and small-scale incivilities, if not taken seriously, will escalate into uncontrollable crime and chaos. Giuliani was hired in 2010 as a security consultant for Rio's Olympics.

These repressive measures are generally justified by a need for increased security. Mega-events are greatly infused by the spectacle of security, and seek to make the state presence more visible in the urban landscape, with the proliferation of police patrols and the multiplication of public interest messages. This conspicuous visibility of law and order helps normalize intrusive security measures, thereby concealing their discriminatory nature and making it acceptable for people to be arrested for the crime of being undesirable.

Filtering access

The popularity and visibility of sporting mega-events has led to growing security concerns on the part of local and national governments, and international sports federations, which fear that host cities may be overcrowded and overburdened and their populations threatened. The result is the implementation of increasingly dramatic measures to keep certain categories of people at bay during the event. Olympic parks and areas surrounding stadiums or other venues are designed to filter access and are turned into territories of exclusion. Marked by a particular brand of urbanism that is at once introverted, aggressive, and slightly paranoid, these sites are characterized by a fortress-like defensive architecture and a spatial layout inspired by military urbanism. Event venues are isolated by the creation of a cordon sanitaire, an unbuilt buffer zone, keeping them at a safe distance from surrounding urban districts. They are protected by a multi-layered safety perimeter and tightly controlled borders, with a series of barriers, in the form of gates, fences, moats or waterways, and few, easily monitored entry points. Other means of filtering access include airport-like security checkpoints, and a vast array of surveillance technologies.

The use of such military-inspired infrastructure is generally supplemented by extensive patrolling, with the massive presence of local law enforcement officers, private security guards, and military police. Fussey and colleagues describe security measures at Olympic parks as a militarization of urban space, which rests upon a policing model that draws heavily on zero tolerance orthodoxies and exceptional forms of penalty.[27] Although actual security threats are difficult to assess, the vast use of military metaphors, and a specialized vocabulary of war by security consultants, help justify the state's recourse to an extensive surveillance apparatus and what appears to be excessive policing.[28]

The filtering system and exceptional security regime which limit access to mega-event territories also signify that such spaces are closed off from public access during the event and that entry is reserved for specific categories of people. Admittance is granted to a selective few, who are either part of the organization or have the rare privilege to hold event tickets. Ticket owners thus enjoy preferential treatment and are granted access on the basis of their close contact to event participants or organizers, their status as members of the press, or their capacity to pay. By limiting both the accessibility and affordability of tickets, certain classes of people are efficiently priced out, and have to remain quietly at home to watch the event on television, thereby preventing a cluttering of public spaces and transportation networks.

Symbolic erasure

A last means of minimizing the visibility of poverty in preparation for the hosting of mega-events is symbolic erasure: a process that amounts to symbolically disqualifying the poor and rendering them discursively invisible. In this strategy, poverty is not only erased from the city's physical landscape but from its virtual or rhetorical representations as well: media reports, tourism propaganda, and mega-event promotional material simply ignore the existence of the poor. The phenomenon is akin to what Stan Cohen calls "denial," which he defines as "the maintenance of social worlds in which an undesirable situation is unrecognized, ignored, or made to seem normal."[29] Media contribute to this lack of recognition by evasion, under-reporting, and cover-up, which, by giving too little importance to an issue and failing to bring it to public attention, prevent society from gaining full consciousness of undesirable situations.

For example, my own field research in Beijing and Rio revealed that the poor and their contribution to society tended to disappear from the media as these cities embarked on event preparation. Problems faced by poor communities went unreported, and official statistics about the extent of urban poverty were underestimated. Apart from media blackouts, both new and old imaging technology was used *selectively* to limit what was to be shown to the world, hiding what was judged either irrelevant or detrimental to the Olympic spectacle, and concealing those aspects that could cause reputational damage. In Beijing, these technologies allowed the projection of photoshopped visions of the urban environment, enhancing some features, erasing others, even at time creatively reinventing reality to maximize the potency of the media-spectacle.[30] Similarly, in Rio de Janeiro, more mundane, less photogenic urban realities that could negatively affect global perceptions of the city and suggest backwardness and underdevelopment were often cropped out, fast-forwarded, or digitally erased in mega-event propaganda.

A particularly graphic example of this occurred in 2011 when major newspapers in Rio de Janeiro ran a full-page advertisement from Petrobras, showing an idealized bird's-eye view of Rio, in which all favelas had been replaced by lush vegetation. In the Brazilian Olympic bid material, venues in Rio's poor Zona Norte are shown as isolated objects, excluding the working-class neighborhoods that surround them. In other sweeping views of Rio, powerful sunrays wash across a portion of the landscape to conveniently erase the presence of favelas. In April 2013, a little over a year before the 2014 World Cup, Rio de Janeiro's favelas suddenly disappeared from Google maps. Google was under pressure from city hall and its tourism board that the word "favela" was replaced by the euphemism "*morro*" or hill. For example, in 2009, Riotur, the local tourism board, had lodged a formal complaint against Google regarding the fact that favelas had been given more visibility and prominence than formal neighborhoods. Google's decision to remove the favelas from Google maps was strongly denounced by the Comite popular da Copa and other citizens groups.

Impacts of image strategies to make poverty invisible

These image construction strategies are neither harmless nor innocent, but pose a sizable threat to urban justice. Their selectivity in the production of urban images divides the city between those who matter and those deemed irrelevant. By privileging representations whose appearance and symbolic references to modernity resonate with the desire, requirements, and expectations of local elites and external actors, they perpetuate patterns of domination and stratification, and reinforce old hierarchies and power disparities at both the local and global level. Mega-events can thus exacerbate pre-existing issues of social justice and inequality and compromise basic rights and freedoms. By promoting social exclusion, the imposition of limits on civil liberties and a tightening of the social control apparatus, they help redefine the rights to participate in society, and affect the constitution of citizenship.

The projection of a flawless and consensual representation of the city, at once efficient, modern, disciplined, and visually appealing, also contributes to the crystallization of an urban vision that is both simplified and unproblematic. Such selective and aestheticized representations of the urban landscape can be extremely alluring for members of the local elite, as they confirm long-held beliefs in the potential of a city unencumbered by impoverished masses. The danger of such exclusionary utopian visions is that they could be taken as projections of the world as it should be by those who still refute the idea of democratic society. By both validating and consolidating their restricted urban ideals, these representations could be used as ammunition to promote more exclusive urban policies, and prompt a backlash against the poor, further marginalizing their actions and de-legitimizing their claims. They carry a dangerous de-politicizing power that can help discredit resistance movements, exacerbate class prejudice, and reinforce segregation.

Resisting the mega-event spectacle

In the recent mega-event literature, much has been said of the spectacle's capacity for demobilization, and of its power to de-politicize space in order to facilitate capital accumulation.[31] Effective mobilization and organized protest have often been hindered by several factors, including fear of repression, the strong consensual power of mega-events and their heavy symbolic weight. For example, in Beijing, the patriotic framing of the Olympics, and appeals to nationalist sentiment, suggested that embracing the Games was not only a civic duty, but also a contribution to the advancement of the motherland. This framing helped to limit protest movements and undermine their legitimacy.[32] Such nationalist appropriation also displaced attention away from human rights violations and helped create a social climate where forced evictions were not only considered acceptable, but necessary.[33] Various forms of censorship or media control provide other impediments to organized resistance. Media outlets with close connections to both state and corporate interests play a part in containing dissent, by banning negative reporting on event preparations, censoring discussions of their adverse impacts, denigrating their opponents, and limiting coverage of eviction disputes, relocation controversies, and other rights violations.

Still, despite the great range of forces that work to deflect or to stifle opposition or criticism, mega-events provide important possibilities for resistance, even in circumstances that can be highly repressive. In a digital world where every phone is a camera and where images or accounts of events can be posted or tweeted almost immediately, mega-events have become more visible than ever as sites of conflict and opposition. Increasingly, the mega-event spectacle has been known to spark protests in host cities, triggering the development of diverse and creative forms of resistance and awakening political involvement that had long been dormant. All around the world, local residents are refusing to remain passive victims of event-led image construction and increasingly take to the streets to protest. These protests in turn now have unprecedented immediacy and a visibility on a global scale.

Symbolic resistance strategies

Indeed, critics of the politics of exclusion in mega-event cities have developed a broad and often innovative range of strategies to challenge event-related abuse. In the case of evictions, for example, and regardless of geopolitical context, the most common measure of resistance is the stand-off, a form of passive resistance carried out by recalcitrant residents who refuse to vacate their house, because they are dissatisfied with the proposed compensation conditions or simply refuse to be sacrificed for the benefit of the event spectacle. Another common way to refuse to be silenced and made invisible involves the occupation of a city's public spaces, via public demonstrations and organized resistance. There were ample examples of such demonstrations in Brazil during the Confederation Cup in 2013 and, again, in the run-up to the World Cup a year later. Fear of violent police repression often dampens mass mobilization and weakens its impacts, yet the struggle to assert public control over space, however temporary, remains a central strategy in popular resistance to mega-events.

There are multiple other, more furtive, and creative strategies for resisting the event spectacle. Activists, especially artists, use a host of oppositional practices that rely on media-savvy hijackings of text, images, and other materials central to the spectacle as weapons of resistance and denunciation. Many tactical approaches of counter-spectacle exploit legal and linguistic gray zones, relying on ambiguity to be less vulnerable to state repression. For example, in Beijing, local residents used a variety of covert modes of resistance to seek redress and turn an oppressive situation to their advantage.[34] Urban images were appropriated, reworked, even sabotaged, to usurp stereotypes, subvert misrepresentations, and contest exclusion. Several of these tactics qualify as what James C. Scott has called "weapons of the weak," those everyday acts of subversion and ordinary forms of resistance devised by the powerless to challenge hegemony, destabilize their oppressor, or simply vent their anger.[35]

Popular practices of linguistic resistance and verbal expressions of symbolic discontent are often reminiscent of those described by Alan Pred.[36] Using wit and irony, opponents resort to multiple forms of oral recalcitrance and linguistic re-workings to unsettle authority and skirt domination. Clever ditties, malicious double entendres, irreverent word games, and other narrative strategies are used to rework slogans, subvert official lingo, and transform dominant discourse into absurdist, derogatory, or cunning expressions. Traveling through the underground grapevine, they spread through word of mouth, Internet blogging, and text messaging. During the 2014 World Cup, the Brazilian blogosphere was replete with these creative strategies of resistance that included caricatures, films, and songs that were widely circulated and ultimately picked up by the foreign media. For example, in Rio, the music band Anarco Funk cleverly reworked classic samba and bossa nova songs to criticize Olympic-related mega-projects and denounce displacement and the masking of poverty.[37] Notably, the band turned Jorge Ben's 1972 success Fio Maravilha, into a derision of Rio's controversial port revitalization project (Porto Maravilha, or Port of Wonders), "marvelous for the bourgeois" (maravilha pra burgues). In another parody, the band took on Rio's new pacification police (UPP) installed in key favelas in preparation for mega-events, asking "UPP for whom?" (UPP para quem?).

Judith Butler insists on the subversive potential of parody, which, once disruptive, becomes domesticated and re-circulated to destabilize and potentially threaten the primacy of hegemonic meanings.[38] Such strategies are reminiscent of tactics promoted by the French Situationists in the 1960s in their response to what Guy Debord called "the society of the spectacle."[39] In Beijing, the power of such creative means of Situationist détournement rested upon the use of ambiguity and double entendre to unmask government pretense and ridicule Olympic organizers' contentions. The deceptively prosaic quality of these resistance strategies and their apparently non-political nature allowed the delivery of a subversive message without fear of repression. Satirical sayings, in particular, were widely circulated. Since the sayings had no known author and tended to circulate informally, they remained free of censorship.[40]

Covert opposition to event-related exclusion can also take a written form, using one of the oldest supports of mass communication: the wall. Such practices are present in the tactical utilization of urban space by graffiti artists, or other forms of street art that Borghini and colleagues call "subvertizing."[41] In many host cities, resistance to event-related transformations has taken the form of a war waged on the walls of neighborhoods awaiting demolition. The anonymity of this mode of communication allows people to powerfully articulate what they would not be able to say in person, and to publicly enunciate what many are silently thinking.

For example, in Beijing, the city's walls bore the evidence of a battle of words fought between local authorities, who painted slogans urging residents to serve the great Olympic cause by complying with eviction orders, and residents who fought back with their own slogans denouncing the unfair eviction process. If official slogans were encoded with the imperative tone of state propaganda, and shamelessly brandished the Olympic spirit in their appeal to compliance, the residents' replies to such a thinly veiled intimidation campaign took the moral high ground to underline injustice, thereby allowing them to retain their integrity while undermining the claims of their adversaries.[42]

In the context of growing media concentration and limited freedom of press, the Internet has become an especially important tactical tool in the battle against the event spectacle. Individuals turn to the Web to share their stories, make their cases heard, and gain moral support from a broader public. Social media serve as privileged sites to disseminate information and exchange strategies, and provide a vast forum for discussion. These platforms help keep the debate alive and exert pressure upon local authorities, event sponsors and organizers, and international sports federations to make mega-events more inclusive and transparent.

While some strategies of resistance to mega-events may appear sub-optimal and their impact limited, they represent important coping mechanisms for the powerless and disenfranchised, affording them a certain sense of control and entitlement. Furthermore, by giving voice to frustrations and fostering the expression of critical and dissenting views in the public realm, these apparently innocuous forms of resistance can register a cumulative effect and complement more traditional forms of protest. Partaking in these symbolic acts helps create an imagined community of resistance that empowers individuals and lays the groundwork for more concrete organized actions. The broad public circulation of such subversive messages may also help open up spaces within which new collectivities may be forged and political agendas refined. If the impact of these weapons of the weak remains incidental, they do represent small moral victories, which allow members of society to maintain their pride, dignity, and right to existence.

Conclusion

This chapter has detailed different ways in which mega-events enable local coalitions of power holders to manipulate urban reality to project an idealized, flawless, and consensual representation of the city, that is at once disciplined and visually appealing and resonates with the desire, requirements, and expectations of both local elites and external actors. Not only do such events cause social, economic, and psychological hardships for many citizens, but they also redefine the terms of belonging to society. While mega-events promoters pitch images of urban solidarity and community, the reality of such events for many of the city's economically marginal citizens is much different. Behind the rhetoric, mega-events can be seen to offer a highly restricted view of urban society, where the poor appear to have no legitimate place. They become structurally irrelevant, unworthy of equal rights and opportunities.

In this context, event-led image construction is typically a powerful instrument of concealment, erasure, and amnesia, concerned with the silencing of dissident voices and the classification of who can or cannot be seen. This socio-aesthetic transformation of the city thus promotes a planning vision that fosters the construction of a consensual image, hostile to conflict and difference, and the de-politicization of the urban landscape, reduced to a mere object of consumption and speculation. The invisibility of urban poverty in this vision becomes a highly political issue. Making poverty invisible does not merely mean visual concealment but also disenfranchisement and silencing as well. On this point, Don Mitchell emphasizes *the right to be seen*, the simple right to be present and visible in public space, as a fundamental right that allows the most economically deprived to exist and participate in society.[43] To hide the poor, to make them invisible, is to attempt to neutralize their voice and to deny them any political weight or citizenship right. To hide poverty is also to perpetuate it, to refuse to face the structural causes of social inequality, and to sustain the myth that the free market is a fair system that can provide for all members of society. In such circumstances, the struggle of the poor to become visible disrupts the conception of universally shared community interests constructed by the mega-event and reveals its inherently ideological character.

Notes

 1 Richards & Palmer, "Why Cities."
 2 Hannigan, J., *Fantasy City.*
 3 Julier, *Urban Designscapes.*
 4 McCann, "City marketing."
 5 Smith, "Reimaging the City."
 6 Deutsche, *Eviction: Art and Spatial Politics.*
 7 Healy, "On Creating the City."
 8 Raco and Tunney, "Visibilities and Invisibilities."
 9 Powell and Marrero-Guillamón, *The Art of Dissent.*
10 Wright, *Out of Place.*
11 Healy, *On Creating the City.*
12 Deutsche, *Eviction: Art and Spatial Politics*, 173.
13 Baudelaire, "The Eyes of the Poor," 52–4.
14 Rabinow, *The French Modern.*
15 Urry, *The Tourist Gaze.*
16 Smith, "Reimaging the city."
17 Garnier, "Scénographies pour un simulacra."
18 Mitchell, "The End of Public Space?"
19 Dimeo and Kay, "Major sports events."
20 Greene, "Staged Cities."

21 Kennelly and Watts, *Sanitizing Public Space.*
22 Rivenburgh, *The Olympic Games.*
23 Black and Westhuizen, "The allure of global games."
24 Williamson, "The 2016 Olympics in Rio."
25 COHRE, *One World, Whose Dream?.*
26 See Broudehoux, "Images of Power"; and "Civilizing Beijing."
27 Fussey et al., 2011, *Securing and Sustaining the Olympic City.*
28 Kennelly and Watts, "Sanitizing Public Space."
29 Cohen, *States of Denial.*
30 Broudehoux, "Images of Power."
31 Ibid.; and Shin, "Unequal cities of spectacle."
32 Broudehoux, "Civilizing Beijing."
33 Broudehoux, "The Social and Spatial Impacts."
34 Broudehoux, "Images of Power."
35 Scott, *Weapons of the Weak.*
36 Pred, "Capitalisms, Crises, and Cultures II."
37 Soifer, *Lyrical Resistance.*
38 Butler, *Excitable Speech.*
39 Debord, *The Society of the Spectacle.*
40 Broudehoux, "Seeds of Dissent."
41 Borghini et al., "Symbiotic postures of commerical advertising."
42 Ibid.
43 Mitchell, "The End of Public Space?"

Bibliography

Baudelaire, Charles. "The Eyes of the Poor." In *Paris Spleen.* New York : New Direction, 1970 [1869], pp. 52–4.

Black, David R. and Janis van der Westhuizen. "The allure of global games for 'semiperipheral' polities and spaces: a research agenda. " *Third World Quarterly,* 25(7), 2004: 1195–214.

Borghini, S., L. Visconti, L. Anderson, and J. Sherry. "Symbiotic postures of commercial advertising and Street Art." *Journal of Advertising,* 39(3), 2010: 113–26.

Broudehoux, Anne-Marie. "The Social and Spatial Impacts of Olympic Image Construction: The case of Beijing 2008." In *A Handbook of Olympic Studies,* Stephen Wagg and Helen Lenskyj (eds.). London: Palgrave Macmillan, 2012.

———. "Civilizing Beijing: Social beautification, civility, and citizenship at the 2008 Olympics." In *The Olympics, Mega-events and Civil Societies: Globalization, Environment, Resistance,* Graeme Hayes and John Karamichas (eds.). London: Palgrave Macmillan, 2011.

———. "Images of Power: Architectures of the Integrated Spectacle at the Beijing Olympics." *Journal of Architectural Education,* 62(1), 2010.

———. 2009. "Seeds of Dissent: The Politics of Resistance to Beijing's Olympic Redevelopment." In *Dissent and Cultural Resistance in Asian Cities,* Melissa Butcher and Selvaraj Velayutham (eds.). London: Routledge, 2009, pp. 14–32.

Butler, Judith. *Excitable Speech: A Politics of the Performative.* New York and London : Routledge, 1997.

Cohen, Stan. *States of Denial: Knowing about atrocities and suffering.* London: Polity, 2001.

COHRE (Centre on Housing Rights and Eviction). *One World, Whose Dream? Housing Rights Violations and The Beijing Olympic Games.* Geneva: COHRE Special Report, 2008.

Debord, Guy. *La société du spectacle.* Paris: Gallimard, 1992 [1967].

Deutsche, Rosalyn. *Eviction: Art and Spatial Politics.* Cambridge, MA and London: MIT Press, 1996.

Dimeo, Paul and Joyce Kay. "Major sports events, image projection and the problems of 'semi-periphery': a case study of the 1996 South Asia Cricket World Cup" *Third World Quarterly,* 25(7), 2004: 1263–76.

Fussey, Pete, Jon Coaffee, Gary Armstrong, and Dick Hobbs. *Securing and Sustaining the Olympic City: Reconfiguring London for 2012 and Beyond.* London: Ashgate, 2011.

Garnier, Jean-Pierre. "Scénographies pour un simulacre: L'espace public réenchanté." *Espace et société,* 3:(134), 2008: 67–81.

Greene, Solomon J. "Staged cities: Mega-events, Slum clearance and global capital." *Yale Human Rights and Development Law Journal,* 6, 2003: 161–87.

Hannigan, J. *Fantasy City: Pleasure and Profit in the Postmodern Metropolis.* London, Routledge, 1999.

Healy, P. "On creating the 'city' as a collective resource." *Urban Studies,* 39, 2002: 1777–92.

Julier, G. "Urban Designscapes and the Production of Aesthetic Consent. " *Urban Studies,* 42(5–6) 2005: 869–87.

Kennelly, Jacqueline and Paul Watt. "Sanitizing Public Space in Olympic Host Cities: The Spatial Experiences of Marginalized Youth in 2010 Vancouver and 2012 London." *Sociology,* 45(5), 2011: 765–81.

McCann, Eugene J. "City marketing." In *International Encyclopedia of Human Geography,* Rob Kitchin and Nigel Thrift (eds.). Oxford: Elsevier, 2009, pp. 119–24.

Mitchell, Don. "The End of Public Space? People's Park, Definitions of the Public, and Democracy." *Annals of the Association of American Geographers* 85(1), 1995: 108–33.

Powell, Hilary and Isaac Marrero-Guillamón (eds.). *The Art of Dissent: Adventures in London's Olympic State.* London: Marshgate Press, 2012.

Pred, A. "Capitalisms, Crises, and Cultures II: Notes on Local Transformation and Everyday Cultural Struggles". in *Reworking Modernity: Capitalisms and Symbolic Discontent,* Pred, A. and Watts, M. (eds.). New Brunswick, NJ: Rutgers, 1992, pp. 106–17.

Rabinow, Paul. *French Modern: The Norms and Forms of the Social Environment.* Chicago, IL: University of Chicago Press, 1995.

Raco, Mike and Emma Tunney. "Visibilities and Invisibilities in Urban Development: Small Business Communities and the London Olympics 2012." *Urban Studies,* 47(10), 2010, 2069–91.

Richards, Greg and R. Palmer. "Why Cities need to be Eventful." In *Eventful Cities.* Oxford: Butterworth-Heinemann, 2010, pp. 1–37.

Rivenburgh, Nancy K. *The Olympic Games, Media, and the Challenges of Global Image Making.* Barcelona: Centre d'Etudis Olimpics (UAB), 2004.

Scott, James C. 1985. *Weapons of the Weak: forms of resistance.* New Haven, CT and London, Yale University Press, 1985.

Shin, H. B. 2012. "Unequal cities of spectacle and mega-events in China." *City,* 16(6), 2012: 728–44.

Smith, Andrew. "Reimaging the city: the value of sport initiatives." *Annals of Tourism Research,* 32(1), 2005: 217–36.

Soifer, Raphael. "Lyrical Resistance: Urban Reform, Social Memory, and the Imagination of Public Space in Rio de Janeiro." Annual Meeting of the American Association of Geographers, Los Angeles, 2013.

Williamson, Theresa. "The 2016 Olympics in Rio: A Community Plays Against the Real Estate Game." *Progressive Planning Magazine*, July 14, 2010: http://www.plannersnetwork. org/2010/07/the-2016-olympics-in-rio-a-community-plays-against-the-real-estate-game/.

Wright, Tamaldge. *Out of Place: Homeless Mobilizations, Subcities and Contested Landscapes*. Albany, NY: SUNY Press, 1997.

Urry, John. *The Tourist Gaze*, 2nd edn. London: Sage, 2002.

8 Sochi 2014

Politics, activism, and repression

Jules Boykoff

When the IOC awarded Sochi the Olympics in 2007, a headline in the Melbourne *Herald Sun* proclaimed, "Russia Wins 2014 Cold War." Russian Deputy Prime Minister Alexander Zhukov waxed that hosting "the 2014 Games will accelerate positive change in our young democracy."[1] The Olympics would also help refurbish Russia's reputation on the global stage. As one academic uncritically put it, the Games were "a huge international 'comeback opportunity' to present a stronger, better, more glamorous image both politically and economically." The Olympics could jumpstart "enhanced global status and identification as a unique and competitive brand."[2]

It quickly became apparent, however, that in order to engineer the Games, a massive fiscal effort would be required, and in a business climate rife with corruption. At the same time, as the Olympic juggernaut rolled over the toes of various political, environmental, and social groups, the coercive capacity of the Russian state was bolstered and refined in order to quell dissent. Sochi 2014 had an avid supporter who was more than willing to both wring the requisite funds from cash-rich oligarchs and tighten up state control: Vladimir Putin.[3] Putin was instrumental in securing the Sochi Games, charming IOC voting members in Guatemala with his unique blend of machismo, braggadocio, and self-assurance. Once Sochi was named host, Putin played an active role in sculpting the Sochi Olympic spectacle.[4]

The Olympics transpire under the white-hot glare of the global media spotlight, and this abets political activism that rises up to challenge the Games and its numerous socio-political ramifications. Security forces and Olympic higher-ups are relatively reluctant to crush dissent or curtail the free speech of athletes, especially while journalists stand with pens and cameras at the ready. Activists benefit from the fact that during the Games the eyes of the world focus on the Olympic city. According to one Pew Research poll before the Sochi Games, 81 percent of respondents said they planned on watching the Olympics.[5] Such a sizable audience presented a unique opportunity for dissident citizens. Perspicacious activists could potentially deflect public attention from the five-ring spectacle and swerve it toward political issues, in a sense, "seizing the Olympic platform." The basic idea, according to Monroe E. Price, is "to find a platform that has proven highly successful in establishing a major constituency for one purpose and then convert that constituency to a different, unintended objective."[6]

The Sochi Olympics provided just such a discursive "platform," ready to be converted into a dais for dissent.

Repressive measures

After winning the right to host the Games, Sochi bid director Dmitry Chernyshenko argued that hosting the Olympics would give Russia a civic boost. He asserted, "There is no doubt, they will help make Russia more internationally orientated, more democratic."[7] However, on-the-ground reality diverged markedly from this rosy prognostication. After Putin returned to the presidency in May 2012, Russia experienced a significant uptick in state repression as Sochi prepared to host the Olympics. Human Rights Watch asserted that "the Russian government has unleashed a crackdown on civil society unprecedented in the country's post-Soviet history." In the lead-up to the Games, the Russian state tightened its grip, thereby "threatening the viability of Russia's civil society."[8]

The Russian Duma legislated an array of measures designed to squelch dissent. In summer 2012, it passed a law that required NGOs engaging in "political activity" and receiving funds from outside Russia to register as "foreign agents," a term rippling with negative connotations from the Soviet era. The law defined "political activity" in extremely broad fashion, that is, any time an NGO

> participates (including through financing) in organizing and implementing political actions aimed at influencing decision-making by state bodies intended to change state policy pursued by them, as well as in the shaping of public opinion for the aforementioned purposes.[9]

The law mandated that "foreign agents" register with the government before engaging in "political activity." Groups that failed to sign on to the government's special registry would have their assets frozen and be vulnerable to administrative and criminal sanctions. Failure to comply could lead to fines of up to approximately US$1,000 (30,000 rubles) for individuals and almost $10,000 (300,000 rubles) for groups.[10] In March 2013, Russian security forces started carrying out unannounced inspections of hundreds of NGO headquarters. Human Rights Watch contended, "The inspections were highly extensive, disruptive, and invasive, and seemed aimed at intimidating NGOs."[11]

Protesters were dissuaded in subtle and not-so-subtle ways. The Russian government installed fines for public "disorder." Even protesters at permitted demonstrations could receive punishments of $660 (20,000 rubles) or up to 50 hours of community labor if "disorder" occurred. For political events carried out without first securing a permit, the penalties were even harsher: more than $9,000 (270,000 rubles) for participating activists and more than three times that for protest organizers. Given the fact that President Putin and his allies in government routinely conflated left-wing dissent with terrorism, often blaming them for fomenting "mass disorder," this law was especially alarming.[12] Oppositionists were often accused of carrying out "extremist" actions. For example, in July 2013, prominent left opposition leader Alexei Navalny was handed a five-year sentence in a prison camp on what the *Guardian* described as "a demonstrably sham charge." In the end, a Russian court suspended his sentence but upheld a questionable conviction for theft.[13]

Beyond this, Russian authorities also aimed to control online space, scouring it for whiffs of dissent. One cyber-law corralled free speech online, giving the government the authority to clandestinely create a blacklist that quickly tallied up around two hundred websites for creating "offensive content."[14] The Russian government took no chances. It placed media—even relatively obscure blogs—under tight scrutiny. The regime blocked online access to LJRossia.org, a blog-hosting website that carried the work of Kremlin critics, placing it on an "Internet blacklist."[15]

Six months before the start of the Games, Putin issued a decree that banned all non-Olympic "gatherings, rallies, demonstrations, marches and pickets" in Sochi between 7 January and 21 March. This created a one-month protest-free buffer on either side of the Games.[16] Then Russian authorities backpedaled, vowing to establish "protest zones," with the closest one in Khosta, a village more than seven miles from the nearest Olympic site. Not a single significant protest was staged in Khosta, where the protest zone was tucked under a highway overpass. The *New York Times* concluded, "If the choice of Khosta as a protest site was meant to make protesting as unappealing as possible, and to ensure that the fewest number of people as possible would notice any demonstrations, then the authorities did their job well."[17] The totality of laws sent political activists and NGOs an unmistakable message: protests that challenged the five-ring spectacle would not be brooked with passive tolerance.

In summer 2013, Russia also passed a law outlawing propaganda of "non-traditional" sexual relations to minors, legislation that most observers translated to be anti-gay.[18] Violators of the law were subject to significant fines—$1,500 for individuals and $30,000 for organizations—while foreigners could be deported. Many activists, and even casual observers, pointed out that the law was incongruent with anti-discrimination principles written into the Olympic Charter.[19] The law galvanized calls to boycott the 2014 Sochi Winter Olympics, as well as a petition to relocate the Games to Vancouver and demands to ban Russia from participating in its own Olympics.[20]

To be sure, repression does not automatically quell dissent. Sometimes state suppression can actually galvanize activism. While in some contexts, in-the-streets political mobilization triggers increased repression, in other instances it actually decreases it, fomenting safety in numbers.[21] However, in the case of Sochi 2014, the coercive structure slotted into place in advance of the Games severely constricted the possibilities for expressing political dissent during the Olympic moment.

Political activism and the Sochi 2014 Games

Despite the structural barriers obstructing their path, a number of activists did use the Sochi 2014 Olympics as a platform for expressing political dissent. Some of these were athlete-activists, but most of them were non-athletes attempting to engage in "piggybacking" off the Olympics to cast light on issues that mattered to them.[22] Many protesters took action outside of Russia, attempting to raise awareness of what was going on inside the host city and country.

In the lead-up to the Sochi Games, numerous individuals spoke out, including many athletes disgruntled with discriminatory laws that they felt did not chime with the Olympic spirit. Activist groups such as Athlete Ally and All Out vigorously pointed out that the Russian anti-gay law sliced against the aforementioned Principle 6 of the Olympic Charter.[23] Andre Banks of the group All Out, told the *Guardian*, "There is a lot more that could be done by the Russian government, the IOC and sponsors. They want this story to go away and have been totally unwilling to make any real concessions regarding the law."[24]

Some people believed an Olympic boycott was the best route forward. English actor Stephen Fry penned an open letter to the IOC and British Prime Minister David Cameron, which stated, "An absolute ban on the Russian Winter Olympics of 2014 in Sochi is simply essential." He suggested the IOC should "Stage them elsewhere in Utah, Lillehammer, anywhere you like. At all costs, Putin cannot be seen to have the approval of the civilized world." Fry compared the 2014 Sochi Games to the 1936 Olympics in Nazi Germany. He argued that Putin was "making scapegoats of gay people, just as Hitler did Jews," and called for the UK to boycott the Games.[25] Harvey Fierstein, the award-winning Broadway performer, wrote an op-ed for the *New York Times* that extended the comparison to Hitler and the 1936 Olympics:

> In 1936 the world attended the Olympics in Germany. Few participants said a word about Hitler's campaign against the Jews. Supporters of that decision point proudly to the triumph of Jesse Owens, while I point with dread to the Holocaust and world war. There is a price for tolerating intolerance.

He argued the IOC "must demand the retraction" of the anti-gay laws "under threat of boycott."[26]

But not everyone supported a boycott. John Carlos—who along with Tommie Smith famously thrust black-glove-clad fists into the Mexico City sky while on the medal stand at the 1968 Olympics as Australian sprinter Peter Norman stood in solidarity—challenged the idea that athletes should sacrifice their chance to speak out on the altar of political principle. He said, "The bottom line is, if you stay home, your message stays home with you." He continued:

> If you stand for justice and equality, you have an obligation to find the biggest possible megaphone to let your feelings be known. Don't let your message be buried and don't bury yourself. To be heard is to be greater than a boycott. Had we stayed home, we'd never have been heard from again.[27]

All the boycott banter, in addition to other critiques wafting through the media ether, led 44 percent of respondents to tell the Pew Research Center it was a "bad decision" to hold the Olympics in Russia.[28]

Feeling the pressure, the IOC made a concession, allowing athletes to speak their minds at press conferences. This allowance actually spotlighted Rule 50 of the Olympic Charter: "No kind of demonstration or political, religious or racial propaganda is permitted in any Olympic sites, venues or other areas."[29] At the same time, this safety valve afforded athletes space to speak out without fearing reprimand of the variety John Carlos and Tommie Smith experienced in 1968 when they were kicked out of the Olympic Village. On the eve of the Sochi Games, Carlos told political sportswriter Dave Zirin and me:

> If I was an athlete today, I wouldn't be concerned about anything other than what's right. You need to follow your conscience, follow your heart, follow your wisdom, and follow your education as to what the plight is. If you feel like you must do something, the only thing you will regret is doing nothing."[30]?

The IOC's improvised press-conference policy made it more feasible to take Carlos's advice to "follow your conscience, follow your heart."

Athlete activism

In the lead-up to the Sochi Olympics, it appeared as if the Games might become a festival of dissent. US President Barack Obama even played a role when he named two out lesbians—Caitlin Cahow and Billie Jean King—to his official delegation.[31] *USA Today* described the move as "a strong message of opposition to Russia's anti-gay laws."[32] A third member of Obama's delegation, figure-skating champion Brian Boitano, came out of the closet two days after Obama selected him. King was forced to stay at home when her mother fell ill, but Boitano and Cahow were outspoken in Russia. Upon arriving in Sochi, Boitano stated:

> We feel very strongly [about] tolerance and diversity. And that's why we're here. Everyone knows why we're here. We've made it obvious and quite public . . . I think Russians know that and I think Americans know that and we're proud to come from a country who supports tolerance and diversity and we stand strong.

Cahow, an Olympic medal winner in ice hockey, spoke directly to the Russian LGBT community: "If there's one person sitting out there watching me on television and realizing that there's someone like them out there and there is the opportunity that one day you may feel safe and you may feel like you can live your life, that's what I want to be able to do."[33]

Athletes participating in the Sochi Olympics also had strong words for the anti-gay law. When the media broached the topic, US figure skater Ashley Wagner said, her voice reportedly quivering, "For me, I have gay family members, and I have a lot of friends in the LBGT community. I'm even so nervous to talk about this . . . I have such a firm stance on this that we should all have equal rights."

US skier Bode Miller went further: "I think it's so embarrassing that there's countries and people who are that ignorant . . . As a human being, I think it's embarrassing." He also targeted Rule 50 of the Olympic Charter when he said, "Politics in sports and athletics are always intertwined even though people try to keep them separate." He added, "Asking an athlete to go somewhere and compete and be a representative of a philosophy and all that different crap that goes along with it and then tell them they can't express their views is pretty hypocritical and unfair."[34] Some US sport honchos were on the same page as Wagner and Miller. Larry Probst, the president of the US Olympic Committee and IOC member, suggested the Olympic Charter should be amended to forbid discrimination based on sexual orientation.[35] Fifty-two Olympic athletes—past and present—signed an open letter to repeal anti-gay laws. The Sochi-bound Australian four-man bobsled team signed on, as did Canadian biathlete Rosanna Crawford and US snowboarder Seth Wescott. They were joined by athletes such as Martina Navratilova, Megan Rapinoe, Robbie Rogers, and Nick Symmonds.[36]

Many athletes who signed the open letter also supported another high-profile action: the Principle 6 Campaign (or "P6 Campaign"). In December 2013, All Out and Athlete Ally teamed up with the clothing manufacturer American Apparel to spearhead the effort. They created athletic gear featuring the exact wording from Principle 6 of the Olympic Charter. Campaigners asserted, "Principle 6, a campaign inspired by the values of the Olympic charter, is a way for athletes, spectators and global supporters to celebrate the Olympic principle of non-discrimination and speak out against Russia's anti-gay laws before the 2014 Winter Olympics in Sochi."[37] One showed support for the campaign by buying and wearing American Apparel gear, which read, "Principle 6: Sport does not discriminate on grounds of race, religion, politics, gender, or otherwise." According to the group's website, "Wearing Principle 6 gear will show support for the Olympic value of non-discrimination and is a tangible way to speak out against the anti-gay laws and violence in Russia leading up to the 2014 Winter Games." It added, "After covering costs, proceeds from merchandise sales will directly benefit LGBT groups in Russia."[38] Longtime Olympic critic Helen Jefferson Lenskyj blasted the group for "reflecting the usual naïve faith in Olympic values" and for being "apparently unaware of the negative implications for any groups that accepted foreign funds without having first registered as 'foreign agents'." She added: "With news of the Principle 6 Campaign readily available online, this well-intentioned plan could endanger the Russian LGBT groups that its organizers were planning to support."[39]

The P6 campaign featured four Olympic athletes participating at the Sochi Games who were "on-site ambassadors": Australian snowboarder Belle Brockhoff, Canadian snowboarder Alex Duckworth, alpine skier Mike Janyk, and the captain of the Australian bobsled team Heath Spence. Brockhoff vowed to publicly rubbish the law. US snowboarder Hannah Teter described the law as "very inhumane" and hinted at Sochi activism, even if that meant breaking rules against dissent. "That's what snowboarders do: We break rules," she stated.[40]

Brian Burke, the director of player personnel for the Sochi-bound US hockey team, dubbed the anti-gay law "repugnant."[41] Burke said, "Olympians, when you pack your skates, pack a rainbow pin. When you practice your Russian, learn how to say, 'I am pro-gay.'"[42] For Burke it was personal: in 2009, his hockey-playing son came out publicly as gay, only to tragically die in a car accident the following year.

Despite all the public criticism that emerged before the Games, athlete protest during the Olympics was minimal. Billie Jean King suggested, "Sometimes I think we need a John Carlos moment," but only a handful of athletes took up the call, and in a series of lower-profile acts.[43] Nevertheless, there were some pronounced instances of athletes taking a political stand on the world stage.

In 1968, IOC President Avery Brundage stated, "You don't find hippies, yippies or beatniks on sports grounds."[44] He hadn't seen the modern incarnation of the Winter Olympics, with snowboarding a popular sport. Turned out, the snowboarders were not passive, apolitical automatons either. Early in the competition, Russian slopestyle snowboarder Alexey Sobolev zipped down the hill on a board featuring a female sporting a balaclava and wielding a knife, an act most interpreted as a bold homage to the high-profile feminist punk-rock performance art collective Pussy Riot. In early 2012, Pussy Riot entered a Moscow cathedral and carried out a confrontational "punk prayer" performance. Three members—Maria Alyokhina, Nadezhda Tolokonnikova, and Yekaterina Samutsevich—were given two-year prison sentences on charges of hooliganism, but Samutsevich was given a suspended sentence in October 2012 and Alyokhina and Tolokonnikova were released from prison in 2013 on the eve of the Games. At the end of his heat, Sobolev flopped onto the snow, posing astride his snow-board. When asked whether his action should be construed as a gesture of solidarity with Pussy Riot, he replied cryptically, "Anything is possible."[45] The act of dissent was somewhat overshadowed by his decision to scrawl his mobile number on his helmet, which generated thousands of texts and calls as well as a fair amount of press attention.[46] The day after Sobalev's cheeky homage, Dutch slopestyle snowboarder Cheryl Maas shoved a rainbow glove—replete with a golden-horned unicorn—toward the television camera after a preliminary run. This was the first open challenge of the LGBT law during the Games. Prior to the Games, Maas, a married lesbian, had slammed the IOC for choosing to stage the Olympics in Russia.[47]

A few days later, US cross-country skier Andrew Newell spearheaded an effort to raise awareness of climate change. He was one of 105 Olympic athletes who signed an open letter prodding world leaders to "Recognize climate change by reducing emissions, embracing clean energy and preparing a commitment to a global agreement at the UN Framework Convention on Climate Change in Paris 2015." Signatories came from Australia, Canada, Estonia, France, Germany, Italy, Norway, Sweden, Switzerland, and the United States.[48] In response *Investor's Business Daily* penned an editorial titled "In the Olympic Spirit, Shut Up and Ski," that slammed Newell and fellow Olympians for "their poor judgment and naiveté" in proliferating "junk science." The publication implored Newell and his colleagues to "suppress their urges to hector the rest of us and express themselves through their athletic performances. We like our Olympics politics-free."[49]

Vladimir Putin, a high-profile climate-change denier who wanted to keep overt politics to a minimum, couldn't have said it better himself.

As the Sochi Olympics transpired, political turmoil engulfed Ukraine. Before the Games had concluded, skirmishes in the streets of Kiev had led to dozens of deaths and injuries. Ukrainian President Viktor Yanukovich fled the country the day before the Games concluded. By early March, a convoy of Russian troops had arrived in Crimea and Crimea's local parliament voted to join Russia. On 7 March, the first day of the Sochi Paralympic Games, rallies in Russia encouraged the people of Crimea to join Russia. On 16 March, the closing day of the Paralympics, the people of Crimea voted to do just that. All this effectively shredded the Olympic Truce. It also inspired Ukrainian skier Bogdana Matsotska to depart Sochi in order to join in solidarity with protesters. The athlete's coach and father, Oleg Matsotskyy, posted on Facebook that "In solidarity with the fighters on the barricades . . . and as a protest against the criminal actions made towards the protesters, the irresponsibility of the president and his lackey government, we refuse further performance at the Olympic Games in Sochi 2014."[50] At a press conference, Ukrainian gold-medal-winning biathlon athlete Olena Pidhrushna requested that reporters offer a moment of silence in respect for the political turbulence in Ukraine. The assembled reporters complied. The episode highlighted how the IOC had wedged open political space at press conferences.[51]

At the Paralympics, Ukrainian athletes put forth principled political protest. Ukraine sent a single emissary to carry the Ukrainian flag at the opening ceremonies while the rest of the squad refused to join the procession, remaining rooted in their stadium seats in dignified solidarity. Also, the Ukrainian cross-country skiing relay team used their hands to cover their silver medals at a ceremony as Russia was bestowed with the gold. One Ukrainian team official argued:

> It is not a political protest, it's us fighting for peace. It's a different kind of protest. We put our hands on our medals because you cannot do anything more . . . If we demonstrate some way else, if we say something, it will not be in the rules of the International Paralympic Committee. So we try to do a silent protest and because we don't want any disqualifications.[52]

At the closing ceremony, the Ukrainian flag bearer, Lyudmila Pavlenko, wore a shirt adorned with the word "peace" in large letters across her chest.[53]

Non-athlete activism

Due to the fortified coercive capacity of the Russian state, activism outside the athlete circuit was also blunted. The activism that did occur revolved around three central areas: environmentalism, the efforts of Pussy Riot, and Circassian genocide on the site of the Games.

Claiming to be "the greenest Games ever" has become bricked into IOC discourse, with promises of "sustainability" emerging as obligatory lingo on the Olympic circuit. Mega-event scholar and critic Christopher Gaffney notes that although moves toward sustainability "can be considered positive in some respects, they are inadequate to deal with the fundamental problem that the events themselves generate."[54] Graeme Hayes and John Horne assert that Olympic sustainability is no mere "benign paradox" of top-down mega-event planning and ground-up sustainable development; it's actually indicative of "a systemic contradiction of advanced late-modern capitalist democracies." They conclude the Olympics are "a fundamentally unsustainable event."[55]

While Sochi 2014 bid materials articulated a bold sustainability agenda, translating ambition into reality proved problematic. The Sochi organizing committee did not operationalize its environmental component until 2009 and became reliant on international consultants, especially from Vancouver. What Martin Müller calls a "dysfunctional governance" arrangement undercut green dreams, with a dearth of high-level support from Russian Olympic plenipotentiaries, sustainability and environment divided into two departments with separate power hierarchies, and the notorious Olimpstroy running the contracting and sub-contracting for Olympic construction. The aspirational "zero waste" Games became "reducing waste" instead.[56] Assessing Sochi 2014 sustainability efforts, Müller noted "the creation and implementation of a national green building standard where none existed before." However, the endeavor was hampered by "over-ambitious commitments" as well as "ineffective governance, an absence of institutional controls, both at the domestic and at the international level, and high time pressure." This

> led to irreversible environmental damage, oversized infrastructure and limited public engagement and benefits. This made the sustainability policies fall far short of the organisers' initial aims and belied the ambitions to harness the Olympics as a vehicle for environmental modernisation.[57]

Public input into the Sochi OCOG's sustainability processes was minimal and expressing dissent that challenged environmental policies was met with state repression. The Russian environmental group Environmental Watch on North Caucasus leveled sharp criticism of the Olympic project for its development in the Sochi National Park and Sochi Nature Reserve. The group documented the loss of biodiversity and the damage done to migratory species and coastal flora. The intense deforestation of mountainsides caused devastating pollution in three rivers: the Achipse, the Laura, and the Mzymta.[58] In response, Dmitry Kozak, the deputy prime minister and Olympic higher-up, countered that the environmentalists were simply trying to "trash" the Olympics rather than opting "to take a constructive stance."[59] As the Games approached, Yevgeny Vitishko—an environmentalist who had been outspokenly critical of Sochi preparations—was slapped with a dubious, preemptive arrest on "petty hooliganism" charges. Vitishko's alleged crime was swearing at a bus stop. As the Games began, he was handed a three-year sentence, ostensibly for spray-painting a fence.[60] When activist David Khakim staged a one-man protest to support Vitishko, he was arrested and sentenced to thirty hours of community service for carrying out an "illegal picket."[61] These cases highlight how little political space existed for expressing dissent in the context of the Sochi Games.

This limited political opportunity structure did not stop the bold, mediagenic, performance art collective Pussy Riot from taking action during the Olympic moment. In December 2013, Maria Alyokhina and Nadezhda Tolokonnikova were released from prison. Partway through the Olympics, ten members of the group—including Alyokhina and Tolokonnikova—were detained by security officials on the peculiar suspicion of stealing a woman's handbag from a hotel, but police opted to drop the charges.[62] When they carried out a guerrilla performance in Sochi, they were attacked by horsewhip-wielding Cossacks. Police officials in street clothes sprayed a mace-like irritant in the activists' faces. As James Compton points out in his chapter in this volume, all this was captured on camera for the world to see.[63] Kozak blamed Pussy Riot for carrying out a "hooligan act," arguing, "The girls came here specifically to provoke this conflict. They had been searching for it for some time and finally they had this conflict with local inhabitants."[64] Activist Semyon Simonov posted online information about Pussy Riot's consistent harassment in Sochi. Previously, Simonov, a local human-rights worker with Memorial—an NGO that documented migrant-worker abuse at Olympic construction sites—was repeatedly questioned by Russian security forces in the lead-up to the Games. He was also denied a spectator passport—an additional security filter needed to enter the Olympic Park—even though he possessed an event ticket.[65]

The media paid attention when Doku Umarov, a high-profile Chechen rebel, implored his fellow militants to "do their utmost to derail" the Olympics, which he viewed as "satanic dances on the bones of our ancestors."[66] Yet, peaceful dissident citizens were also protesting the fact that Sochi 2014 was transpiring on blood-soaked land: these were Adygean nationalists, or Circassians. The Sochi Games occurred on the 150-year anniversary of the Circassians' forced removal from the Black Sea littoral by Tsar Alexander II, an event that scholar Matthew Light describes as a "violent ethnic cleansing of the indigenous inhabitants." He notes that "many Circassian activists today would use the term 'genocide'."[67] The downhill ski slope in the Yasnaya Polyana mountain area is site of a brutal nineteenth-century battle in which the Russians violently pacified the local population; Yasnaya Polyana translates to "red meadow" due to the bloodstained fields the battle left in its wake.[68] New Jersey-based Circassian Dana Wojokh, asked me, "Would you have an Olympics in Darfur? Would you have an Olympics in Auschwitz? No, so why Sochi?"[69]

Wojokh, teamed up with fellow Circassians to jumpstart the activist group No Sochi 2014. Zack Barsik, an active member of the group, told me. "For 150 years, Circassians around the world always wanted their rights to be heard and their grievances to be addressed, and once Sochi popped up, it crystallized into the perfect platform for Circassians to try to bring to the world the plight that we've been experiencing."[70] According to political scientist Sufian Zhemukhov, since 2005 the modern Circassian movement has been revitalized around three "shared strategic goals"—"recognition of the genocide, repatriation of the diaspora, and unification of the territories." In regards to the Olympics, Circassians were not monolithic, but exhibited a diversity of opinions, from cancellation of the Games to unconditional support.[71]

Between 2008 and 2014, No Sochi 2014 carried out more than a hundred demonstrations, from Istanbul to Israel, from Germany to Jordan, and from New York to the Caucasus.[72] On May 21, 2012, the anniversary of Circassian surrender to Tsarist forces in 1864, No Sochi 2014 mobilized a worldwide day of action in Brussels, Istanbul, and New York in an effort to raise awareness of the Circassian plight.[73] A few months later, No Sochi 2014 took its show on the road to London where it convened at the Albert Memorial in Kensington Gardens, directly in front of the Sochi House, the official Sochi 2014 Winter Olympics hotspot, where for £30 (US$45) one could consume the pro-Putin version of the upcoming Games. Just outside, No Sochi 2014 activists—donning traditional Circassian clothing—presented an alternative narrative that included the genocide of the Circassian people. Blending anti-Olympics chants and Circassian history, they presented their case to passersby and members of international media.[74]

In Russia, Circassian activists organized demonstrations in Nalchik and Maykop—cities in the same region as Sochi—to protest the Games. Russian police rounded up dissident citizens and arrested leader Asker Sokht. Intimidation rippled through Russia, with many Circassians not wanting to go on record for fear of government reprisal.[75] No Sochi 2014 held solidarity demonstrations across the scattered diaspora. On the night of the Sochi 2014 opening ceremony, more than two hundred activists descended on Times Square in New York. "We had to have a physical protest," said Wojokh. Barsik added, "Everyone was in solidarity: Georgians, Armenians, Polish, Ukrainians, Estonians, Lithuanians, Latvians. Anyone who had previous experience with Russian imperialism and occupation supported us." Wojokh noted that because it wasn't possible to go to Sochi, "The Internet and specifically Twitter was the way to get our message out there." She added that the group organized events "wherever there was a Circassian who could hold up a sign," but that "most of our action—and most of our success—came with contacting media outlets and journalists who might have an angle to tell our story."[76] The No Sochi 2014 website was hacked as the Olympics got underway, but activists pressed ahead with their message.[77] As Wojokh noted, the Olympics were

> the perfect platform for us to talk about the issues that are facing the Circassian world: issues of repatriation, issues of our identity crisis as Circassians in diaspora and even in the homelands, the rights that we do not even have in the homeland, and the assimilation we are facing with the loss of our language, the loss of our culture by living in diaspora and elsewhere.[78]

An Olympic pivot?

As the Sochi Olympics drew to a close, Olympics booster Dimitry Kozak asserted the Games were an unbridled success for "the new Russia. The Games have turned our culture, our people into something that is a lot closer, more appealing and more understandable for the rest of the world." Kozak said there was not a single thing he would have changed about Olympic preparations, noting, "You can see that Russia has kept its word. Russia managed to prove to itself and the rest of the world that we are capable of making the impossible, possible."[79]

Clearly, not everyone agreed with this sunny assessment. The Sochi Olympics were the most expensive in the history of the modern Games. Athletes and activists questioned the legitimacy of Russia's anti-gay law. Some challenged the IOC for its moral judgment and wishy-washy standards. Environmentalists disputed Olympic sustainability rhetoric. Circassians used the Games as a platform for spotlighting repressive political history. But the political atmosphere in Sochi—and Russia more generally—was not propitious for political activists who wanted to challenge the predominant logic that the Olympics were a positive development for the country. The political opportunity structure in Sochi meant dissident citizenship was extremely limited.

A political opportunity structure can be broken down into six central tenets:

1   the openness of the political institutions of the host city and country;
2   the solidity of elite alliances in support of the Games;
3   the presence or absence of elite allies for activists to work with;
4   the ability and willingness of security forces to clamp down on dissent;
5   the presence of international pressures that aid the activist cause; and
6   the receptivity of the mass media.[80]

With Olympic activism, demonstrators typically face an uphill battle. Even in democratic host cities, elites across the political spectrum tend to sing from the same Olympic hymnal. Security forces set up to fight terrorism are there to quash dissent. And the Games are popular across the globe.

But as we have seen, in Russia, the political opportunity structure was especially unpropitious. Even with a relatively controversial host, everyday people were hesitant to politicize the Games. The month before Sochi 2014 commenced, a CBS poll asked, "Do you think political expression should have a role in the Olympic games because it can bring attention to important issues, or do you think political expression should not have a role in the Olympic games because the attention should be on the events and the athletes?" Respondents overwhelmingly condoned the IOC's brand of apoliticism, with 82 percent stating that political expression and the Olympics should not mix. Only 13 percent of those polled believed the Games were a reasonable platform for raising political issues while 5 percent were unsure.[81] In the context of the Olympics, the wider social receptivity of groups challenging dominant five-ring power relations is complicated.

Nevertheless, the 2014 Sochi Olympics may change the political-economic equation. Sochi's $51 billion price tag has had a ripple effect on subsequent Olympic bidding. Voters in Krakow, Munich, Stockholm, and Switzerland all rejected the Games, leaving Beijing and Almaty, Kazakhstan as the two remaining candidates to host the 2022 Winter Olympics. High costs were a centerpiece of discussion in each locality's referendum.[82] And skepticism extends beyond the Winter Games. Dan O'Connell, president of the group backing Boston's bid for the 2024 Summer Olympics, observed, "The Olympic brand has been damaged by the oligarchs. Sochi is an embarrassment to the Olympic movement."[83]

The IOC is experiencing a slow-motion crisis and the new President of the IOC—Thomas Bach of Germany—appears to be aware of it. His "Agenda 2020" plan to reform the Games takes aim at the problems that surfaced in Sochi.[84] Bach even recently acknowledged the inherently political nature of the Olympic Games, remarking at the 2014 Asian Games, "In the past, some have said that sport has nothing to do with politics, or they have said that sport has nothing to do with money or business." He continued, "And this is just an attitude which is wrong and which we cannot afford anymore. We are living in the middle of society and that means that we have to partner up with the politicians who run this world."[85] If the Olympics pivot in a new direction, the 2014 Sochi Games will likely be a key explanatory factor.

Notes

1 Wilson, "Russia Wins 2014 Cold War," 105.
2 Ostapenko, "Nation Branding of Russia," 60–61.
3 Boykoff, "Celebration Capitalism."
4 Orttung and Zhemukhov, "The 2014 Sochi Olympic Mega-Project," 184.
5 Pew Research Center, "Public Skeptical."
6 Price, "On Seizing the Olympic Platform," 89.
7 *Hobart Mercury*, "Russia's Winter Ecstasy," 57.
8 Human Rights Watch, "Laws of Attrition," 1.
9 Ibid, 14.
10 Ibid, 14–17.
11 Ibid, 25.
12 Hahn, "Russia in 2012," 221; Weir, "Russian Activists Sound Alarm": David M. Herszenhorn and Andrew E. Kramer, "Russian Protesters Challenge Permit Law," *Boston Globe*, 16 December 16, 2012: http://bostonglobe.com/news/world/2012/12/16/couple-thousand-demonstrators-march-moscow-unsanctioned-protest/ANwYEoofs5wsfiakq67E7H/story.html.
13 Weir, "Putin Warns of Growing Terror Risks as Kremlin Arrests Opposition Leader," *Christian Science Monitor*, October 17, 2012: http://www.csmonitor.com/World/Europe/2012/1017/Putin-warns-of-growing-terror-risks-as-Kremlin-arrests-opposition-leader; Michael Idov, "Putin rival's sentence forces the question: what next for opposition?," *Guardian*, July 18, 2013: http://www.theguardian.com/world/2013/jul/18/putin-rival-sentence-alexei-navalny-opposition; "Alexei Navalny Freed by Russian Court but Conviction for Theft Is Upheld," *Reuters*, October 16, 2013; http://www.theguardian.com/world/2013/oct/16/alexei-navalny-freed-russian-court/.
14 Elder, "Censorship Row over Russian Internet Blacklist," *Guardian*, November 12, 2012: http://www.guardian.co.uk/world/2012/nov/12/censorship-row-russian-internet-blacklist.
15 Greenslade, "Russia Blocks Access to Blog Site," *Guardian*, February 11, 2014: http://www.theguardian.com/media/greenslade/2013/feb/11/censorship-russia.

16 "Sochi, Sport and Security: Russia Bans Protests During Winter Olympics, Limits Access," *Russia Today*, August 24, 2013: http://rt.com/news/sochi-protest-ban-olym pics-931/.

17 Herszenhorn, "A Russian Protest Zone Where Almost No One Registers a Complaint," *New York Times*, February 14, 2014, A12; Jules Boykoff and Dave Zirin, "Sochi Games Are Apt Venue for Athlete Activism," *San Francisco Chronicle*, January 24, 2014, A20.

18 Kramer, "Russia Passes Bill Targeting Some Discussions of Homosexuality," *New York Times*, June 12, 2013, A5.

19 Lenskyj, *Sexual Diversity and the Sochi 2014 Olympics*, 81.

20 "Gay Rights in Russia: Facts and Myths," *Russia Today*, August 2, 2013: http://rt.com/ news/russia-gay-law-myths-951/; Sean Ingle, "Sebastian Coe and David Cameron Dismiss Winter Olympics Boycott Idea," *Guardian*, August 10, 2013: http://www. theguardian.com/world/2013/aug/10/sebastian-coe-winter-olympics-boycott;   Martin Pengelly, "Obama and Fry Have History on Their Side," *Guardian*, August 8, 2013: http://www.theguardian.com/commentisfree/2013/aug/08/obama-fry-russia-olympics-gay-laws.

21 Tilly, "Repression, Mobilization, and Explanation," 224–5.

22 Price, "On Seizing the Olympic Platform," 89.

23 For more on All Out, see: https://www.allout.org and for more on Athlete Ally, see: http://www.athleteally.org.

24 Gibson and Walker, "Olympians Urge Russia to Reconsider 'Gay Propaganda' Laws," *Guardian*, January 30, 2014: http://www.theguardian.com/sport/2014/jan/30/olympic-athletes-russia-repeal-anti-gay-laws.

25 Gibson and Luhn, "Calls to Boycott Winter Olympics over Laws 'that treat gays as Hitler did Jews'," *Guardian*, August 8, 2014, 9.

26 Fierstein, "Russia's Anti-Gay Crackdown," *New York Times*, July 22, 2013, A19.

27 Zirin, "Boycott Sochi?" *Grantland*, August 1, 2013: http://grantland.com/features/gay-rights-sochi-boycott-movement/.

28 Pew Research Center, "Public Skeptical of Decision."

29 International Olympic Committee, *Olympic Charter*, 93.

30 Boykoff and Zirin, "Sochi Games Are Apt Venue for Athlete Activism."

31 "Obama Names Billie Jean King as One of Two Gay Sochi Olympic Delegates," *Associated Press*, December 17, 2013: http://www.theguardian.com/sport/2013/dec/ 18/obama-names-gay-delegates-sochi-olympics.

32 Whiteside, "U.S. Sochi Group Sends 'Respectful' Statement: Including Gay Athletes Adds to Heat on Russian Anti-Gay Law," *USA Today*, December 18, 2013, 1C.

33 Brennan, "U.S. Delegation Delivers Strong Message in Sochi," *USA Today*, February 7, 2014: http://www.usatoday.com/story/sports/olympics/sochi/2014/02/07/winter-games-putin-obama-boitano-gay-propaganda/5275387/.

34 Whiteside, "Wagner, Miller Slam Russia's Anti-Gay Laws," *USA Today*, October 1, 2013, 3C.

35 Whiteside, "USOC Favors Charter Fix," *USA Today*, 2 October 2013, 7C.

36 Gibson and Walker, "Olympians Urge Russia to Reconsider 'Gay Propaganda' Laws," *Guardian*, January 30, 2014: http://www.theguardian.com/sport/2014/jan/30/olympic-athletes-russia-repeal-anti-gay-laws.

37 See "What Is Principle 6?" at http://www.principle6.org.

38 Ibid.

39 Lenskyj, *Sexual Diversity and the Sochi 2014 Olympics*, 83.

40 See: "Who Is Already Part of the Principle 6 Campaign?": http://www.principle6.org; Boykoff and Zirin, "Sochi Games Are Apt Venue for Athlete Activism."

41 Brigidi, "Sochi 2014: Brian Burke Calls Russia's Anti-Gay Law 'Repugnant'," *SB Nation*, August 27, 2013: http://www.sbnation.com/nhl/2013/8/27/4664566/brian-burke-russia-anti-gay-law-olympics-2014.

42 Zirin, "Sochi Games Are Apt Venue."

43 Whiteside, "Wagner, Miller Slam Russia's Anti-Gay Laws."

44 Brundage, "Address: 67th Solemn Opening Session, Mexico City, Mexico."

45 Dillman, "A Pussy Riot Homage? Alexey Sobolev's Olympics Board Raises Questions," *Los Angeles Times*, February 6, 2014: http://articles.latimes.com/2014/feb/06/sports/la-sp-on-pussy-riot-alexey-sobolev-olympics-20140206.

46 Jones, "Snowboarder Gets Thousands of Texts after Writing Cell Number on Helmet," *USA Today*, February 7, 2014: http://ftw.usatoday.com/2014/02/snowboarder-alexey-sobolev-sochi-olympics.

47 Ziller, "Out Snowboarder Cheryl Maas Displays Rainbow Glove in Sochi," *SB Nation*, February 7, 2014: http://www.sbnation.com/2014/2/7/5389570/cheryl-maas-rainbow-glove-lgbt-sochi-olympics-snowboarding.

48 "US Ski Team Member Andrew Newell & 105 Winter Olympians Call for Climate Action," *Protect Our Winters*, February 10, 2014: http://protectourwinters.org/newell-2890#sthash.jb2gXzLx.21crWIKx.dpbs.

49 "In the Olympic Spirit, Shut Up and Ski," *Investor's Business Daily*, February 14, 2014, A14.

50 Pinelli and Hula, "Sochi Scene – Mountain Report; Ukraine Fallout; Putin on Hockey," *Around the Rings*, February 20, 2014: http://aroundtherings.com/site/A__46105/title__Sochi-Scene-Mountain-Report-Ukraine-Fallout-Putin-on-Hockey/292/Articles.

51 Hula, "Gold Medal Matchup Set; Moment of Silence for Ukraine," *Around the Rings*, February 21, 2014: http://aroundtherings.com/site/A__46130/title__Gold-Medal-Matchup-Set-Moment-of-Silence-for-Ukraine/292/Articles.

52 Boykoff and Zirin, "The Sochi Paralympics, Ukraine, and the Olympic Truce," *The Nation*, March 16, 2014: http://www.thenation.com/blog/178865/sochi-paralympics-ukraine-and-olympic-truce#.

53 "Sochi Paralympics: Games End with Colourful Ceremony," *BBC*, March 16, 2014: http://www.bbc.com/sport/0/disability-sport/26602384.

54 Gaffney, "Between Discourse and Reality," 3929.

55 Hayes and Horne, "Sustainable Development, Shock and Awe?" 761.

56 Müller, "(Im-)Mobile policies."

57 Ibid. 16.

58 Environmental Watch on North Caucasus, "Sochi 2014: Independent Environmental Report."

59 "Russian Ecologists 'Trashing' 2014 Sochi Olympics – Deputy PM," *RIA Novosti*, March 12, 2010: http://en.ria.ru/sports/20100312/158174256.html.

60 Amnesty International, "Russia: Civil society activist arrested ahead of start of Sochi Olympics," February 3, 2014: http://www.amnesty.org/en/news/russia-civil-society-activist-arrested-ahead-start-sochi-olympics-2014-02-03; Shaun Walker, "Sochi Environmentalist Jailed for Three Years for Spray-Painting a Fence," *Guardian*, February 12, 2014: http://www.theguardian.com/environment/2014/feb/12/sochi-environmentalist-jailed-painting-fence-revenge.

61 Walker, "Police Detain 'Illegal Picket' Protesters at Sochi Winter Olympics," *Guardian*, February 17, 2014: http://www.theguardian.com/world/2014/feb/17/police-detain-illegal-picket-protesters-sochi-winter-olympics.

62 Walker, "Pussy Riot Members among Group of Activists Arrested in Sochi," *Guardian*, February 18, 2014: http://www.theguardian.com/music/2014/feb/18/pussy-riot-members-arrested-sochi-winter-olympics; Gessen, *Words Will Break Cement.*

63 Also see, Roth, "Members of Russian Protest Group Attacked by Cossacks in Sochi," *New York Times*, February 20, 2014, A4.

64 "Deputy Prime Minister Dmitry Kozak Defends Pussy Riot Treatment in Sochi," *Independent*, February 18,2014; http://www.independent.co.uk/sport/olympics/winter-olympics-2014-deputy-prime-minister-dmitry-kozak-defends-pussy-riot-treatment-in-sochi-9146392.html.

65 Human Rights Watch, "Silencing Activists, Journalists Ahead of Sochi Games," August 7, 2014: http://www.hrw.org/news/2013/08/06/russia-silencing-activists-journalists-ahead-sochi-games; Nataliya Vasilyeva "Activists in Court over Access to Sochi Games," *Associated Press*, January 31, 2014: http://bigstory.ap.org/article/activists-court-over-access-sochi-games-0.

66 Vasilyeva, "Rebel Leader Urges Fighters to Derail Sochi Olympics," *Associated Press*, July 4, 2013: http://www.bostonglobe.com/news/world/2013/07/03/chechen-rebel-calls-for-attacks-sochi-games/gSi3MVpifXu86X9VApWUDO/story.html.

67 Light, "Migration, 'Globalised' Islam and the Russian State," 211.

68 Light, "Sochi and the Northwest Caucasus – II."

69 Personal interview, July 29, 2012.

70 Personal interview, October 21, 2014.

71 Zhemukhov, "The Birth of Modern Circassian Nationalism," 506.

72 Personal interview with Zack Barsik, October 21, 2014.

73 Bullough, "Sochi 2014 Winter Olympics: The Circassians Cry Genocide," *Newsweek*, May 21, 2012: http://www.newsweek.com/sochi-2014-winter-olympics-circassians-cry-genocide-64893.

74 Boykoff, *Activism and the Olympics,* 171.

75 Watson, Gena Somra and Dina Filippova, "Russia Arrests Leader of Circassian Ethnic Minority," *CNN*, February 17, 2014: http://www.cnn.com/2014/02/16/world/europe/russia-arrest/ Nalchik sits in the south of Russia, east of Sochi, while Maykop is to the north of the Olympic city.

76 Personal interviews with Dana Wojokh and Zack Barsik, October 21, 2014.

77 Bacchi, "Sochi Winter Olympics: Circassian Protest Website NoSochi2014 Hacked on Games' Eve," *International Business Times*, February 7, 2014: http://www.ibtimes.co.uk/sochi-winter-olympics-circassian-protest-website-nosochi2014-hacked-games-eve-1435553.

78 Personal interview, October 21, 2014.

79 Hula, "Kozak Says Sochi Broke 'Ice of Skepticism,' Offers New Sochi Cost," *Around the Rings*, February 22, 2014: http://aroundtherings.com/site/A__46133/title__Kozak-Says-Sochi-Broke-%60%60Ice-of-Skepticism%60%60-Offers-New-Sochi-Cost/292/Articles.

80 Boykoff, *Activism and the Olympics*, 27.

81 CBS News Poll, January 15–19, 2014: http://www.pollingreport.com/olympics.htm.

82 Boykoff, "A Bid for a Better Olympics," *New York Times*, August 14, 2014, A23.

83 Quinn, "Boston's $4.5B Olympic Plans Include a Temporary Stadium, Beach Volleyball on Common, Additional $5B in Infrastructure," *MassLive*, October 17, 2014: http://www.masslive.com/news/boston/index.ssf/2014/10/boston_olympic_plans.html.

84 International Olympic Committee, "IOC President Thomas Bach Announces Composition of Olympic Agenda 2020 Working Groups," May 22, 2014: http://www.olympic.org/news/ioc-president-thomas-bach-announces-composition-of-olympic-agenda-2020-working-groups/231913.

85 Bodeen, "IOC's Bach Says Sports and Politics Do Mix," *Associated Press*, September 20, 2014: http://www.miamiherald.com/news/business/article2179027.html.

Bibliography

Boykoff, Jules. *Activism and the Olympics: Dissent at the Games in Vancouver and London* (New Brunswick, NJ and London: Rutgers University Press, 2014).

———. "Celebration Capitalism and the Sochi 2014 Winter Olympics." *Olympika: The International Journal of Olympic Studies* Vol. 22 (2013): 39–70.

Brundage, Avery. "Address: 67th Solemn Opening Session, Mexico City, Mexico," Avery Brundage Collection, 1908–75, Box 246, Reel 143, October 7, 1968, International Centre for Olympic Studies, London, Ontario.

Environmental Watch on North Caucasus. "Sochi 2014: Independent Environmental Report." March 18, 2014: http://bankwatch.org/sites/default/files/Sochi-Environmental Report-EWNC-Mar2014.pdf

Gaffney, Christopher. "Between Discourse and Reality: The Un-Sustainability of Mega-Event Planning." *Sustainability*, Vol. 5 (2013): 3926–40.

Gessen, Masha. *Words Will Break Cement: The Passion of Pussy Riot* (New York: Riverhead Books, 2014).

Hahn, G.M. "Russia in 2012." *Asian Survey*, Vol. 53, No. 1 (2013): 214–23.

Hayes, Graeme and John Horne. "Sustainable Development, Shock and Awe?: London 2012 and Civil Society." *Sociology*, Vol. 45, No. 5 (2011): 749–64.

Herszenhorn, David M. and Andrew E. Kramer. "Russian Protesters Challenge Permit Law." *Boston Globe*, December 16, 2012: http://bostonglobe.com/news/world/2012/12/16/couple-thousand-demonstrators-march-moscow-unsanctioned-protest/ANwYEoofs5wsfiakq67E7H/story.html.

Hobart Mercury (Australia). "Russia's Winter Ecstasy Black Sea Resort Wins Olympic Bid." July 6, 2007.

Human Rights Watch. "Laws of Attrition: Crackdown on Russia's Civil Society after Putin's Return to the Presidency," April 2013: http://www.hrw.org/reports/2013/04/24/laws-attrition-0.

International Olympic Committee. *Olympic Charter*, Lausanne, Switzerland. September 9, 2013: http://www.olympic.org/documents/olympic_charter_en.pdf.

Lenskyj, Helen Jefferson. *Sexual Diversity and the Sochi 2014 Olympics: No More Rainbows* (New York: Palgrave Macmillan, 2014).

Light, Matthew. "Migration, 'Globalised' Islam and the Russian State: A Case Study of Muslim Communities in Belgorod and Adygeya Regions." *Europe-Asia Studies* Vol. 64, No. 2 (2012): 195–226.

———. "Sochi and the Northwest Caucasus – II." *Global Brief: World Affairs in the 21st Century*, April 12, 2010: http://globalbrief.ca/blog/2010/04/12/sochi-and-the-northwest-caucasus—ii/.

Müller, Martin. "(Im-)Mobile policies: Why Sustainability Went Wrong in the 2014 Olympics in Sochi." *European Urban and Regional Studies* (February 7, 2014): 1–19.

Orttung, Robert W. and Sufian Zhemukhov. "The 2014 Sochi Olympic Mega-Project and Russia's Political Economy." *East European Politics* Vol. 30, No. 2 (2014): 175–91.

Ostapenko, Nikolai. "Nation Branding of Russia through the Sochi Olympic Games of 2014." *Journal of Management Policy and Practice*, Vol. 11, No. 4 (2010): 60–63.

Pew Research Center. "Public Skeptical of Decision to Hold Olympic Games in Russia." *Pew Research Center for the People and the Press*, February 4, 2014: http://www.people-press.org/2014/02/04/public-skeptical-of-decision-to-hold-olympic-games-in-russia/.

Price, Monroe E. "On Seizing the Olympic Platform." In *Owning the Olympics: Narratives of the New China*, Monroe E. Price and Daniel Dayan (eds.) (Ann Arbor: University of Michigan Press, 2008), pp. 86–114.

Tilly, Charles. "Repression, Mobilization, and Explanation." In *Repression and Mobilization*, Christian Davenport, Hank Johnston, and Carol Mueller (eds.) (Minneapolis and London: University of Minnesota Press, 2005), pp. 211–25.

Weir, Fred. "Russian Activists Sound Alarm at Soaring Fines for Civil 'Disorder'." *Christian Science Monitor*, June 5. 2012: http://www.csmonitor.com/World/Europe/2012/0605/Russian-activists-sound-alarm-at-soaring-fines-for-civil-disorder.

Wilson, Jim. "Russia Wins 2014 Cold War." *Herald Sun* (Australia). July 6, 2007.

Zhemukhov, Sufian. "The Birth of Modern Circassian Nationalism," *Nationalities Papers*, Vol. 40, No. 4 (July 2012): 503–24.

9   The World Cup, the security state, and the colonized Other

Reflections on Brazil, Russia, South Africa, and Qatar

Grant Farred

The 2014 World Cup in Brazil was foreshadowed from the outset by concerns about Brazil's ability to successfully stage the competition and was superseded by the specter of World Cups to come. The numbers vary, but at least nine workers are reported to have died in the process of constructing stadiums—and related buildings—for the World Cup. The run-up to the competition featured widespread criticism and protests within Brazil and, as late as the eve of the opening game, sources reported some 40 percent of Brazilians opposed the World Cup, citing government corruption and a preference for funds to be allotted to education and health rather than to a sports mega-event. Several of the stadiums built, such as the one in Manaus, in the heart of the rain forest (Amazonas state), are condemned to have little use after the tournament. The local Manaus team, Nacional Futebol Clube (known as "Nacional"), plays to crowds of, at best, three to four thousand, so the stadium was destined to become a white elephant from the very beginning: gaudy, visible, and with no apparent purpose (see Chris Gaffney's chapter in this volume). In other words, you can build it, but they won't come.

The construction of these stadiums and related "renewal" projects, along with policing the protests against them, set significant political forces in motion and raised a number of important issues. These were often local in character, highly specific to Brazilian ambition and Brazilian history, but they also referenced similar forces at play, and issues at stake, in other World Cups held in the recent past and yet to be held in the future. This essay explores the interplay between World Cup ambitions, the continued growth of the high-security state and issues of colonial and racial difference, drawing examples from the recent World Cup in Brazil, the South African World Cup in 2010, and future World Cups in Russia in 2018 and Qatar in 2022.

The security state and the management of dissent

It has become obvious that mega-events create increasing opportunities for the expansion of state power and surveillance. If major sports events, post-9/11, have been marked by increasing security—with arms manufacturers making a killing (the pun is unavoidable) by providing material support to police and military units in nations or cities hosting such events—then it is important to properly identify the nature of the threat. Increased militarization is intended to safeguard sports venues, spectators and, of course, tourists, from local antagonisms as well as from "terrorist attacks" (which are internal or external in derivation).

In truth, however, new and more effective modes of security are more likely to be aimed at the local population than any terrorist threat. For the last year or more before the World Cup, under the banner of "pacification," the Brazilian police engaged in bringing Rio's favelas to order by attacking both dissent originating there and, with (some) public support, seeking to bring organized crime under control, thereby making the favelas safer and, in some instances, promoting gentrification.[1] Policing was also directed to suppressing protests beyond those by activists who insisted that Brazil could make better use of its resources than host the World Cup. The concern for security also meant tighter policing over protests against deracination, the treatment of unions, transportation costs, and inadequate infrastructure to deal with the needs of the poor. In other words, the police focused on suppressing local opposition and stymieing unrest that could destabilize or seem to reflect badly on the host nation; a handy dry run for the 2016 Olympics. Clearly, this program of "pacification" worked, at least insofar as it kept the specter of major protests from the world's cameras for the duration of the World Cup itself. Or, at least it worked to keep the visual evidence of protest to a minimum in the several media modes that make it fairly easy to transmit images of any kind in our high-tech era. When critics of the 2014 event wrote, then, that "this World Cup may well be remembered less for the events on the pitch than the events on the streets,"[2] they did so, it turns out, with a sense of wistful—and unfounded, one regrets to say—political optimism. If the run-up to World Cup 2014 featured global coverage of social unrest, when all was said and done, the actual event was mega-event business as usual.

After the prospect of disruption dissipated, the world was once again free to attend to matters on the pitch, from the questionable refereeing to the surprise (and welcome, one should add) performance by unfancied teams (Chile, Costa Rica, Columbia and, after a dour performance in their opening match, Algeria; the US too, gave yet another spirited showing) and the grandiose failures of traditional European power houses (Spain, Italy, England); not forgetting, of course, Luis Suarez's form as goal poacher (against England) and as "cannibal." Suarez first earned this sobriquet in the Netherlands during his time there with Ajax. It is a practice, his biting opponents, he has now twice repeated—once in England, for his former club Liverpool against Chelsea (2013) and now for Uruguay against Italy in the 2014 World Cup. The bite that was tweeted and circulated "virally" around the world became a World Cup meme, more universally visible than representations of political protest.

It is true that the specter of opposition was never entirely quelled in Brazil, but, like South Africa in 2010, it was superbly managed. Despite the protests and the (relatively) widely shared unease about Brazil's decision to host the World Cup, one wonders—now especially in light of the "globalization" of the "Charlie Hebdo event" (with ripple effects in places as far apart as Cameroon and the Middle East)—about the security concerns that threaten to plague the World

Cup when Russia hosts in 2018. These concerns are discussed in detail in Jules Boykoff's chapter in this volume; however, it is worth reiterating the intensity of the "pacification program" adopted by the Putin government in regard to the 2014 Sochi Winter Olympics (which included euthanizing stray dogs in Sochi). Sochi is one of the eleven host cities for the 2018 World Cup) and one can only imagine the scrutiny that Russia will be subjected to when its turn arrives in 2018. The Sochi 2014 "pacification" program was aimed, simultaneously, at two kinds of nationals: those identifiable within the Russian Federation, who made their opposition visible as Russian citizens, and those who operated under conditions of greater stealth. While still, technically, Russian citizens, ethno-nationalist groups, and the Chechnyans, were understood to constitute a far graver and more violent threat to the state and the Winter Games it was hosting—and, of course, the World Cup that Russia is due to host.

It is impossible to conceive that the "threat" which derives from the Caucasus—assigned, loosely speaking, the name of "Islam" (as in "terrorism," "Islamic anger" at its nineteenth-century displacement from what is today southern Russia, and so on)—will have been satisfactorily resolved by then. Given the long durée of the Chechen "question"—which cannot but raise questions about other "questions" that turn on predominantly Muslim populations—it is likely that the 2018 World Cup will further elevate the high level of security that characterized the Sochi Winter Olympics. Given this unsettled state of things, we must approach the Russian Federation as a political bloc that is at once aggressive toward its neighbors, especially the Ukraine (annexing Crimea, and involved, whether directly or not, in violent struggles in eastern Ukraine with the city of Donetsk currently a key battleground), and internally vulnerable (the Caucasus, and "local" opponents, from Alexei Navalny to Pussy Riot); or, in the logic of realpolitik, aggressive precisely because it recognizes its vulnerabilities.

The 2018 World Cup will be hosted, then, in anticipation of violence against the event. Because it is a global event, it invites—it instigates, it provides an international stage for—the very violence it sets itself against. This is the paradox of all sports mega-events in the twenty-first century: they are *autoimmune*: they contain within themselves the very conditions for their own destruction. Everything needed to keep the body politic alive—commerce, culture, the desire to belong fully to the world—is precisely what can and, almost inevitably, will transform that organism that is the nation. It is their very globality that, their organizers hope, showcases them as international venues for (other) cosmopolitans. It is in the very staging of these sports extravaganzas that the host nation opens itself up to the world that makes them vulnerable to the world—from within and from without—the world the host nation wishes to impress, the world they wish to draw to themselves. It is in and through that act that autoimmunity—the self-protection that is, simultaneously, the kernel of self-destruction—manifests itself. The host nation invites, literally, in equal measure, praise (celebration as the site of pleasure and nationalist success) and disaster (the unleashing of forces aiming to attack the state because the state has acted against certain aggrieved constituencies in the past).

Autoimmunity as such animates a set of strategic questions, all of which are critical to the success of the 2018 World Cup. Will Moscow and St. Petersburg, Sochi and Kalingrad, be safe from "terror" for players, officials, and fans, given Russia's renowned intransigence and its nominal gestures (releasing dissidents— politicians such Navalny and artists such as Pussy Riot, the latter of whom were treated with a "firm hand" for their actions around Sochi) on the eve of Sochi Winter Olympics? If the presence of tanks around the stadia and on the streets of South Africa's major cities, Cape Town, Johannesburg, Durban, was a fact of life during the 2010 World Cup, what kind of public reassurances will police the stadiums in Moscow, St. Petersburg, Vladivostok? After all, a city such as Vladivostok is close to China and North Korea, nations with whom Russia has an uneasy relationship. The answers to such questions will surely be given in the form of further militarization, something that has already become *de rigueur* for the World Cup. Escalating militarization is what we can expect to see for all such extravaganzas, now and in the future: the host nation flaunting its highly developed security apparatus (there were more members of the British Army on patrol in London at the 2012 Olympics than there were British troops in Afghanistan)[3] in a bid to keep its citizens and its economic assets safe (among which the tourist industry ranks highly in the time of the sports extravaganza). Moreover, the military hardware acquired to protect the global sport mega-event is never condemned to the arms dustbin in the wake of the event. It is, rather, put to political and military use against restive or historically vulnerable populations (as the case in Ferguson, MO, made so dramatically visible): those who oppose the state from both inside and outside.

In a salient way, it might be possible to argue that Islam (implicitly, as the source of violence, intended against the Russian state) and allegations of corruption have established themselves as central themes for the two World Cups that will follow Brazil 2014. From the moment it was awarded the 2022 tourney, Qatar found itself the target of intense critique. The issues have been wide-ranging. Although allegations of corruption in the bidding process and within FIFA have been a major theme, there have also been concerns expressed about environmental safety, which has led to question about the physical health of workers involved in stadium construction, players and officials, to say nothing of the fans: is it safe for workers to build arenas in 45 degree C heat? Can teams play in the extreme heat in Qatar in June and July? Then there is the matter of World Cup history, where hosting venues are required to offer more than a single viable site: currently, outside of Doha, Qatar does not seem to have much on offer, while Russia, for its part, has proposed eleven venues, stretching the length and breadth of the country.

Furthermore, because of the extreme heat, Qatar is proposing to play in domed rather than open-air stadiums so as to minimize the health concerns for players, referees, and spectators. If games were, for the first time, interrupted for water breaks in Manaus, in the heart of the rain forest in northern Brazil, domed stadia might be the only safe solution in 2022. Playing indoors will give an entirely new dimension to the World Cup, as if the competition were, literally, being shut off from the rest of the local, national, and international population. The World Cup in a bubble, a very expensive and safe bubble, but this gives exclusivity a wholly new—and disenfranchising—meaning. Playing in a domed stadium would mean shutting out the environment, reducing the local context to a kind of late-capitalist "nowhere-" or "anywhere-ness." So, for all its historic significance of the first World Cup in the Middle East/Gulf region, the competition could simultaneously be anywhere—context is reduced to nothing, a potentially remarkable accomplishment, both philosophically and politically—and only in this one place that has the resources to stage so distinct a World Cup. The World Cup, staged not only in a region that has never hosted it, but hosted in an entirely unprecedented way and under conditions heretofore never encountered. Before it even takes place, Qatar is already memorable.

Because of the extreme climatic conditions, the prospect of hosting the 2022 World Cup outside of its traditional time spot of the Northern Hemisphere's summer (June–July) months, has been raised, leaving open the possibility of an unprecedented December World Cup, when the weather would be cooler in Qatar. Playing in December will be more conducive to the game and it will certainly help to improve player safety. This has met with widespread opposition by European officials, who do not want their domestic schedules disrupted—UEFA seems determined to protect the normal schedule for the lucrative Champions League and domestic competitions as well as the traditional winter break in countries such as Germany and Spain. For the UEFA officials, an "unseasonal" World Cup is akin, as Shakespeare's Hamlet might have it, to a (football) "time out of joint," a response, surely to the strong hints that "something is rotten in the state of Qatar."[4] All the same, in addition to the health concerns of the players, the officials, and the public—that is, the spectators and those who perform immediate and ancillary tasks to keep the World Cup games running—there is the matter of keeping those in the tourist, transportation, and supply industries, to name just three, safe. If there was already in Brazil, for the first time in a World Cup, a water break, Qatari conditions will certainly require even greater vigilance.

2022 is not 2010: on relationality and the postcolonial other

In his book, *Poetics of Relation*, the Caribbean author and philosopher, Édouard Glissant, argues:

> we need to figure out whether or not there are other succulencies of Relation in other parts of the world (and already at work in an underground manner) that will suddenly open up other avenues and soon help to correct whatever simplifying, ethnocentric exclusions may have arisen from such a perspective.[5]

The ongoing criticism of Qatar's successful 2022 bid represents not so much a contrast with, as an intensification of, the treatment afforded South Africa when it hosted the 2010 World Cup. 2010 was a historic event but there were, as has become customary, the usual criticisms of the bidding process, cost overruns, the deracination of local communities (especially the most vulnerable constituencies), corruption and tension within South Africa.[6] This is to say nothing about the lack of security in South Africa, which played on the fear of (implicitly and explicitly racialized) violence against international visitors.

South Africa was, of course, not the first time that the World Cup was assigned a nation outside of the Europe-Americas axis.[7] That honor belonged to Asia, to South Korea and Japan in 2002. That was a historic tournament, because it was also the first jointly hosted tourney. Although the World Cup was held in France a year after a major recession in Asia in 1997, the tournament was awarded to Japan and Korea during a time of remarkable economic expansion and reflected the ambition of the host countries to better position themselves in global markets as well as widespread international recognition of the growing power and importance of Asian economies.

South Africa also sought the World Cup for reasons of global recognition and economic ambition. However, 2010 possesses its own signality. It marked FIFA's first turn to the decolonized black world. This was made all the more memorable and venerable for it being South Africa, a nation newly emerged, just a decade earlier, into a non-racial democracy from its apartheid past. For all rhetorical intents and purposes (to ignore, just for a moment, the resident racialized populations of Brazil, Chile, Uruguay, and Argentina), then, 2010 stands as the inaugural "black" World Cup. The Other, not too long ago colonized and subjugated, had finally emerged into full global enfranchisement—overlooking, for a moment, the widespread abjection that continues to obtain in the postcolonial world. Nevertheless, South Africa enjoys the status of exceptional African nation—accounted for, no doubt, by its advanced integration into the Western economy, materially as well as discursively. It seems unlikely that the World Cup will return to Africa anytime soon. The most populous nations, such as Egypt and Nigeria, appear too strife-ridden and "unstable" to host. South Africa, by virtue of its superior infrastructure and its resources stands as the singular "stable" democracy in the continent: the exception that proves the malaise and unsuitability of the continent to organize such an event a second time. South Africa will bid again to host more sporting mega-events, based—implicitly—on these grounds: it is an African nation and the continent deserves a regular opportunity to host "world-class" events; it is a suitable venue precisely because it does not conform to the stereotypes of an African nation, although it bears many resemblances to its African neighbors, including near and far governmental corruption and incredibly high levels of inequality.[8]

On this ground, the difficulty that immediately presents itself is, in a word, *difference*. Why is it that South Africa was, in the main (local opposition and institutional—FIFA's processes notwithstanding), an event mostly welcomed by the international community and Qatar is already, before its coming into itself, the subject of opprobrium, discontent, dissatisfaction, and a slew of allegations? After all, the two regions (if South Africa might be allowed to function, metonymically, itself a problematic designation, as a particular form of colonization) share, broadly, a history of colonization and, most importantly, a peripheral relation to

FIFA. What this difference provokes is the demand for an explanation, not only, as just delineated, of exceptionality. The dominant argument might be that South Africa is the African nation that can host because it conforms to Western modernity because of its signal place in the world's political imagining—first the ethical struggle against white minority rule, followed by the strange, and hugely beneficial (economically and culturally speaking), afterlife of apartheid.

What difference between 2010 and 2022 demands is the thinking, as Édouard Glissant might insist, of relationality. South Africa and Qatar are distinguished by how one event in one place (nation) reveals what Glissant so poetically names the "succulencies of Relation" to "other parts of the world," an "a priori critique," "already at work in an underground manner."[9] Or, to recall the phrase from a famous Algerian who failed as a goalkeeper but succeeded as a philosopher, "They must have had it in their heads all along." This is Jacques Derrida indicting Vichy France, and not Nazi Germany, for the disenfranchisement of the Algerian Jews in 1940.[10]

The "origin" of difference, then, points to that which—already—exists. It is not new, it should not surprise us, and yet it does. In order to apprehend difference, it is necessary to begin with what is "already at work in an underground manner." Yet, the manner in which this process works is not in the least "underground." It is the secret that we all share. It is that body of knowledge available, publicly, to all of us and yet we do not name it so that we are all culpable in giving life to the secret, all equally party to keeping the secret "safe," if not from disclosure (impossible, since the secret is that which is known), then from appropriate disruption into a new mode of circulation.[11]

It is only preliminary, and as such wholly insufficient (if politically necessary) to begin with questions about how Doha stands in relation to Cape Town or Johannesburg. How are those of us in the West to think these distinctly different responses to World Cups hosted by the Other? What politics of difference—the politics of the "break"—obtains in our political unconscious? The answers will be at best predictable, at worst misleading. Most obviously, Qatar is an Islamic country located in the Middle East, in a time when Islam is widely read as a global signifier of "terror." Qatar is also a small oil-rich nation, home to an advanced economy that is massively (and disproportionately) prosperous. Within Qatar, the city of Doha is a gleaming, high-tech center of medical advances and culture. (As art dealers are finding out, Doha now sets the prices in the international market.) If anything, Qatar is (by far) a more "ordered" society than South Africa, in significant measure because it is not as racially diverse—or ethnically divided—as South Africa.

This does not mean, of course, that there are no stratifications, based on issues such as race and ethnicity (skin color, place of origin, level of education, command of "international" languages such as English, and so on) and religion. Most of the Nepali and Indian immigrants and temporary workers are not Muslim; they are more likely to be Hindus or Buddhists[12] Nepal is the birthplace of Buddha: in an Islamic society does this make them more vulnerable? And, what of the Sunni–Shia tensions that are rife in the region? Qatar is more than 70 percent Sunni.

Does this affect how certain Muslim immigrants are treated? All societies, of course, have internal manifestations of difference and there is no reason to believe that Qatar is any different, especially because of its determination to protect both its culture and what can only be labeled the "Qatari brand." At the very least, as international labor observers have found, Qatari capitalism is no less exploitative or pernicious than any other. High-profile advocacy organizations, such as Amnesty International, or the International Confederation of Trade Unions (ITUC), have gone further, suggesting that conditions for migrant workers in Qatar can approximate a form of modern slavery.[13] Intense international lobbying has brought modest gains; for example, Qatar allowed the formation of the first trade union in the emirate in 2012. But, amidst repeated promises of reform from Qatari officials, there has been little change to labor laws that allow authorities a wide range of powers incompatible with international worker rights; these include the right to unilaterally cancel work visas, deny workers the opportunity to change employers, and withhold travel documents.

With almost 90 percent of the Qatari population designated "foreigners," established residents see the Gulf state as particularly vulnerable. For them, it is the condition of autoimmunity in the Gulf writ large. Qatar's fast-growing economy needs foreign workers (which it seems to draw from all over the world in addition to Asia and Africa) to maintain the pace of infrastructure development (and to keep most of the society functioning), but Qatar will not extend citizenship rights to imported workers for fear of its small native population (some 300,000 Qataris who "host" almost 1.5 million foreigners performing various functions in their economy) being overwhelmed by the non-natives. An absolute monarchy ruled by the Al-Thani family, Qatar is the richest country in the world per capita. Most Qataris believe that this is reason enough to limit citizenship and, with that, claims upon this tiny nation's vast wealth.

In both South Africa and Qatar, then, the issue of *the foreigner* is a matter of contention, but far more intensely (if not as violently, yet, as in South Africa) in the Gulf state. Qatar's economy is built on migrant labor. Remembering, as just noted, that "migrant" itself is a term that bears reflection, particularly in relation to how "citizenship" and national belonging operates in Qatari society. This is to say nothing of what the place of birth or origin means for the foreigner in various societies—from the Muslim in France, to the Indian or Nepalese laborer in Doha. James Dorsey, a football fan who follows the labor situation in Qatar closely, writes, "Proponents of a radical reform of Qatar's sponsorship or kafala system that puts workers at the mercy of their employers have argued that Qatar needs to introduce a uniform minimum wage and authorize collective bargaining."[14] In following its ambition to belong fully to the world, to establish itself as properly modern (as not simply a society sustained by its oil and natural gas reserves with an increasingly voracious appetite not only for conspicuous consumption but also for international recognition), Qatar has become dependent on non-native labor. The consequence of this is that the citizens are a minority (albeit a very wealthy minority) in their own country. Qatar's is a national unconscious haunted by the specter of its own vulnerability: how long can the citizen keep the immigrant under control? How long can the quasi-feudal "kafala system" stay in place in the face of international criticism? How long before the world, in the form of trade unions and international NGOs campaigning for worker's rights (humane living conditions, freedom of movement, the right to retain one's travel documents, and so on), entirely disrupts this orderly but inordinately vulnerable society? Qatar 2022: the World Cup funded by nationalist capital, but built primarily by imported and, yes, exploited labor.

For its part, South Africa also has a blemished post-apartheid record as regards its hostile and sometimes violent treatment of foreigners from other African nations. South Africans have coined the term *"amakweri-kweri"* for black foreigners from other African nations; never, saliently, does the term *"amakweri-kweri"* apply to the white European or the North American. A substantial number of black foreigners hail from nations such as Zimbabwe, many of whom are fleeing persecution in their own nation (Robert Mugabe's unending tyranny), or Kenya (where violence periodically, and brutally, erupts), or Somalia (the most glaring example of the contemporary failed modern nation-state, whose violence has dispersed its population the world over, from Cape Town to Minneapolis),[15] or Nigeria, a nation fracturing at its very borders, fracturing into and because of its troubled relationality with its neighbors. The root of Nigeria's difficulty, at the time of writing, is the radical Islamist movement, Boko Haram, which is wreaking havoc with not only northern Nigeria but with all the countries in the region— from Cameroon to Chad.

In football time, twelve years is the blink of an eye, but it is a crucial period in the life of the game. The 2010–2022 nexus provide the bookends to a historic era in international football and FIFA history: *it is the time of the postcolonial subject* (which applies, it must be said, in its own way to South Korea, and Japan, too). It is, as has been suggested, best understood as the time which requires us to locate the very complex Gulf-Africa relations at the core of our thinking of the way in which the world's game, *"joga bonito,"* the "beautiful game," as the Brazilians say, makes immanent a set of political relations that are not always in the forefront of our thinking. The prospect of 2022, already positioned as the event of political difficulty before us, returns us, at once despite and because of itself (because of its resonant historicity), to its ideological and historic antecedent: South Africa. Qatar 2022 is the event of international consternation that cannot, will not, stand by itself.

The force of the "relation" is such that its resonances far exceed itself. The Qatar World Cup brings 2010 back into view as the political disruption that provokes 2022, its true political successor. This demands a new mode of thinking the World Cup. Brazil and Russia, as has been discussed, each have their own evocations, much as they will surely offer singular provocations. But they are merely, relatively speaking, bridges to the salient ways in which 2010 is indubitably linked—and links us—to 2022. The way to Doha, to the Gulf, in footballing terms, must wend its relational way through Cape Town. In itself, such a conundrum—understood as "ethnocentric exclusions"—bears thinking about because, as Glissant argues, in a discussion about Faulkner's work, the "relation is tragic."[16]

Moreover, as Glissant insists, important for us, Faulkner's writing is "somehow theological." And the theological is what we have had "in our heads all along," however we configure it. Islam and the West; Sunni and Shia at war, literally, with each other; the struggle against Islamic radicalism, not only in France or Germany or the US but in places such as Nigeria or Niger, returns us to the violent history of colonialism and the various articulations that underwrote that project.

The signification of race

To speak of colonialism necessarily raises the question of race. Embattled FIFA President Sepp Blatter (who announced in June 2015 that he would resign in the wake of an escalating corruption scandal) has never been prone to insightful or progressive musing. Yet Blatter felt it necessary to name racism as a factor in the widespread criticism that accompanied FIFA awarding the 2022 World Cup to Qatar: "Once again there is a sort of storm against Fifa relating to the Qatar World Cup. Sadly there's a great deal of discrimination and racism and this hurt me."[17]

The bureaucrat has heeded the poet. Blatter has, it might be said, taken Glissant's advice and "opened up other avenues" along and through which to mobilize "racism" as a political shield. Awarding the World Cup to South Africa, in all its historicity—beginning with the iconic visage of Nelson Mandela and ending, if that is the correct term, with the "miracle" of the transition from white minority rule to post-apartheid democracy—made "race" an impermissibility. "Race" was the word that could not be spoken; any critique lacking substance—that is, empirical "proof"—"opened" its speaker up to charges of the impermissible. "Racism," or "neo-colonialism," or "neo-liberalism," a concept that has—however much (little, in truth) ideological purchase the term still possesses—simultaneously become synonymous with "neo-colonialism" and is a euphemism for the term. The history of South Africa converted the 2010 World Cup into (its own) effective prophylactic against race.

Qatar in 2022, however, enjoys no such insularity. Instead, what Blatter's protestations, whatever their expedience, demand is the question about how race—and "racism"—function in relation to Qatar. If the issue of race functions as the repressed, that which could not be spoken, it is mobilized in this instance to protect Qatar from interrogation. In the terms of Blatter's logic, any criticism of Qatar (and its imputed misdeeds) must be understood not as legitimate concerns about the process of bidding practice, itself highly controversial yet lucrative for FIFA, nor about Qatar's own internal racial tensions, but as an attempt to improperly impugn both the process and the beneficiary.

In the process of leveling the charge of racism against his critics, however, Blatter effectively transforms Qatar into the space that is, conceptually and politically, almost indistinct from blackness (that is, from the event of the first "black"—African—World Cup). At the very least, Qatar becomes the site of the Other—in an almost classical way, as if it were sporting capitalism's equivalent of Edward Said's concept of Orientalism.[18] Racism can only function in relation to an object and the object, for all its proximity—its approximating, its resembling—the Self, is definitively not the Self. Here Glissant's notion of poetic relation finds a strange, and strangely haunting, corollary: "The poet's word leads from periphery to periphery, and, yes, it reproduces the track of circular nomadism; that is, it makes every periphery into a center."[19] The repressed, as we know, is precisely that which cannot be kept from view and it returns, more powerful and disruptive than its original articulation.

So it is in relation to race and the World Cup. The discourse of race and racism was *verboten* in 2010 when its historicity demanded full voice. After all, why was 2010 the first time an African country hosted the tournament? Such a question could not be addressed without an account of European colonialism and its violence—there was no African country sovereign "enough" in 1930 to undertake such a project. Uruguay, of course, could do so, because independence had come to Latin America—racism in tow—a full two centuries earlier. In this way, South Africa and Qatar are in relation to each other, addressing each other—despite their discreteness, their geographical differences and specificities, their temporal sovereignty—"periphery to periphery."

It is race which translates them into relation, and makes them address each other, in a time completely "out of joint." It is race, after the fact (and yet not, as I have suggested) for South Africa and with the force of a future anteriority for Qatar, which "centralizes" them. It does not do so, moreover, discretely. It produces a coherence through and because of racism: the black African World Cup and the Gulf World Cup—the intensely discrete and resonant singularity of the Other. The Other is always, as Glissant's poet well knows, in relation to all Others. That is the force of Occidentalism: in its determination to make the *Other* Other, it must refuse (deny) the Other any singularity. The force of Occidentalism is that it makes (all) the Other(s) one; the effect of that suturing is, paradoxically, not to render all Others the same but to un-suture one Other from an-other Other; and, even more importantly, it is because of Occidentalism's desire to "flatten" difference that the singularity—the oneness of the Other, its ipseity, if you will— of the Other emerges. The effect of this emergence is to make all Others singular (distinct, un-suturable) in relation to every other Other.

Blatter's invocation of racism lets loose more than just the ghost of racism— that is, of course, a live presence in FIFA's world. The organization has adopted the slogan, "Stamp out Racism," or, as it is more commonly rendered, "Say No to Racism." In addition to supporting sanctions for racist acts, FIFA has also opted for more dramatic public relations gestures, such as organizing a match in the name of Nelson Mandela in 2007, between an "All African" XI and a "Rest of the World" XI.[20] Various prominent clubs, such as FC Barcelona, have also promoted anti-racism in their own footballing terms. Barcelona recently campaigned under the slogan "Put Racism Offside," complete with a thoughtful pose by Barcelona and Spain central defender Gerard Piqué. Yet, racist acts, as Piqué well knows, occur routinely in Spanish stadiums and, indeed, in stadiums all over Europe. Italy[21] and Spain were the most egregious violators in the 2013/14 season. Piqué's own teammate, Dani Alves, was subjected to a series of racist taunts in a 2014 match with Villareal, at the latter's El Madrigal stadium. At one point, a Villareal fan threw a banana at Alves. Bananas are meant as a symbol of black players' relation to monkeys, signifying that black players belong to a lower order of being. Alves, adroitly, picked up the banana and took a bite out of it, almost ironizing the racist gesture.[22]

Blatter's use of the term "racism" gives the practice a multivalent life (it assumes predictable guises and entirely unexpected formations) because he cannot, and will not, define racism. The work of the term "racism," as used by Blatter, is not to act against those who indict the Other, but, rather, *to immunize the Other* (Qatar, in this instance, or South Africa in the bidding process for 2010) against charges that implicate the Self (FIFA and, of course, Blatter himself). Blatter's charge of "racism" reverberates, then, as a politically expedient—and rhetorically hollow—mobilizing of a term. Blatter invokes the term to silence, not to address, the extent to which racism is rooted in world football, at all levels, in every possible way that affects the playing and administration of the game. Blatter's speaking racism, then, makes the injunction—designed to serve as an indictment—a matter for skepticism.

This is a forced relation that makes of the charge "racism" a signifier that is at once empty and intensely resonant. It is an empty signifier because it has no meaning in this context. Blatter's charge, which is, in truth, a defense against (his) critics (and those who want to see FIFA clean up corruption in the organization), has no meaning except the mobilizing of a charged term: "racism" is employed not against racist acts but as a way to ward off critiques—and challenges to Blatter's FIFA presidency. This is, arguably, the function of the empty signifier: it is, by its very nature, susceptible to misuse (it is ripe for abuse); it can be made to do any rhetorical work that the speaker desires. And yet, of course, the force of the empty signifier is that it is never, historically, empty (i.e., evacuated of meaning, without a tradition, or a series of resonances that it addresses) so that it always possesses the power of evocation. There is always "something" tangible, politically tenable (it "applies"/refers to something other than itself), to the empty signifier; it is, for this reason a force to contend with, an articulation capable of mobilizing, of re-ordering (frequently, but not always, through disruption) relations.

In this way the empty signifier—or, rather, the empty signifier that is the signifier awaiting its (re-)signification, i.e., the signification that comes after its "original," unshakeable "first" speaking—is decidedly not empty. It resonates in and by itself. It is always, as if magnetically, inexorably, in the process of being "filled" with meaning; meaning is, as it were, "drawn" to it. (Is meaning in search of the empty signifier? Does meaning need an "unoccupied" philosophical space in order to come into itself?) The empty signifier is always on the cusp, being recruited to one political task (some form of ideological work) or another. All emptiness is temporary, and possibly even illusory, which makes every empty signifier resonate intensely with potentiality—at once the rhetorician's dream and nightmare. The empty signifier is always the signifier that is potentially to hand, available for conscription; and, as has been delineated, complicated in its availability because the empty signifier is never what it seems. The empty signifier never indicates an end in itself; it always inaugurates a thinking of the political; and, as such, it implicates—holds to account—any and every speaking.

It is for this reason that the empty signifier must always be thought in relation to, awkwardly phrased, the irrepressible "somethingness" of emptiness. It never stands by itself and it is in its putative emptiness that the signifier concatenates: it draws other signifiers—other definitions of race and racism—to it. In this instance, this means that Blatter's blustery invocation of racism is necessarily insufficient. (The emptiness is, arguably, in search of nothing so much as—its—substance, as its substantiation; that is, as its fully vested political self.) The empty signifier is in circulation and it relates, "periphery to periphery" in our instance, to those signifiers with which it shares what might be named a "root meaning." The empty signifier draws other like signifiers (and signifieds, of course) to it, as much as it is drawn to those self-same signifiers. As if to suggest that it might confound the laws of physics, the empty signifier reveals the magnetism of emptiness—iterating once more that there is a solid (political) substance at its core. Consequently, the empty signifier has a ghostly quality: it haunts those signifiers in its "set," as much as it is haunted by those signifiers; the empty signifier sets something in motion, possessed as it is of an incipiently potent political force.

When Blatter uses the term "racism" so expediently, it animates the concept and Qatar proceeds, rapidly, from its status as the first Gulf or Middle Eastern and, yes, the first predominantly Muslim nation, to something "newly" politicized. It can no longer stand as it would like: the historic host of the World Cup (first in its region; first among a "theological" community, in Glissant's terms). Blatter's mobilization of the discourse of racism has the effect of racing the Gulf nation. To speak race, whatever the intentionality, is to give the term, its history, and several other histories, new life. It is in this way that the relationality of 2022 to 2010 is especially thought-provoking because racism, for all its agreed-upon meanings and visceral evocations, always demands translation. Racism cannot stand by itself, as itself; it must spoken—as it is, as it is imagined to be—as "racism"—the "empty" signifier—again; then, we are turned to face the politics of race, colonialism, new and old imperialisms, yet again.

Racism 2010 cannot be applied, ad hoc or in toto, to racism 2022. How does African-ness (and we name this, and not in the least apologetically, blackness) stand in relation to Gulf/Middle Eastern Muslim-ness? The black African (who could also be Muslim, or Maghrebian) was immunized against racism in 2010 but the revocation of racism—a post ipso facto-ness that always had an a priori life—in this "later" context now converts every invocation of racism into a loaded, intensely resonant signifier. The Oriental Other cannot be equivalenced to the sub-Saharan African, but they are bound by this signifier. Following this logic, the comparative silence around racism in 2010 (which of course also includes the build-up to the South African World Cup) was nothing so much as a putative silence, a silence awaiting nothing so much as its own—unexpected, but, inevitable—articulation. In this way, Blatter is both the source of the event of racism (re-turning; turning us to it anew) and entirely incidental to it. His speaking animated racism; his speaking was incidental; it would, at some conjuncture or other, spoken "itself," spoken for itself; it would, inevitably, have spoken.

Above all else, this is what Blatter's "defense" of Qatar's successful bid does. It saliently gives racism a recognizable form, a structure around which critiques can be politically organized and discursively shaped. It ironically unleashes into political life the discursive significance of race, racism, slavery, colonialism, neoliberalism, and their relations to FIFA—an organization that is at once all-powerful and susceptible to the force of incidental speaking. All conversations about race and racism in World Cup football must now run between these two, as Glissant might say, "peripheral poles." The football World Cups of 2010 and 2022 draw us, in our thinking on race/racism in/and football, not away from each other, but fully into the orbit of their relationality. What is it that was *not* said, that was made impermissible, by 2010? How are we to speak *now*, in a moment that appears removed but is not, bound as these peripheries (joined in/by their—respective—status as precedent-setting: South Africa and Qatar, each a first) are to each other? How are we to speak of race, both retrospectively and prospectively? In his expedient mobilization of race, there is at least one thing for which we should be, discursively, grateful. We should acknowledge the philosophical gift that Sepp Blatter has inadvertently given us.

Notes

1 Davis, "Brazil: Poor Face Iron Heel."
2 McMichael, "The World Cup as Pacification."
3 Graham, "Olympics 2012 Security."
4 The extent to which the European leagues are entirely geared to their traditional fall-winter season is notable during the African Cup of Nations, held biennially and always during January. Because of the high number of African players (or, those players who qualify to play for African nations) in European leagues, this affects a huge number of clubs but there is no accommodation made. How, then, will the European leagues make adjustments for a December World Cup?
5 Glissant, *Poetics of Relation*, 21.
6 In this regard, see the critiques offered by political organizations such as the Durban Shack Dwellers—see Abahlalibase Mjondolo.
7 With the exception of 1994, when the World Cup was held in the USA, the host has been either a European nation—Italy, Germany, twice, 1974 and 2006, France, England—or a Latin American one—Chile, Brazil, also twice, 1950 and 2014, and Argentina in 1978.
8 According to the World Bank, South Africa is the most unequal society in the world. See Kiersz, "Here are the Most Unequal Countries."
9 Glissant, *Poetics of Relation*, 21.
10 Derrida, *Monolingualism of the Other*, 15.
11 This argument about the "body" of difference recalls Mudimbe's assertion in *The Idea of Africa*: "The body which lives or survives as the transcript of the metamorphosis is still that which testifies to the break," 135.
12 In a scathing critique of Qatari treatment of workers, the Nepali ambassador to Qatar, Maya Kumari Sharma, described the emirate as an "open jail." Cited in Pattisson, "Revealed: Qatar's World Cup Slaves."

13 Amnesty International, *No Extra Time*; the International Confederation of Trade Unions (IUTC) Special Report, *The Case Against Qatar*.
14 Dorsey, "Gulf Human Rights Declaration Increases Heat on Qatar to Act on Migrant Workers' Rights."
15 The relation between South Africa and Somali refugees has become the stuff of exiled Somali writer Nuruddin Farah's fiction. Most recently see "The Start of the Affair."
16 Glissant, *Poetics of Relation*, 21.
17 Cited in Gibson, "Sepp Blatter Launches Broadside."
18 Said, *Orientalism.*
19 Glissant, *Poetics of Relation*, 29.
20 See FIFA's self-assessed history, "FIFA Against Racism."
21 There are widely reported incidents of racism in Italian football. Recent examples include frequent taunts directed toward the black Italian striker, Mario Balotelli and a high-profile incident in which Kevin Prince-Boateng (of AC Milan) walked off the pitch after encountering racism from the fans of Pro Patria, causing the game—a friendly match between the two clubs—to be abandoned.
22 But not quite. Alves's response to the thrown banana, and its supportive repetition by other footballers, prompted considerable debate. For a discussion of the issue in the British press, see the report by Prenderville, "Spanish Police Arrest Fan."

Bibliography

Abahlalibase Mjondolo. *Home of the Ahahlalibase Mjondolo Schackdweller's Movement South Africa*: http://abahlali.org/.
Amnesty International *No Extra Time: How Qatar is Still Failing on Worker's Rights Ahead of the World Cup*, November 2014: http://www.amnesty.org/en/library/info/MDE22/010/2014/en.
Davis, M. "Brazil Faces Iron Heel Ahead of World Cup." *Green Left Weekly*, July 13, 2013: https://www.greenleft.org.au/node/54296.
Derrida, J. *Monolingualism of the Other Or The Prosthesis of Origin*, translated by Patrick Mensah. Stanford, CA: Stanford University Press, 1998.
Dorsey, J. "Gulf Human Rights Declaration Increases Heat on Qatar to Act on Migrant Workers' Rights." *Huffington Post*, December 17, 2014: http://www.huffingtonpost.com/james-dorsey/gulf-human-rights-declara_b_6342322.html.
Farah, N. "The Start of the Affair." *New Yorker*, December 22 and 29, 2014.
FIFA. "FIFA Against Racism: A Decade of Milestones": http://www.fifa.com/aboutfifa/socialresponsibility/news/newsid=1384919/.
Gibson, O. "Sepp Blatter Launches Broadside Against the 'Racist' British Media." *Guardian*, June 9, 2014: http://www.theguardian.com/football/2014/jun/09/sepp-blatter-fifa-qatar.
Glissant, É. *Poetics of Relation*, translated by Betsy Wing. Ann Arbor: University of Michigan Press, 1997.
Graham, S. "Olympics 2012 Security: Welcome to Lockdown London." *Guardian*, March 12, 2012.
International Confederation of Trade Unions (IUTC). Special Report: *The Case Against Qatar*, March 16, 2014: http://www.ituc-csi.org/ituc-special-report-the-case?lang=en.
Kiersz, A. "Here are the Most Unequal Countries in the World." *Business Insider*, November 8, 2014: http://www.businessinsider.com/gini-index-income-inequality-world-map-2014-11.

McMichael, C. "The World Cup as Pacification." June 18, 2014: http://www.theconmag.co.za/2014/06/18/the-world-cup-as-pacification/.

Mudimbe, V.Y. *The Idea of Africa*. Bloomington : University of Indiana Press, 1994.

Pattisson, P. "Revealed: Qatar's World Cup 'slaves'." *Guardian*, September 25, 2013: http://www.theguardian.com/world/2013/sep/25/revealed-qatars-world-cup-slaves.

Prenderville, L. "Spanish police arrest fan after banana was thrown at Barcelona's Daniel Alves." *Mirror*, April 30, 2014: http://www.mirror.co.uk/sport/football/news/dani-alves-banana-racism-incident-3477994.

Said, E.W. *Orientalism*. New York: Pantheon Books, 1978.

Part III

Economies of events and experiences

10 The urban impacts of the 2014 World Cup in Brazil

Christopher Gaffney

Introduction

The costs of hosting the FIFA World Cup have increased exponentially since the turn of the twenty-first century. While municipal and federal governments invested in stadium infrastructure for previous tournaments, such as Italy 1990 and France 1998, by today's standards the scope and scale of investments were comparatively small. Beginning with Japan/Korea 2002 when the hosts combined to build or renovate twenty stadiums, there has been an escalating impact on host cities as local, regional, and federal governments use the World Cup to meet the infrastructural and technical demands of FIFA and to push through projects aimed at "legacy development." This chapter explores the impacts on Brazilian cities of hosting the World Cup. My analysis stems from observations developed during a long engagement with scholars, activists, and media in Brazil as well as a longitudinal study that dealt with the urban impacts of the World Cup on all twelve host cities.[1]

"Winning" the Copa?

Brazil was the only candidate to host the 2014 World Cup. This unique situation was the result of a short-lived policy of host-continent rotation that FIFA President Joseph Blatter instituted after the controversial awarding of the 2006 World Cup to Germany over South Africa. Blatter had been a major proponent of bringing the tournament to Africa and, in response to last-minute horse-trading within the FIFA executive committee in support of Germany, he established a rotation system that would see the World Cup move from Europe, to Africa, to South America, and then to North America. Since at least 2000, then, Brazil was the likely host for the 2014 World Cup. This rotation system was later abandoned, but not until after Brazil had been officially awarded the 2014 World Cup in October 2007.

The lack of competing bids for Brazil 2014 ensured a lack of transparency relative to the contractual obligations, infrastructure developments, costs, and responsibilities assumed by the federal government, potential host cities and the Brazilian Football Confederation (CBF). On July 31, 2007, Ricardo Texeira, the since-disgraced and defrocked president of the CBF, handed a 900-page candidature dossier to FIFA President Sepp Blatter. The dossier included 18 potential host cities and a series of interventions in transportation, communication, security, hotel, tourism, and stadium infrastructure. At least five cities were guaranteed as hosts: Salvador, Belo Horizonte, Rio de Janeiro, São Paulo, and Porto Alegre. Another 13 were disputing as many as seven positions: Manaus, Belém, Natal, Fortaleza, Recife, Brasília, Curitiba, Florianopolis, Campo Grande, Cuiabá, Rio Branco, Goiania, and Maceio. The candidature dossier was never seen again.

Although FIFA made the official announcement that Brazil would host the 2014 World Cup in October 2007, it was not until May 2009 that twelve host cities were finalized in a closed-door evaluation process. Even after the hosts were chosen, it would not be until mid-2010 that they entered into contractual agreements with FIFA to develop "host city agreements" and accompanying "responsibility matrices." The choice of host cities appears to have been more based on the Brazilian political landscape than the technical merits of the candidates.[2] For example, the Brazilian government deliberately chose to pursue the maximum number of host cities and to use the World Cup as a vehicle for stimulating investment in Brazil's largest cities. As early as 2009, the Federal Ministry of Planning had identified that many of the host cities were superfluous to the necessities of the tournament and that the World Cup could be realized with as few as six cities. FIFA preferred to have between eight and ten host cities. In conversations with FIFA officials, I was informed that the Brazilian government wanted to have as many as 15 host cities. The direct federal investment in Brazil's largest cities has served to maintain an unbalanced urban hierarchy as well as overspending on non-essential infrastructure.

The decision to include or not include a city in the list of hosts would have implications for the ability of cities to gain federal financing for projects, as well as their capacity for undertaking large-scale infrastructure projects. For instance, the dispute to host the World Cup in the Amazon region between Belém and Manaus was won by the latter. Belém was therefore excluded from a federally financed urban mobility package and tourist promotion, but was also not responsible for delivering on a host city agreement with its financial and spatial repercussions.

Because political considerations at the national level heavily influenced the contest to become a host city, the impacts of the World Cup were less evident in unsuccessful cities than the successful candidates. This is a double-edged sword, as Manaus was temporarily in the international media and tourist spotlight, received millions in federal financing for infrastructure and built a new stadium, but the city was unable to complete its urban mobility projects and is now faced with a white elephant stadium that consumes R$50 million of the annual city budget in maintenance.[3] By contrast, Belém might be in a better long-term financial position for not having hosted the World Cup. Unfortunately, the proposals for urban transformation hidden in the 2014 World Cup bid book will never allow us to compare these comparative urban trajectories.

Equally important to the analysis of urban impacts is to evaluate whether or not the World Cup on its own can be considered a major catalyst of urban intervention, or whether or not the proposed urban interventions were scheduled before the event.[4] Ideally, host cities would have been able to incorporate the demands of hosting the World Cup into pre-existing planning agendas. While every case is different, the majority of projects proposed appear to have been addendums to planning agendas that used the "hook" of the World Cup for emergency implementation. However, even within each city there are variations between the projects. For instance, the renovation and expansion of airports falls under the classification of urban impacts, yet none of the World Cup host cities had these projects scheduled prior to 2007, because the airports in Brazil are owned and managed by the federal government. Another element to consider are projects associated with Brazil's federally financed Accelerated Growth Programs (PAC I and PAC II). Many World Cup projects had been scheduled through PAC but had not moved beyond the planning stage, and the time pressures of the football showcase gave them the push they needed to come into fruition.

Critical to the manner in which the Brazilians pursued their urban interventions for the World Cup is to grasp the extraordinary influence that civil construction firms have on urban planning agendas.[5] In Brazil generally, and in large cities particularly, civil construction firms, transportation consortiums, and real-estate firms are the largest campaign finance contributors.[6] Because of the emergency or exceptional nature of the World Cup projects (see Vainer, this volume), all of the public works associated with Host City Agreements and the Responsibility Matrices associated with them were subject to a specific conjuncture of rules for the contracting process. Known as RDC (Regime Diferenciada de Contratação— Differential Contracting Regime), World Cup infrastructures were exempt from the *Law of Budgeting Directives*, which would make more difficult the identification of inflationary budgeting and price gouging.[7] Host cities were also granted an exemption from the *Law of Fiscal Responsibility*, which ensures that municipal governments operate with balanced budgets. This opened the possibility of nearly unlimited deficit spending on pet projects for host cities.

In 2007, FIFA produced a report that called into question the necessity, scope, and breadth of the interventions proposed by all levels of the Brazilian government, noting that: "[A]ir and urban transport infrastructure would comfortably meet the demands of the 2014 FIFA World Cup."[8] The report went on to state: "[O]f the 18 prospective host cities presented by the bid LOC, only four require brand-new stadiums: the Zagallo Arena (Maceio), the Estrela dos Reis Magos (Natal), the Recife/Olinda Arena (Recife) and the Bahia Arena (Salvador)."[9]

Despite FIFA's optimistic evaluation, the scope and scale of investments for the 2014 World Cup were the most extensive in the history of the tournament. The ambitious agendas of the Brazilian federal government, and of the host states and cities, make it nearly impossible to describe the impacts in their entirety. There is also the problem of transparency in contracting and in the completion of the projects. By some estimation, more than half of all World Cup-related projects were not completed on time.[10] The delays, incomplete projects, and overpriced infrastructure were a source of conflict that marked the Confederations Cup in 2013.[11] The social impact of such projects, including approximately 170,000 forced removals, is discussed amply by other authors but cannot be separated from the present discussion.[12] In the passages that follow, I note thematic elements that were present in nearly all of the host cities, while discussing their local particularities.

Porto Alegre and the shifting tones of dialogue

Since the advent of the World Social Forum in the 1990s, Porto Alegre's municipal government has been known for innovative social policies, such as participatory budgeting and having an open dialogue with the population. Yet, as Brazilian cities have adopted models of urban entrepreneurialism, there has been a steady erosion of democratic channels of communication. Indeed, Porto Alegre's hosting of the World Cup revealed the degree to which the formerly progressive government ceded control over city planning agendas to development coalitions.

Of particular concern in Porto Alegre were the ways in which municipal and state authorities treated low-income communities that suddenly found themselves in the way of infrastructure projects. The major interventions were centered on the expansion of the Salgado Filho International Airport and the expansion of road and "buffer infrastructure" around the Beira-Rio Stadium. As Lucimar Sequeira suggests, Porto Alegre has gone through an accelerated shift in the way that urban space is produced, above all in the real-estate sector. This has most negatively influenced the most vulnerable residents because the major disputes are over urbanized land, the localization of infrastructure, urban mobility, and recreational facilities.[13]

In the cases of three communities threatened with eminent domain (compulsory purchase) removal, the municipal and state governments did not interact with residents in accord with existing legislation. In all instances, once a family had entered into the formalized process of resettlement, basic services were cut off even though the family remained in situ.[14] As happened in other World Cup cities, once a family had been resettled, the government would destroy the property, leaving behind the ruins, thereby creating health and safety hazards and reducing the value of the remaining homes. To make matters worse, for residents that remained behind in a community slated for removal next to the Porto Alegre airport, the noisy public works projects could only operate between 1 a.m. and 6 a.m., when the airport was not in use.

In general, residents who found themselves in the way of World Cup infrastructure projects suffered from the inability or disinterest of the city government to implement the legal instruments that had been created for their protection. In the long struggle for territorial rights in Brazil, the poor have made significant gains—this was especially true in Porto Alegre. However, it would appear in the current conjuncture that thousands of low-income families are living in a permanent state of crisis because municipal government has been subordinated to the interests of developers. Pushing the poor to the periphery in favour of infrastructure projects for the World Cup meant that, "the municipal government of Porto Alegre has not managed to guarantee the right to the city to low income residents."[15]

Curitiba: from urban poster child to dysfunctional planning syndrome

Curitiba is another Brazilian city that found the international spotlight for its nominally progressive urban transportation policies. Touted as the "green example" for other medium-size cities to follow, Curitiba's fame has resulted from decades of urban marketing combined with a signature transportation system and relative wealth within the Brazilian urban hierarchy.[16]

Yet, the World Cup challenged Curitiba's reputation for efficient and egalitarian urban planning. While not as ambitious as Cuiabá or Porto Alegre in its urban interventions, the Responsibility Matrix of Curitiba initially included a suite of transportation projects, tourist infrastructure, airport renovations, and a stadium upgrade. As the World Cup drew nearer, it became clear that almost none of the projects would be completed on time and they were successively withdrawn from the Responsibility Matrix. Eventually, the final results included a suspension bridge, a road-widening project, a reformed bus terminal and a traffic-monitoring center.[17]

Accompanying these projects was the Arena da Baixada, the last stadium to be delivered to FIFA for the World Cup and a stunning example of project mismanagement. As one of three private stadiums included in the World Cup, the Curitiba proposal was also the least expensive. However, in order to economize even more, the stadium owner, Club Atletico Paranaense (CAP), decided that it would act as the manager and general contractor of the stadium upgrading process. This decision proved disastrous when inevitable cost overruns associated with an ambitious retractable roof project forced CAP to seek emergency financing from the state of Paraná and the federal government.

CAP was overly mortgaged because it had agreed to pay one-third of the originally budgeted R$180 million reform, which had since risen to R$240 million. In order to receive money to complete the stadium on time, the state had to act as the guarantor of a loan from the Federal Government. This was accomplished because the emergency conditions of the World Cup placed the private stadium reform in the realm of the "public interest." An additional R$24 million was added to the project in order to install the retractable roof, which because of the chronic delays, was vetoed by FIFA.[18] However, the money stayed in the project budget even through the roof was not completed.[19] While the stadium was delivered just in time for the World Cup, the state of Paraná is on the hook for the repayment of a R$24 million loan to the federal government.

São Paulo: political conjunctures produce urban impacts

The São Paulo World Cup stadium opened up a new zone of valorization and verticalization in the poor eastern periphery of the city. While clearly tied into a more traditional urban policy frame of using the tournament to pursue long-term objectives, the construction of a new stadium and multi-modal transportation line in the Itaquera region resulted from many months of political wrangling.

The initial project for São Paulo included an R$150 million reform of the historic Pompedeu Stadium of São Paulo FC in the wealthy Morumbi region of the city, an upgrade to the regional and international airports, and the creation of a monorail line to the Morumbi region. However, the political landscape of the Brazilian Football Confederation pitted the president of São Paulo FC Juvenal Juvêncio against the president of the CBF and the president of Corinthians FC, Andrés Sanchez. As debate heated up in the press and in the boardroom, then-President Lula, a fervent supporter of Corinthians (and close friend of the Odebrecht construction firm) interceded behind the scenes and the CBF announced that the yet to be built Itaquera Stadium would host the opening match of the World Cup.[20]

After more than a year of negotiations, the São Paulo city government, Corinthians and Odebrecht signed a contract to deliver a stadium with an initial price tag of R$820 million. A stadium financing package of R$420 million was put together through a municipal level Building Investment Fund (Fundo de Investimento Imobiliário, FII) and through the provision of Certificates of Incentive for Development (Certificado de Incentivo ao Desenvolvimento, CIDs). The remaining financing came through a R$400 million loan from the Brazilian National Development Bank (BNDES), which had opened lines of credit for stadium financing in all host cities.[21]

The combination of influences from national-level political figures (Lula) and opaque relations with civil construction firms (Odebrecht); the internal dynamics of the CBF (Juvêncio vs. Sanchez); the willingness of the city government to create special financing measures (FII and CID), and the potential for real-estate valorization in São Paulo's east side led to creation of an "East Zone Development Pole" that would receive a further R$548,507,000 of investment from the city and state of São Paulo.

This resulted in a rapid increase in real-estate prices in the region, which created immense downward pressure on favela residents from developers. In many cases, residents were known to be working on the stadium project yet were forced from their homes as a result of World Cup-related projects.[22] In addition, the late start of the project, and the unwillingness of Odebrecht to collateralize an extra R$200 million loan to complete the stadium, forced an increase in costs (which benefited Odebrecht) and created immense time pressures to complete the stadium.[23] In a tragic incident just months before the World Cup, a crane lifting the stadium roof collapsed, killing two workers. São Paulo's Civil Police later indicted seven Odebrecht functionaries and two from the crane operating company, citing a lack of procedural oversight.

Taking projects out of the drawer in Cuiabá

Cuiabá was the smallest World Cup host city and as a consequence suffered the most extensive interventions. Capital of the state of Matto Grosso, Ciuabá is the southern terminus of an important soy-production region and it was the political influence of the state's governor, Blair Moggi, that brought the World Cup to the city.

As with the urban restructuring projects in other cities, such as Recife and São Paulo, Matto Grosso government officials and industry used the World Cup to institute a series of urban mobility projects to direct future expansion of the city. In particular, the development of bus rapid transit (BRT) lines, duplication of roadways, and the installation of a light rail line (VLT) in the center and airport regions will have profound impacts on real-estate development and residential patterns in the metropolitan region. In the short term, Cuiabá was the city that most suffered with the magnitude of construction projects, as none of the proposed interventions were ready in time for the World Cup. Pre-existing difficulties with traffic congestion in the city were magnified because all of Cuiabá's projects began in the same week in 2012.

The extension of Cuiabá's road and VLT network to the north and north-east of the city into a sparsely vegetated hinterland will allow developers to acquire inexpensive territory that is currently under-provided with adequate sewerage, electricity, and other key infrastructure. The localized provision of infrastructure by the city government will also allow the rapid valorization of these territories, generating conflicts over land use, exclusionary residential landscapes, and the use of eminent domain to acquire transportation right of ways. The production of a closed-condominium residential landscape will increase the use of automobiles, while encouraging the already established patterns of mall-based consumption and urban fragmentation.

One of the most salient elements of Cuiabá's urban planning regime for the World Cup was the rapid approval of projects that did not pass through pre-existing democratic channels. To the contrary, the development, approval, and implementation of Cuiabá's urban restructuring moved through a complex parallel governmental structure called the Secretário Extraordinario da Copa do Mundo do Matto Grosso (SECOPA).[24] The more than R$1.5 billion invested in transportation infrastructure will forever alter the dynamics of the city, yet few of the projects were planned before Cuiabá was named as a host city in 2009. While each of the 26 projects underway in Cuiabá needs to be analyzed on its own merits, the general trend has been to create a temporary governmental authority to carry off projects that benefit a narrow range of public interest without opening democratic channels. It may be, as the projects are completed, that Cuiabános will see some relief for their daily transportation headaches. However, as of mid-2015, none of the proposed projects had been completed, leaving the city without a functional transportation network and significantly more in debt than before.

Privatization, removals, and resistance in Rio de Janeiro

Because Rio de Janeiro will also host the 2016 Summer Olympics, it is the most complex of the World Cup cities to evaluate. Rio's municipal government has pursued sports mega-events as a development strategy for two decades and each successive event brings changes to urban and social structures that impinge on future events. For instance, the 2007 Pan American Games served as a template for the 2016 Olympic bid, and the 2013 Confederations Cup was an operational test for the World Cup. While the demands of all these events are different, there are consistencies in the privatization of public lands, forced removals of low-income communities, and public resistance to these projects.

The privatization of the Maracanã sporting complex has been highly symbolic and hotly contested. The Maracanã was built in 1950 and had served as Rio de Janeiro's principal football ground until its closure for renovation in 2010. The state of Rio de Janeiro had administered the Maracanã for several decades and while the stadium was in need of repair, the sporting complex as a whole served as a public space and recreational facility.[25] Beginning with the FIFA World Club Championship in 2000 and continuing through the 2016 Olympics, planning for the stadium occurred through a series of political machinations that bypassed earlier legal requirements for public audiences, conferred privilege to government insiders, and eventually, removed the stadium complex from public administration altogether.[26]

This led to the stadium's internal architecture being carved out and replaced with a standardized seating arrangement, eliminating the *genus loci* of one of the world's most historic sports venues.[27]

In the process of privatizing the Maracanã, two of Rio's Olympic training facilities were also closed down, an indigenous settlement forcibly removed, and a top-performing public school threatened with demolition.[28] A nearby favela was slated for demolition, so that the land could be used as a parking lot.[29] While the demolitions took place and the community was destroyed, the parking lot project never moved forward. In all of these instances, strong resistance came from the Comitê Popular da Copa e das Olimpíadas—RJ that worked with the affected groups to articulate public actions and media strategies against the government-led projects.[30]

As part of the World Cup and Olympic interventions, the city government has embarked upon an ambitious 150-km Bus Rapid Transit building spree that will connect Rio's nominal Olympic zones. By some estimates, more than 30,000 people will be removed from their homes during this ongoing process. As with other World Cup hosts, the city government has not followed appropriate legal measures for the removal of low-income communities, yet when it comes to wealthy property owners, the mayor has on occasion personally directed negotiations.

Rio de Janeiro has also suffered more than most cities from real-estate inflation associated with mega-events. Research has shown that Rio de Janeiro's real-estate values increased well above the average for World Cup hosts and this has generated a series of urban knock-on effects such as gentrification, involuntary displacement, and increased traffic congestion.[31] These tendencies have been exacerbated by the installation of a vast military apparatus to dominate key territories formerly under the command of drug traffickers.[32] In short, Rio can be considered the poster child for dysfunctional urbanism associated with short-term projects that cater to sports mega-events.

Creative destruction and the destruction of creativity in Salvador

As FIFA noted in their 2007 inspection report, Salvador was in need of a stadium upgrade. Just after the report was published, part of the upper stands of the Fonte Nova Stadium crumbled and seven people fell to their deaths, while thirty more were severely injured. The stadium was subsequently closed. As with many Brazilian stadiums constructed in the high-modernist era of the 1960s, the Fonte Nova Stadium was part of a larger public space that provided swimming, Olympic sports, and other facilities for community events. When the stadium was condemned, the entire complex was also closed as the city government decided how to prepare for the World Cup.

The official investigation into the Fonte Nova Stadium disaster revealed a gross lack of investment in maintenance, which can be considered typical of many of Brazil's large public stadiums. A similar disaster had happened in the Maracanã in 1993. Yet, like the Maracanã, the Fonte Nova Stadium was considered an important mark of Brazilian architecture as it expressed significant achievements in the use of materials, created space for the realization of diverse cultural forms, and expressed a progressive ideology that encouraged public investment in public recreational facilities.[33] Rather than acknowledge the collapse of a section of stands as evidence of governmental mismanagement, the administration of Salvador suggested that the entire Fonte Nova complex was outdated and needed to be demolished to make way for a "modern, multi-use arena." As the city government moved forward with their plans for demolition, significant resistances emerged.

Critics argued that the debates surrounding the stadium were not inclusive, that multi-million dollar contracts had been conceded without having discussed the project with the public, that poor communities around the stadium complex were being expelled from their homes, and that a significant architectural and cultural patrimony was being destroyed. The State Council of Culture, the Department of Architecture of the Federal University of Bahia, and other cultural institutions publicly opposed the demolition of the stadium. The UFBA Polytechnic University worked with a private company to demonstrate that it was possible to attend to FIFA's stadium requirements while preserving the Fonte Nova. All of these institutions and their expert opinions were ignored and the Fonte Nova complex was imploded on August 29, 2010.

In what is now known as the Itaipava Arena Fonte Nova, there are no athletic facilities, no public swimming pool, no gymnasium, or public meeting facilities. In effect, the multiple uses of the stadium complex have been reduced. In addition to the R$591 million spent on reconstruction, the stadium complex has been given to a consortium comprised of the civil construction firms OAS and Odebrecht through a public-private partnership for a period of 35 years—the effective life span of the stadium. That is to say, once the stadium is in need of renovation, it will return to the state.

If the Fonte Nova was once an important marker in the development of a progressive urban politics and architectural achievement, the Arena Fonte Nova can also be considered an important temporal and spatial marker of Brazilian urban governance in the twenty-first century. Instead of pursuing creative, cost-effective solutions to an interesting architectural problem, the city government has opted for a model of creative destruction that has effectively excluded the population from active participation in sport (on "creative destruction," see Gotham, this volume). In the Arena Fonte Nova, the absence of recreational facilities and the exclusionary urban model that FIFA-standard stadiums imply has uncoupled the stadium from the needs of the people and from democratic urban planning regimes.

Natal, Manaus, and Brasília: the march of the white elephants

Once the World Cup host cities were chosen, it was clear that at least four cities would have trouble with the viability of their stadiums. Natal, Manaus, Brasília, and Cuiabá, discussed earlier, are four cities that have not traditionally placed football teams in Brazil's top divisions and whose football clubs have average attendances of less than three thousand per match. While each city had a pre-existing stadium, to meet FIFA requirements city administrators destroyed the existing structures in order to build a state -of-the-art stadium from scratch.

While Manaus and Brasília are very different cities, their World Cup initiatives make for an interesting comparison. Both cities initially proposed improvements to their urban transportation network but were unable to get the projects off the drawing board. In the case of Manaus, a proposed monorail that would connect the port region to the stadium was abandoned after an investigation by the Federal Auditor's Office (Tribunal de Contas da União—TCU) found incomplete documentation and suspicions of overpricing.[34] The effective abandonment of any urban transportation projects in October 2013 left the largest city in the Amazon without any investments in local infrastructure, although many dozens of families were removed from their homes to make way for the projected interventions.

In Brasília, several projects were intended to remake the mobility structure of the Plano Piloto, including a R$1.55 billion investment in light rail that would connect the administrative center and north residential sector to the airport. Early plans presented by the Federal District planning authority for the World Cup demonstrated a commitment to building bicycle lanes to increase sustainable transportation in Brazil's capital city. Still, according to the National Institute of National Historic and Artistic Patrimony (IPHAN), which evaluates all interventions into Brasília's preserved Plano Piloto, there were indications of fraud in the contracting process of the VLT and an environmental impact study had never been conducted. The Justice Tribunal of the Federal District annulled the contracts for the VLT and Brasília did not attempt a different project because there would not be enough time to implement it before the World Cup.[35] Following the canceling of all urban mobility projects, the Brasília Local Organizing Committee boasted that theirs would be the only host city to realize all of its projects within a 2-km radius.

The World Cup interventions in Natal were relatively limited and tended to favor the growth of private-sector housing as part of a larger process of restructuring growth dynamics in the city. The ability of government officials to obtain long-term subprime loans for infrastructure developments meant that Natal's World Cup infrastructure would be based in the expansion of road networks to zones of elite residential expansion. One of these roads led between the hotel and tourist zone to the Arena das Dunas Stadium.

As with Manaus and Brasília, Natal does not have a football team with a large following. After destroying the pre-existing stadium with public money, the Natal World Cup stadium was built by OAS, using a R$396.5 million loan from BNDES and R$26.5 million of private financing. The state of Rio Grande do Norte entered into a private-public partnership (PPP) with OAS, which will manage the property for twenty years, and will have to maintain and operate it. The PPP takes some of the onus off the public purse as attendances for football matches only pay for 32 percent of the annual maintenance costs.[36] Similar to other formerly public stadiums, the Arena das Dunas was constructed to serve primarily the needs of the World Cup with very little forethought given to later uses. The state has effectively given over a large public space to a private company to exploit for low rent over two decades. The creation of a shopping mall structure and atmosphere in stadium space will be the inevitable result, creating exclusionary and consumptive spaces of leisure.

Fortaleza: a new wave of city marketing

Despite the fact that Brazil receives fewer than 6 million international tourist visits a year, many of the World Cup cities structured their urban interventions to attend to this potential growth sector. The municipal government of Fortaleza is particularly notable for a discursive framing that identified the World Cup as a "unique opportunity" to exhibit the region's tourist charms to the world (read: Europe). This framing centered on the consolidation of the image of the city as a host for conferences and international events, and for national-level entertainment and leisure activities. To this end, the municipal and state governments invested R$623 million in the demolition and reconstruction of a "multi-use" stadium (Castelão) and the R$486.51 million Ceará Convention Center.

Fortaleza's strategy of targeting high-profile interventions to attract tourists fits very well with current models of entrepreneurial city governance and trends in city marketing. In addition to the stadium and convention center, the state of Ceará invested R$275 million in a 12.7-km light rail line that runs through the historic and touristic center of Fortaleza. Both city and state governments were dedicated to delivering the projects on time and on budget, something that distinguished Fortaleza from other host cities. This may have been a strategy to demonstrate the efficiency of governmental operations in order to attract investments, but it did provide good publicity, as Fortaleza was the only city to meet FIFA's deadlines.

The concentration of transportation projects in Fortaleza has benefited the real-estate sector along their trajectories and concentrated investment in relatively wealthy areas of the city. As Fortaleza implemented three BRT lines and pursued road-widening programs, thousands of people were forced from their homes. As with every other World Cup host city, legal norms for disappropriation and relocation were not followed and significant resistances to these projects arose. The public agents responsible for negotiating with residents who opposed the projects engaged in a deliberate misinformation campaign.[37]

Unfortunately, the urban interventions in Fortaleza, attended to a very narrow sector of the local population and to national and foreign visitors. As these projects were implemented, low-income communities were not afforded the same quality of treatment as the more expensive and visible projects for the World Cup. For example, financial compensation packages for families dislocated by transportation lines were laden with complex bureaucracy, were slow to be paid out and did not reflect market value for housing. At the same time, massive public works were fast-tracked and completed in time for the events. Consistent with other cities, the majority of Fortaleza's highly visible projects do not attend to the critical problems of urban mobility that plague the metropolitan region.[38]

Recife: World Cup stadium as *Boi de Piranha*

Recife represents one of the classic cases of using the hook of the World Cup to carry off larger urban agendas. While many are familiar with the "white elephant" metaphor for stadiums that cost more to maintain then they provide in return, the Recife stadium represents the *Boi de Piranha* ("sacrificial cow"). When crossing a piranha-infested river, Brazil's ranchers send the weakest cow of the herd across first, allowing it to be devoured by the rapacious fish. As the piranhas attack, the remainder of the herd passes safely upriver. In this sense, the Arena Pernambucano has served as a *Boi de Piranha* to distract public attention from the transfer of public lands to a private development consortium.

Recife has three principal football teams, each with its own stadium. The largest, Estádio do Arruda of Santa Cruz FC has a capacity of 60,000 and could have undergone minor reforms to meet FIFA's demands for the World Cup. Yet, instead of investing in stadiums in the consolidated metropolitan area near centers of population, the state government of Pernambuco chose to locate a new stadium on a greenfield site in the suburb of São Lourenço da Mata, 20 km from the center of Recife. This decision prompted a series of urban interventions that will continue to have impacts on the expansion of the Recife metropolitan region towards the interior of the state.

Two of the principal interventions chosen for the Arena Pernambucano were the development of a series of BRT lines that would link the stadium and its future real-estate development with the center of Recife. Once again, duplication of highways and the development of BRT lines resulted in the removal of hundreds of lower-income residents and commercial interests. The emergency planning regimes for these interventions have created life-emergencies such as housing loss and neighborhood dislocation for residents who did not benefit from open dialogue with state or city governments relative to the processes of disappropriation and compensation.

If the development of the Arena Pernambucano was unnecessary, it forced the development of urban infrastructures to feed temporarily the demands of the World Cup. These demands would be later justified by the development of the Cidade da Copa (World Cup City), a 240-hectare real-estate project headed by Odebrecht that will have seven thousand residences, a university campus, a museum, theatre, an indoor sports arena, a shopping center and office buildings. Promoted as "Latin America's first intelligent city," the Cidade da Copa involved a transfer of public property to Odebrecht in the form of a 33-year concession. According to media reports, the new neighborhood would be able to receive up to a hundred thousand people in new recreational facilities and a complex of state government offices would be installed in the region.[39]

The project of the Cidade da Copa involves many of the same factors and actors that are driving fragmented and privatized urbanization in the rest of Brazil. The government has ceded public lands and subsidized construction costs to Odebrecht, which will be in charge of developing a high-end residential landscape that will be filled with civil servants and the "creative class." In order to bring service workers in from the metropolitan region, BRT lines were implemented and car lanes duplicated.[40]

The investment in the Arena Pernambucano was in the neighborhood of R$520 million, but this pales in comparison to the potential profits that will be realized from the concession of public lands to Odebrecht. In addition to expanding the metropolitan footprint, the exclusionary nature of the Cidade da Copa will reinforce worrying trends towards residential fragmentation, socio-economic polarization, and hyper-security that define current trajectories in Brazilian urbanism.[41] However, as of this writing, the Cidade da Copa real-estate project has yet to coalesce but was projected to have its first phase initiated in 2015.[42]

Belo Horizonte: collapsing into path dependency

Belo Horizonte and Cuiabá were the host cities that most intervened in the urban fabric based on urban transportation projects associated with the World Cup. In Belo Horizonte, the decision to implement three BRT lines and to expand two roadways, as well as to construct several highway overpasses, has resulted in a radical modification of the public transportation system. Following the model established by Curitiba in the 1980s, Brazil's national transportation policy has been one that subsidizes the use of BRTs to solve chronic problems of urban mobility in dense capital cities.[43] As has been made clear in other places where BRTs have been implemented, they are relatively cheap to implement but also open more space for cars and continue dependence on buses and road-based transportation.

Belo Horizonte invested R$841.3 million on BRT lines and R$364.2 million on road-duplication projects. While it is as yet too early to evaluate the functional impact of these projects on urban mobility in the metropolitan region, the investments were concentrated in the city center—an area relatively well-served by public transportation. As is well known from other examples around the world, BRTs alone are inadequate structural solutions for urban mobility and are better used as part of a suite of interventions.[44] One of the reasons for not placing them in city centers is that they create impermeable barriers, create air and noise pollution, and cannot expand their capacity over time. Unfortunately, the ease of implementation, the large public subsidies available to cities and the influence of bus and car manufacturing companies has ensured that BRT lines will be the dominant form of public mobility in Belo Horizonte.

Belo Horizonte was also the site of the only major infrastructure disaster that occurred in projects associated the World Cup. On July 4, 2014, a newly constructed highway overpass collapsed, killing two and injuring dozens. Early indications were that the overpass had been hastily and poorly constructed, with little oversight on the part of city government as developers hurried to complete the projects in Belo Horizonte's Responsibility Matrix. The collapse of the overpass was overshadowed by Brazil's stunning loss to Germany in Belo Horizonte's privatized Minerão Stadium. The rush to build roads in Brazilian cities continues a form of urban development that benefits vested interests in the automobile and civil construction sectors. The linking of these projects to the World Cup increased their costs, reduced oversight, and resulted in tragedy.

Conclusion

The Brazilian government estimates spending for the 2014 World Cup at R$28 billion, but the numbers are conflicting and incomplete. Of the four government or industry-based transparency websites, none are able to produce the same input costs for stadiums or to even agree on stadium capacity.[45] The details of each city's interventions are equally confusing as the contracting process, payments, and completion of the projects are difficult to follow without close accompaniment of each project. I have outlined some general trends evident in host cities that apply in specific situations based on my reading of their relative importance in the local context. Notably, these include privatization of formerly public spaces, gentrification, displacement and the continued influence of Brazil's civil construction firms in planning agendas.

In this overview, I have left out important factors such as hotel development, Fan Fest Zones, militarization and security apparatuses, real-estate speculation, and urban governance regimes that I have discussed in other places.[46] While there were inevitably positive results from the massive public outlay for World Cup-related infrastructure (job creation, capital circulation, communication technologies, etc.), we need to question seriously how these projects distributed wealth, access, and power in Brazilian cities. Unfortunately, the existential condition of hosting mega-events is one of impending crisis, late delivery, overblown budgets, and tight contractual obligations. As early as 2010, FIFA was clamoring for the Brazilians to take more seriously their delivery time frames.[47] Ironically, the narrative of lateness and incomplete projects dominated the media framing of the World Cup, which distracted attention from the procedural challenges, high costs, and the necessity or utility of the projects themselves.[48] Yet, there is a strong case to be made that the condition of permanent crisis, emergency, and exception led to a weakening of Brazilian democratic institutions, the deterioration of public spaces, and the increased polarization of Brazilian society.

Notes

1 Some of this research appears in de Queiroz Ribeiro, *The Metropolis of Rio de Janeiro*. The three-year research project was hosted at the Universidade Federal do Rio de Janeiro (UFRJ) and involved nine research teams across Brazil. The chapter also draws on information contained in the "Responsibility Matrix" that each host city published online on various government websites, detailing the infrastructure projects to be associated with the World Cup.

2 Hori, "Exclusão de Cidades Sedes."

3 Instituto Humanitas Unisinos, "Estádio de Manaus Poderá Se Pagar Em 198 Anos"; Watts, "Brazil after the World Cup."

4 Prouse, "The Jock Doctrine."

5 Campos, *Estranhas catedrais*.

6 Lopes, "Os Donos Do Rio."

7 Lima, "Mudança Na LDO Afrouxa Controle de Obras Da Copa."

8 FIFA, *Inspection Report for the 2014 FIFA World Cup*.

9 Ibid., 28.

10 Morais, "Só 45% Das Obras Da Copa Ficarão Prontas, Diz Estudo."

11 Brum, "Curitiba Ajusta Prazos Para Driblar Atrasos Em Obras"; Reuters, "Atrasos em obras da Copa 2014 causam estouros no orçamento"; Konchinski, "Governador Liga Aumento de 87% Do Custo Do Maracanã Ao "Imponderável"; Watts, "Brazil's World Cup Courts Disaster as Delays, Protests and Deaths Mount."

12 De Queiroz Ribeiro, Cesar and Alves dos Santos Junior, "MegaSporting Events in Brazil"; Mascarenhas et al. *O jogo continua: megaeventos esportivos e cidades*; Fundação Instituto de Pesquisa Economica, *Impactos Socio-Economicos Dos Jogos Pan-Americanos Rio 2007*.

13 Sequeira, "A Questão Da Moradia Em Tempos de Copa Do Mundo Em Porto Alegre."

14 Marko, "Audiencia public expoe inseguranca deas comunidades com as obras da copa"; Barros, "Chave Por Chave: Sem Casa Nova, Ninguém Arreda O Pé."

15 Sequeira, "A Questão Da Moradia," 21.

16 Sánchez, *A Reinvenção Das Cidades Para Um Mercado Global*.

17 Firkowski, "A Copa Em Discussão (3:31)."

18 Konchinski and Almeida, "Estádios de Curitiba E Manaus Desistem de Projetos Por Prazo Da Copa."

19 Dantas and Segalla, "Arena Da Baixada."

20 Warth, "Com Lula, Corinthians E Odebrecht Assinam O Contrato Do Itaquerão – Esportes."

21 Ibid.

22 Lopes, "Passamos Um Dia Na Ocupação Copa Do Povo, Em Itaquera."

23 Itri, "Custo Para Levantar E Operar O Itaquerão Vai Superar R$ 1 Bilhão."

24 See the website http://www.mtnacopa.com.br/index2.php?sid=353 for a complete list of the five levels of governamental structures put in place to carry off Matto Grosso's World Cup projects.

25 Gaffney, *Temples of the Earthbound Gods*; Anon., "Futuro do Maracanã é questionado em debate no Rio."

26 Castro, "Consórcio Que Reúne Odebrecht, AEG E Eike Batista Ganha Licitação Do Maracanã."

27 Dias Comas, "Neimeyer E O Maracanã, 1936–2011."

28 Dolzan, "Protesto Bem-Humorado Marca Um Ano de Fechamento Do Célio de Barros."

29 Berta, "Favela Do Metrô."
30 Articulação Nacional das Comitês Populares da Copa, *Megaeventos E Violações de Direitos Humanos No Brasil.*
31 Gaffney, "Forjando Os Anéis."
32 Freeman, "Raising the Flag over Rio de Janeiro's Favelas."
33 Fernandes, "Está Errado Demolir a Fonte Nova."
34 Farias, "Sem Mobilidade Urbana, Manaus Aposta No Turismo Como Legado | Amazônia Real."
35 Coelho, "VLT Saiu Da Matriz Da Copa Por Decisão Da Justiça, Diz GDF."
36 Carvalho, "Os Planos Da OAS Para a Arena Das Dunas Depois Da Copa."
37 Pinheiro, et al. "Os Impactos Da Copa Do Mundo Da FIFA 2014 Em Fortaleza."
38 Ibid., 110.
39 Segalla, "Pernambuco Terá "Cidade Da Copa."
40 Articulação Nacional das Comitês Populares da Copa, *Megaeventos E Violações de Direitos Humanos No Brasil* .
41 Queiroz Ribeiro et al., "MegaSporting Events in Brazil."
42 Sandes, "Mundial Termina Sem Cidade Da Copa."
43 Ministerio das Cidades, "Manual de BRT, Guia de Planejamento."
44 Mejía-Dugand et. al., "Lessons from the Spread of Bus Rapid Transit in Latin America"; Baumann and Matheson, "Infrastructure Investments and Mega-Sport Events"; Ross, "Bus Rapid Transit Is a Toolbox, Not a Package."
45 Gaffney, "The Traumas and Dramas of Post-Cup, Pre-Olympic Brazil."
46 Gaffney, "Securing the Olympic City"; Gaffney, "A World Cup for Whom?"; Gaffney, "The Barriers to Entry"; Gaffney, "Global Parties, Galactic Hangovers."
47 Phillips, "Brazil World Cup in Disarray as Construction Falls Way behind Schedule."
48 Ley, "2014 World Cup: Will Brazil Be Ready?"; Ransom and Vickery, "Finishing Rio's Maracanã Stadium: A Race against Time"; Naddo, "Fifa Convoca Reunião de Emergência Para Tratar Atrasos No Maracanã."

Bibliography

Anon. "Futuro do Maracanã é questionado em debate no Rio." *Portal 2014*, 2012: http://www.portal2014.org.br/noticias/10772/FUTURO+DO+MARACANA+E+QUESTIO NADO+EM+DEBATE+NO+RIO.html.

Articulação Nacional das Comitês Populares da Copa. *Megaeventos E Violações de Direitos Humanos No Brasil*. Rio de Janeiro, 2012: http://comitepopulario.files.word press.com/2012/06/dossie_megaeventos_violacoesdedireitos2012.pdf.

Barros, Ciro. "Chave Por Chave: Sem Casa Nova, Ninguém Arreda O Pé." *Pública*, 2013: http://www.apublica.org/2013/02/chave-por-chave-porto-alegre-copa-2014/.

Baumann, Robert, and Victor Matheson. "Infrastructure Investments and Mega-Sport Events: Comparing the Experience of Developing and Industrialized Countries." College of the Holy Cross, Department of Economics Faculty Research Series, Paper No. 13-05, 2013.

Berta, Ruben. "Favela Do Metrô: Ex-Moradores Ainda Estão Em Fase de Adaptação." *O Globo*, September 5, 2012: http://oglobo.globo.com/rio/favela-do-metro-ex-moradores-ainda-estao-em-fase-de-adaptacao-4857134.

Brum, Adriana. "Curitiba Ajusta Prazos Para Driblar Atrasos Em Obras." *Gazeta do Povo*, January 22, 2011: http://www.gazetadopovo.com.br/esportes/conteudo.phtml?tl=1&id= 1089219&tit=Curitiba-ajusta-prazos-para-driblar-atrasos-em-obras.

Campos, Pedro Henrique Pedreira. "*'Estranhas catedrais': as empreiteiras brasileiras e a ditadura civil-militar, 1964–1988.* Niterói, Rio de Janeiro: EdUFF, 2014.

Carvalho, Juia. "Os Planos Da OAS Para a Arena Das Dunas Depois Da Copa." *Exame*, 2014: http://exame.abril.com.br/negocios/noticias/os-planos-da-oas-para-a-arena-das-dunas-depois-da-copa.

Castro, Carolina Oliveira. "Consórcio Que Reúne Odebrecht, AEG E Eike Batista Ganha Licitação Do Maracanã." *O Globo* (Rio de Janeiro), September 5, 2013: http://oglobo.globo.com/esportes/consorcio-que-reune-odebrecht-aeg-eike-batista-ganha-licitacao-do-maracana-8342004.

Coelho, Mario. "VLT Saiu Da Matriz Da Copa Por Decisão Da Justiça, Diz GDF." *Congresso em Foco* (Brasília), January 20, 2014: http://congressoemfoco.uol.com.br/noticias/vlt-saiu-da-matriz-da-copa-por-decisao-da-justica-diz-gdf/.

Dantas, Tiago, and Vinicius Segalla. "Arena Da Baixada: R$ 99 Mi Mais Cara, Um Ano de Atraso E Gambiarra Para Ficar Pronta a Tempo." *UOL Esporte*, August 28, 2013: http://viniciussegalla.blogosfera.uol.com.br/2013/08/28/arena-da-baixada-r-99-mi-a-mais-um-ano-de-atraso-e-gambiarra-para-ficar-pronta-a-tempo/.

Dias Comas, Carlos Eduardo. "Neimeyer E O Maracanã, 1936–2011." *ARQTEXTO*, 17 (2011), 16–63.

Dolzan, Márcio. "Protesto Bem-Humorado Marca Um Ano de Fechamento Do Célio de Barros – Esportes – Estadao.com.br." *Estadão*, 2014: http://www.estadao.com.br/noticias/esportes,protesto-bem-humorado-marca-um-ano-de-fechamento-do-celio-de-barros,1116579,0.htm.

Farias, Elaíze. "Sem Mobilidade Urbana, Manaus Aposta No Turismo Como Legado | Amazônia Real." 2014: http://amazoniareal.com.br/copa-2014-sem-mobilidade-urbana-manaus-aposta-no-turismo-como-legado/.

Fernandes, Ana. "Está Errado Demolir a Fonte Nova." *A Tarde* (Salvador, Bahia), June 25, 2010, section Opinão: http://jeitobaiano.atarde.uol.com.br/?p=2263.

FIFA. *Inspection Report for the 2014 FIFA World Cup*: http://www.fifa.com/mm/document/affederation/mission/fwc2014_brazil_bid_inspection_report_en_24491.pdf.

Firkowski, Olga. "A Copa Em Discussão (3:31)." Universidade Federal do Paraná, 2014: www.copaemdiscussao.com.br.

Freeman, James. "Raising the Flag over Rio de Janeiro's Favelas: Citizenship and Social Control in the Olympic City." *Journal of Latin American Geography*, 13 (2014): 7–38: http://dx.doi.org/10.1353/lag.2014.0016.

Fundacao Institutu de Pesquisa Economica. *Impactos Socio-Economicos Dos Jogos Pan-Americanos Rio 2007* (Brasilia: Ministerio dos Esportes, 2009): https://i3gov.planejamento.gov.br/balanco/2%20-%20CIDADANIA%20E%20INCLUSAO%20SOCIAL/7%20-%20Esporte/1%20-%20Documentos/Pan%20e%20Parapanamericano/BGF%20-%20Jogos%20Pan%20e%20Parapanamericanos%202007%20-%20FIA%20-Estudo%20de%20Impactos%20Socioecon%F4micos%20dos%20Jogos.pdf.

Gaffney, Christopher. "A World Cup for Whom? The Impact of the 2014 World Cup on Brazilian Football Stadiums and Cultures." In Paulo Fontes and Bernardo Buarque De Hollanda (Eds.), *The Country of Football: Politics, Popular Culture, and the Beautiful Game in Brazil.* London: Hurst & Co. Ltd, 2014, pp. 189–208.

———. "Forjando Os Anéis: A Paisagem Imobiliária Pré-Olímpica No Rio de Janeiro." *E-Metropolis*, 15 (2013): 8–24.

———. "Global Parties, Galactic Hangovers: Brazil's Mega-Event Dystopia." *Los Angeles Review of Books*, October 30, 2014: 45–55.

———. "Securing the Olympic City." *Georgetown Journal of International Affairs*, 13 (2012): 75–82

———. "Segurança Publica E Os Mega-Eventos Esportivos No Brasil' (unpublished Public Lecture presented at the Os impactos dos mega-evenots espotivos nas metrópoles brasileiras, Clube da Engenharia, 2013): http://prezi.com/hrjd9qfjepjb/?utm_campaign=share&utm_medium=copy.

———. *Temples of the Earthbound Gods: Stadiums in the Cultural Landscapes of Rio de Janeiro and Buenos Aires*, 1st edn. Austin: University of Texas Press, 2008.

———. "The Barriers to Entry." *Hunting White Elephants*, 2011: http://www.geostadia. blogspot.co.uk/2011/03/barriers-to-entry.html.

———. "The Traumas and Dramas of Post-Cup, Pre-Olympic Brazil." *Roar Magazine*, August 25, 2014: http://roarmag.org/2014/08/brazil-world-cup-olympics/.

Hori, Jorge. "Exclusão de Cidades Sedes." *Copa2014.org*, July 9, 2009: http://www.copa2014. org.br/blog/inteligencia-estrategica/index.php/2009/09/07/exclusao-de-cidades-sedes/.

Instituto Humanitas Unisinos. "Estádio de Manaus Poderá Se Pagar Em 198 Anos." *Instituto Humanitas Unisinos*, 2012: http://www.ihu.unisinos.br/noticias/507238-estadiodeman auspoderasepagarem198anos.

Itri, Bernardo. "Custo Para Levantar E Operar O Itaquerão Vai Superar R$ 1 Bilhão." *Folha online*, October 19, 2012: http://www1.folha.uol.com.br/esporte/1171583-custo-para-levantar-e-operar-o-itaquerao-vai-superar-r-1-bilhao.shtml.

Konchinski, Vinicius. "Governador Liga Aumento de 87% Do Custo Do Maracanã Ao 'Imponderável'." *UOL Copa do Mundo 2014*, 2013: http://copadomundo.uol.com.br/ noticias/redacao/2013/05/08/governador-liga-aumento-de-87-do-custo-do-maracana-com-o-imponderavel.htm.

———, and Pedro Ivo Almeida. "Estádios de Curitiba E Manaus Desistem de Projetos Por Prazo Da Copa." *UOL Copa do Mundo 2014*, 2013: http://copadomundo.uol.com.br/ noticias/redacao/2013/11/25/estadios-de-curitiba-e-manaus-abandonam-projetos-por-prazo-da-copa.htm.

Ley, Robert. "2014 World Cup: Will Brazil Be Ready?" *Outside the Lines*, 2012: http:// espn.go.com/video/clip?id=espn:7972440.

Lima, Daniela. "Mudança Na LDO Afrouxa Controle de Obras Da Copa." *Folha de São Paulo*, March 7, 2010: http://www1.folha.uol.com.br/fsp/poder/po0307201014.htm.

Lopes, Débora. "Passamos Um Dia Na Ocupação Copa Do Povo, Em Itaquera." *VICE Brasil*, 2014: http://www.vice.com/pt_br/read/passamos-um-dia-na-ocupacao-copa-do-povo-em-itaquera.

Lopes Pinto, João. "Os Donos Do Rio." *O Dia* (Rio de Janeiro), July 11. 2014: http://odia. ig.com.br/noticia/opiniao/2014-07-11/joao-roberto-lopes-pinto-os-donos-do-rio.html.

Marko, Katia. "Audiencia public expoe inseguranca deas comunidades com as obras da copa." *De Olho na Cidade*, April 2011, 1.

Mascarenhas, Gilmar, Glauco Bienenstein, and Fernanda Sánchez. *O jogo continua: megaeventos esportivos e cidades*. Rio de Janeiro: EdUERJ, 2011.

Mejía-Dugand, Santiago, Olof Hjelm, Leo Baas, and Ramiro Alberto Ríos. "Lessons from the Spread of Bus Rapid Transit in Latin America." *Journal of Cleaner Production*, 2012: http://dx.doi.org/10.1016/j.jclepro.2012.11.028.

Ministerio das Cidades. "Manual de BRT, Guia de Planejamento." 2008: http://multimidia. brasil.gov.br/biblioteca/manual_brt.pdf.

Morais, Afonso. "Só 45% Das Obras Da Copa Ficarão Prontas, Diz Estudo." *Congresso em Foco*, 2014: http://congressoemfoco.uol.com.br/noticias/so-45-das-obras-da-copa-ficarao-prontas-diz-estudo/.

Naddo, André. "Fifa Convoca Reunião de Emergência Para Tratar Atrasos No Maracanã." *Terra na Copa*, 2013: http://esportes.terra.com.br/futebol/copa-2014/,16c9313e8c54d3 10VgnVCM5000009ccceb0aRCRD.html.

Phillips, Tom. "Brazil World Cup in Disarray as Construction Falls Way behind Schedule." *Guardian* (Rio de Janeiro), 13 July 2010, section Football: http://www.theguardian. com/sport/blog/2010/jul/13/brazil-world-cup-2014-delays.

Pinheiro, Valéria, Clarissa Sampaio Freitas, Cleiton Nogueira, and Alexandre Pereira. "Os Impactos Da Copa Do Mundo Da FIFA 2014 Em Fortaleza." In *Os impactos da Copa do Mundo e das Olimpíadas no Brasil*. Rio de Janeiro: Letra Capital Editora, 2015, pp. 101–20.

Prouse, Carolyn, "The Jock Doctrine." *Jacobin*, 2014: https://www.jacobinmag. com/2014/10/the-jock-doctrine/.

De Queiroz Ribeiro, Luiz Cesar, *The Metropolis of Rio de Janeiro: A Space in Trasnition*. Rio de Janeiro: Letra Capital Editora, 2014.

———, and Orlando Alves dos Santos Junior, "MegaSporting Events in Brazil: Transformation and Commodification of the Cities." In *The Metropolis of Rio de Janeiro: a space in transition*. Rio de Janeiro: Letra Capital Editora, 2014, pp. 249–62.

Ransom, Nicola, and Tim Vickery. "Finishing Rio's Maracana Stadium: A Race against Time." *France24*, June 16, 2013: http://www.france24.com/en/20130515-2013-05-15-rio-de-janeiro-brazil-maracana-football-world-cup-2014-fifa/.

Reuters. "Atrasos em obras da Copa 2014 causam estouros no orçamento." *Terra na Copa*, 2011: http://esportes.terra.com.br/futebol/brasil2014/noticias/0,OI5383336-EI10545,00. html.

Ross, Benjamin. "Bus Rapid Transit Is a Toolbox, Not a Package." *Greater Greater Washington*, 2013: http://greatergreaterwashington.org/post/20093/bus-rapid-transit-is-a-toolbox-not-a-package/.

Sánchez, Fernanda. *A Reinvenção Das Cidades Para Um Mercado Global*. Chapeco, Santa Catarina: Argos, 2010.

Sandes, Giovanni. "Mundial Termina Sem Cidade Da Copa." *Jornal do Commercio* (Recife), July 2, 2014): http://jconline.ne10.uol.com.br/canal/economia/pernambuco/ noticia/2014/07/02/mundial-termina-sem-cidade-da-copa-133881.php.

Segalla, Vinicius. "Pernambuco Terá 'Cidade Da Copa', Com Previsão de Conclusão Em 2025." *UOL Esporte*, 2011: http://esporte.uol.com.br/futebol/copa-2014/ultimas-noti cias/2011/08/24/pernambuco-tera-cidade-da-copa-que-sera-concluida-depois-de-2020. htm.

Sequeira, Lucimar. "A Questão Da Moradia Em Tempos de Copa Do Mundo Em Porto Alegre." In *Impactos da Copa em Porto Alegre*. Porto Alegre: Ed UFRS, 2014, pp. 3–23.

Warth, Anne. "Com Lula, Corinthians E Odebrecht Assinam O Contrato Do Itaquerão – Esportes." *Estadão* (São Paulo), September 3, 2011: http://esportes.estadao.com. br/noticias/futebol,com-lula-corinthians-e-odebrecht-assinam-o-contrato-do-itaquerao,768080.

Watts, Jonathan. "Brazil after the World Cup: Almost back to Business as Usual." *Guardian*, December 29, 2014: http://www.theguardian.com/football/blog/2014/ dec/29/brazil-after-world-cup.

———, "Brazil's World Cup Courts Disaster as Delays, Protests and Deaths Mount." *Guardian*, February 16, 2014, section World news: http://www.theguardian.com/ world/2014/feb/16/brazil-world-cup-disaster-delays-protests-deaths.

11 China meets Korea

The Asian Games, entrepreneurial local states, and debt-driven development

Hyun Bang Shin

Less than two weeks after the closing of the 2010 Shanghai Expo, Asians shifted their gaze to mainland China, this time, the opening of the 2010 Asian Games in Guangzhou. This was the second Asian Games to be held in mainland China, the first one being the 1990 Beijing Asian Games. The 2010 Asian Games in Guangzhou, the capital of Guangdong Province, was a more regional event than the 2008 Beijing Olympic Games or the 2010 Shanghai Expo. Nevertheless, the Guangzhou Asian Games provided an opportunity for the host city, and by extension Guangdong Province, to attain added global reputation and to strengthen its position in the Asia-Pacific regional economy. Guangzhou's hosting of the Asian Games also exhibited a unique trait of China's localism, albeit negotiated with the central state.[1] Since the late 1970s, China's local states had been given greater power during the period of economic decentralization in terms of expanding their grip on territorial economic activities. Local states also exhibited a certain degree of state entrepreneurialism to maximize economic gains through an active use of state agencies.[2] The rise of local autonomy, however, was achieved under the auspices of the Party State that ensured the political centralization to bring about national security, territorial integrity, and sociopolitical stability.

On the day of the closing ceremony of the Guangzhou Asian Games, the Games flag changed hands, ultimately reaching the then mayor of Incheon, the city that was the next host of the Games taking place four years later. The 2014 Incheon Asian Games was the third Asian Games for South Korea: Seoul, the national capital, had them in 1986 and Busan, the second largest city of the country, in 2002. Previously, Incheon fell from grace when it had to give up the host city status for the 1997 National Games due to poor preparations. The 2014 Asian Games was a chance to erase the dishonor. For Incheon, the 2014 Asian Games would also have been a means to revitalize its sluggish economy. Incheon developed rapidly as one of the major industrial centers during the country's rapid economic development guided by the developmental state. About one-third of Incheon's gross regional product is still generated by secondary industry (e.g. manufacturing, mining, etc.), but the city's economy has been trailing behind Busan and had been recently overtaken by Ulsan. From the early 1990s, South Korea implemented a number of measures to liberalize its economy and also to promote decentralization.[3] Local elections were also adopted to allow the direct election of mayors and provincial governors, but there is a strong presence of the central state, a legacy of the developmental statism. Nevertheless, enhanced local autonomy provided the foundation of a prominent rise of regionalism and place-based growth politics. State entrepreneurialism, one of the key characteristics of the South Korean developmental state, has become a more distinctive character-istic of South Korean local states, when the central state itself was going through mutations vis-à-vis neoliberal pressures.[4]

In this regard, the two Asian Games were embedded in political economic contexts that showed both similarities and differences. Notable differences arose given the domination of the Party State in Mainland China, on the one hand, and the mutations of the South Korean developmental state on the other hand.[5] Yet, the experiences of hosting the Asian Games by Guangzhou and Incheon also testi-fied to the importance of local states proactively pursuing economic development through an active mobilization of resources to make productive investments. By juxtaposing the experiences of Guangzhou and Incheon in their preparation for the Asian Games, this chapter aims to show how both cities attempted, some-times successfully and at other times unsuccessfully, to make use of the Asian Games to realize their developmental aspirations by investing heavily in the built environment. These attempts included fast-tracking the development process by launching ambitious mega-projects as part of channeling capital into the second-ary circuit of the built environment.[6] As the chapter shows, these efforts were unfortunately speculative and debt-driven, placing a heavy burden on each city's future developmental prospects.

Local state entrepreneurialism and urban development

Developmental statism has been associated with the rise of Asian tiger economies such as South Korea, Taiwan, Singapore and Hong Kong in the twentieth century under conditions that were influenced not only by the domestic politics dominated by authoritarian states, but also by the prevailing geopolitical economy such as the Cold War and armed struggles in the region.[7] Entrepreneurialism underpins developmental statism, which is characterized by the state's active intervention in the economy to maximize capital accumulation. State institutions worked hand-in-hand with private business interests to excavate new business opportunities. Public corporations were often set up to assume the risk of venturing out into a new industrial sector or to address collective consumption (e.g., housing). A developmental state was not only a market regulator but also an active entrepre-neurial participant in the market.

In times of democratization and liberalization, such as the rise of local elections as witnessed in South Korea from the 1990s, local states tend to exhibit a more acute entrepreneurial orientation, as local politicians running for elections espouse place-based interests to appeal to their constituencies. As cross-border activities and the influence of transnational capital grow, entrepreneurial local states at the municipal level may adopt "glurbanization" strategies "to secure the most advanta-geous insertion of a given city into the changing interscalar division of labour in the world economy."[8] Growth politics thus prevail, but this has inherent limitations when the local coffer is heavily dependent on central government subsidies.[9]

In Mainland China, the initiation of market reform has resulted in the trans-formation of the central and local states in the way they relate to the economy and the society. Restructuring of the state and its rescaling through decentraliza-tion provided local states with a stronger grip on territorial economies, gradually overcoming (though not diminishing entirely) the constraints of the vertical hier-archy of work-units inherited from the planned economy era. Earlier discussions of how the nature of the local state transformed during the reform era resulted in several studies that highlighted both the developmental and entrepreneurial roles of the local state. For instance, Jean Oi examined the rise of township and village enterprises and their integration in the county-level economy in Shandong and Tianjin, arguing that local county governments displayed local state corporatism, treating "enterprises within their administrative purview as one component of a large corporate whole."[10] Local governments showed both entrepreneurial and governmental roles, transforming into "*economic* actors, not just administrative-service providers."[11] As economic actors, local states exercised entrepreneurship, taking risks and absorbing benefits, which then led to the rise of "a corporatist strategy to pool resources and debt."[12] Duckett referred to state entrepreneurialism to examine the business-oriented activities of municipal departments of Tianjin, discussing how the state administrative bureaucracy adjusted to market-reform policies. Her main focus was on the establishment of new enterprises by state bureaux, and how these enterprises retained bureau personnel and governmental functions, essentially paving the way for "bureaucrats in business."[13]

The entrepreneurial nature of China's local states has become more pro-nounced due to their strong growth imperatives, which relied heavily on spatial strategies implemented by local states to drive "productive investment" in the secondary circuit of capitalist accumulation; that is, investment in fixed assets and collective consumption. While the local state's financial capacity became some-what restricted when the central Chinese state promulgated tax reform in 1994, local governments were given the power to administer the transaction of land-use rights from the state (as the ultimate owner of urban land) to end-users such as developers. This provided the basis for local states becoming de facto landlords in the emerging land (use right) market and for their accumulation of land-related income as part of extra-budgetary revenues that contribute heavily to financing local development.[14]

These processes in turn laid the foundation for the exercise of entrepre-neurial urban and regional policies by local states to expand their land assets. Development zones were set up as zones of exception across the country by local states, prompting Wu and Phelps to argue that

> The political economy of Chinese municipal entrepreneurialism has, on the whole, been altogether more complete in terms of the state's control of the land-development process, the supporting infrastructure, and, as a conse-quence, the location of that growth.[15]

You-tien Hsing discusses how urban governments have concentrated their resources on establishing "new towns" (*xincheng*).[16] The latter is identified as being promoted under the banner of "urban operation and management" (or *chengshi yunying*), which involves developers as key partners of urban development and aims at producing "property values" through following "the logic of the real-estate market."[17]

It is in this context of local state entrepreneurialism that this chapter comparatively discusses the experiences of pursuing mega-event hosting by major regional cities such as Guangzhou and Incheon. The existing literature has shown that mega-event hosting tends to be favored by growth advocates (i.e., businesses, politicians, or their joint coalition) as a means to address wider developmental agendas that include not only the attraction of investment capital and experts, but also a local state's productive investment in fixed assets. Some projects may get a green light to be fast-tracked (e.g., transportation projects or urban beautification), while some other projects may be pursued "even if they have little relevance to a sporting event."[18] The fact that local states pursue economic development in an entrepreneurial way does not necessarily mean that they would only target transnational capital for its inward investment. To a varying degree, local states are dependent fiscally on the central state, and this characteristic is more pronounced in times of mega-event hosting, when the local state usually enters into negotiation with the central state to leverage as many national resources as possible.[19]

Major events such as the Olympic Games and the FIFA World Cup also make it compulsory for the central government to pledge a certain level of financial input into the Games preparation in order to make sure financing responsibility is apportioned between the host city and the central government, although the actual share of the central government contribution is up to further negotiation. In summary, mega-events are regarded as attractive strategies by both central and local states for their pursuit of political and economic interests. For local states that are relatively freed from the central state's key concern for national security, territorial integrity, and sociopolitical stability, their entrepreneurial characteristics would be even more pronounced when it comes to the use of mega-events to advance their development aspiration.

Spatial manifestation of regional developmental aspirations

Event promoters in Guangzhou and Incheon saw the use of the Asian Games as a means to facilitate spatial restructuring and make productive investment in the built environment to accumulate fixed capital. For Guangzhou, the city's development vision evolved throughout the 1990s to aspire to become an international central city in the Asia-Pacific region.[20] This places Guangzhou, and by extension Guangdong Province in direct competition with neighboring economies such as South Korea and Taiwan. In fact, Guangdong's economy has already overtaken those of Singapore, Taiwan, and Hong Kong in terms of the gross regional product. It is catching up fast with that of South Korea. The gross regional product of Guangdong was a little less than two-thirds of that of South Korea in 2010, but reached about three-quarters three years later. Guangzhou's gross regional product in 2010 was three times larger than that of Incheon.

The Guangzhou municipal government produced an important strategic development plan in 2000. However, in 2004, soon after having successfully bid for the 2010 Asian Games, the municipal government announced a revised plan known as the "Outline of Urban Planning and Construction for Guangzhou's 2010 Asian Games." The 2004 plan also facilitated the development of the Pearl River New Town along its new central axis that is identified as the site for the city's new central business district (CBD), as well as other new towns across the city to serve as new regional cores.[21] The construction of this brand new CBD was a municipal effort that has spanned nearly two decades, and the Asian Games turned out to be a significant facilitator for its completion. Guangzhou's keen interest to promote the new CBD was expressed in the city's decision to have the Asian Games' opening ceremony outside the main stadium on Haixisnha Island, positioned along the Pearl River at the southern end of the new CBD (see Figure 11.1).

Furthermore, domestically, Guangzhou's use of the 2010 Asian Games and related developmental activities could be understood as the rise of the Pearl River Delta region, often dubbed as the "factory of the world," in its competition with other city-regions such as the Beijing-Tianjin city-region and the Yangtze River Delta city-region. The need to direct national resources more towards the Pearl River Delta city-region was further justified by deploying a unique set of "center" and "periphery" discourses, framing the development of Guangdong Province simultaneously as *advanced* (in comparison with its own past and other regions) and *lagging* (in comparison with what it should be). Such a strategy also provides the rationale for a strenuous negotiation with the central Chinese state to consolidate Guangzhou's leadership position within the Pearl River Delta city-region vis-à-vis Shenzhen and the neighboring special administrative regions of Hong Kong and Macau.[22]

This was particularly pronounced in the 2008 "Outline of the Plan for the Reform and Development of the Pearl River Delta region" (hereafter 2010 Outline), produced by the National Development and Reform Commission in consultation with the provincial government four years after Guangzhou won the host city status for the 2010 Asian Games. It is noteworthy to state that all these efforts, especially at the provincial level, were under the leadership of influential political figures who rose to prominent positions in the vertical hierarchy of the Chinese Party State: the party secretary of the province, i.e., the top political figure, was Dejiang Zhang between 2002 and 2007, succeeded by Yang Wang between 2007 and 2012, both of whom were promoted to vice-premiers in the central government.

In line with a number of development projects to transform the city, the Guangzhou municipal government further established its ambitious plan to promote city-wide urban redevelopment projects. The municipality was already showing keen interests in transforming its city-scape by tackling a large amount of "dilapidated" housing stock, as one of the media reports suggested:

> According to the Guangzhou Land and Housing Management Bureau, the total registered size of dilapidated housing in Guangzhou reached 911,000

Figure 11.1 The venue of the Asian Games' opening ceremony with the brand new
Guangzhou Tower in the background (top) and the view of the new CBD
(bottom); photographed by the author in 2011.

square metres by the end of 2004. In 2005, another 57,000 square metres
were newly added to this . . . The Guangzhou municipal government decided
that these dilapidated houses will be the key to the city's old city redevelopment works in the coming years. It was also put forward that the redevelopment of dilapidated houses in the city was to be completed before the 2010
Asian Games.[23]

The new ambitious plan to redevelop the city targeted in particular what the
municipality defined as the "Three Olds," that is, old inner-city neighborhoods, old

brownfield sites, and old urbanized villages. The urban redevelopment policy was initially advocated and announced by the provincial government of Guangdong in 2009, and put into practice in Guangzhou in the same year. A special bureau was opened in February 2010 to oversee the progress and supervise municipal-wide "Three Olds" projects, helping the government to implement so-called "environmental improvement" projects that covered 318 square kilometers. More than one-third of the target areas was to go through wholesale demolition and reconstruction over the next ten years or so.[24] A number of redevelopment projects were streamlined to be completed in time for the opening of the 2010 Asian Games. For instance, a planning official in one of the old city districts in Guangzhou, indicated that the district government received about 220 million yuan from the municipal government for the city's Games-related environmental improvement projects, and another 380 billion yuan for the waterside renovation along the creeks in the district, all to be completed before the Asian Games.[25]

In the case of Incheon, the initiative to strengthen investment in the built environment was led by its mayors, who have been directly elected in local elections since 1995. The two mayors who were influential in urban politics in the city and who reigned successively until 2010 were all from the right-wing political party, which ruled South Korea for most of its industrialization period until the 1990s. These mayors advocated urban policies that emphasized state-led development. They aspired to expand the capacity of the municipality to design and implement a number of real-estate and infrastructure projects, which were centered on accumulating land assets through reclamation as a means to secure revenue sources.[26] Although an opposition party candidate with a more liberal stance took the mayoral seat for the first time in 2010, the boosterish policies begun under the previous mayors were difficult to overturn, including preparation works for the Asian Games that had fixed and irreversible deadlines.

In Korea, Incheon's primary concern was to come out of the shadow of the economic and political influence of neighboring Seoul, the national capital city, and to transform its earlier reputation as a manufacturing center into a city of high-tech and international business. Incheon's gross regional product (at current prices) was only about one-fifth of that of Seoul.[27] For Incheon, its developmental aspiration was embedded not only in the context of the declining economic position of the city within South Korea, but also in the context of its regional future threatened by rapidly developing China across the sea. Bidding for the Asian Games therefore reflected Incheon's enthusiasm "to help elevate South Korea's third largest city onto the world map as a new economic hub of Northeast Asia."[28]

Similar to Guangzhou's desire to build the Pearl River New Town as the city's new CBD, Incheon also aimed to build an international center of business and finance, focused on the use of reclaimed land adjacent to South Korea's international gateway, the Incheon International Airport. This ambition emerged back in the early 2000s when Shanghai, only about two hours away by flight from Incheon, was seeing the initial completion of the development of Pudong.[29] The ambition was also closely entwined with the then national policy to promote the country as a North-east Asian business hub centered on high-tech and global service industries including finance and logistics.[30] This ambition resulted in the designation of the new Incheon Free Economic Zone (IFEZ) as a zone of exception in August 2003, aimed "to attract investments and offer world class business environment that guarantees high returns for investors."[31] Bolstered by this, the then mayor Sang-soo Ahn, who was elected in 2002, propagated a successful bid in 2007 for the 2014 Summer Asian Games. As the section chief in urban design at the metropolitan government said:

> the previous mayor wanted to promote Incheon as an urban brand globally, and the sporting mega-event was combined with the IFEZ . . . By having the Asian Games, Incheon would be known to the Asian population, raise its position in the region, and attract the attention from emerging economies including China and encourage their investment.[32]

Moreover, at the time of running for re-election in 2006, Ahn made a hundred key election pledges, of which ninety were urban and regional development projects that centered on mega-scale real-estate projects. These were mostly to redevelop existing historic urban cores, and to develop new towns, as well as to concentrate resources on the IFEZ and the Asian Games-related facilities.[33] Revenues from selling reclaimed land to investors and developers were meant to pay for subsequent infrastructure development, as well as state-led redevelopment in existing urban cores.

The Asian Games and other development projects were all streamlined to raise the international profile of Incheon and, in return, attract further investment. The seeds were initially sown in the establishment of the 2020 Incheon Urban Master Plan, which received the final approval in May 2006 by the Ministry of Construction and Transport at the central government. The preparation of the 2020 Urban Master Plan was given a full thrust under the leadership of Mayor Sang-soo Ahn, whose first four-year term commenced in July 2002. At the time of preparing the 2020 Urban Master Plan, Incheon was already proposing an ambitious plan to increase the total metropolitan population from 2.62 million people in 2005 to 3.5 million by 2020.

This was downsized by the Central Urban Planning Committee of the Ministry of Construction and Transport during the approval process. However, only two years after the approval of the 2020 Urban Master Plan, a new proposal was put forward by the Incheon metropolitan government to revise the previous plan and prepare a 2025 Urban Master Plan. Led again by Mayor Sang-soo Ahn, who successfully ran for his second term in the 2006 local election, the metropolitan government argued that the revision was necessary, as Incheon was awarded in April 2007 the right to host the 2014 Summer Asian Games. The proposal for the 2025 Urban Master Plan put forward for public consultation was even more ambitious, setting the planned size of the total municipal population to reach 4 million.[34] About 1.2 million people were meant to be migrating from outside Incheon by 2025, to be accommodated by various development projects envisaged in the proposal for a new master plan.

All these were put together to promote Incheon globally and place the city on the global investor's map, helping it to achieve its openly pronounced aspiration to become (somewhat over-ambitiously) one of the world's top ten cities. These objectives were to be assisted by "mega-scale development projects, changes to the transportation system, and urban redevelopment projects for a balanced development of existing urban areas."[35] Incheon also organized a World Urban Fair (later officially named the "Global Fair & Festival") in 2009. The aforementioned IFEZ constituted one of the major growth poles for Incheon, and itself became a major mega-project for the metropolitan government's drive to transform Incheon into a city of multiple centralities and global prominence. The IFEZ was given multiple roles, destined to become sites for international business and finance, high-tech knowledge industry, culture, tourism, leisure, a transportation hub centered on the existing international airport, and upmarket residential estates. The IFEZ alone was planned to accommodate 9 million new residents.[36] To showcase the newly emerging IFEZ, the Asian Games also saw the allocation of some of the strategic events, such as the triathlon and beach volleyball, to the Songdo Free Economic Zone, an epicenter of Incheon's aspiration to become a regional center in the East Asian region.[37] New development areas, such as the Songdo International Business District, saw the accommodation of and the opening of the Games' media centre.[38]

Debt-driven speculative development

During the years of preparing for the Asian Games, the developmental aspiration held by the governments of Guangzhou and Incheon translated into various urban redevelopment, beautification, and infrastructure projects. These projects naturally required the mobilization of large financial resources, eventually placing a heavy burden on local government. The Guangzhou and Incheon governments dealt with the financial situation in differing ways, reflecting the divergences by which urban political economy was structuring state actions despite their differentiated modes of establishing state entrepreneurialism. However, the common thread was the fact that these projects were largely speculative and debt-driven.

In the case of Guangzhou, the city's Games-related finance showed some similarities with the way in which Beijing spent its money for the 2008 Olympic Games.[39] That is, much more money was spent on infrastructure provision and beautification. As an expert at the Guangzhou Asian Games Organizing Committee pointed out, as far as the Asian Games were concerned, the public facilities that received the greatest emphasis would have been "the transport, which is definitely the most important."[40] An earlier report suggested that about 122.6 billion yuan was spent on the Asian Games and the related urban projects (see Shin 2012). About 90 percent of the total expenditure were thought to have gone into infrastructure and urban redevelopment projects, while the remaining 10 percent were to pay for the operation costs of the Games. The suggested total amount of spending by Guangzhou for the Games preparation was larger than the total annual budget of Guangzhou in 2011 (103.8 billion yuan).[41]

An academic with frequent experiences of providing policy consultation services for the municipal government suggested in an interview with the author that the Guangzhou Asian Games came as a huge opportunity to make things possible in a shortened amount of time:

> Actually, I think direct organising is not too much money, but the infrastructure change or construction is an opportunity for the city, so they take this opportunity. and, also they always use this word "to take the opportunity from the event," because the economic, the industrial development and planning is also based on this. And, also the urban planning is based on this . . . They consider money as not quite a problem.[42]

In particular, local government finance is heavily dependent on land-related revenues generated by selling land-use rights as part of expanding extra-budgetary revenues that have become a major source of local finance since the 1994 Tax Reform.[43] In Guangzhou, the debt issue was also raised but it is not clear what impact this may have on municipal development, as most developmental projects in China had in fact been debt-driven and speculative, in particular by means of using state investment companies often known as local government finance vehicles (LGFVs), to issue bonds or borrow from financial institutions on behalf of local governments. In the case of local states in Mainland China, concerns were raised about the possibility of a large amount of local debts incurred by LGFVs, i.e., public enterprises set up by local governments to issue bonds or borrow loans. It is reported that the total amount of borrowing by LGFVs across the country totaled 17.89 trillion yuan, which would amount to about one-third of China's GDP.[44]

While the debt situation was not rising prominently at the time of the Asian Games preparations, it became a concern about two years later. For instance, a deputy with the Guangzhou People's Congress named Nanshan Zhong accused the municipal government of having invested far too much on the Games preparation, and claimed that after the Games, the city was left with a huge debt that reached 210 billion yuan.[45] His claim was quickly rebuked by the director of the city's finance bureau, questioning the source of such figures. However, at the end of December 2012, Guangzhou revealed that its excessive debt level reached 241.4 billion yuan by mid-year 2012,[46] or about 233 percent of Guangzhou's budget for government expenditure for the year 2011 (103.8 billion yuan), which may have sounded an alarm bell for many observers.[47] On July 30, 2013, Guangzhou further revealed that "it needs to pay loans worth almost 26.1 billion yuan this year. That is 19.37 percent of the city government's projected income for this year."[48]

Similar concerns about Incheon's financial health were raised by some council members, but at the time of Incheon's bid, these concerns were not extended to the Asian Games. The whole city celebrated the award of the Games when Incheon comfortably defeated Delhi in Kuwait in April 2007. On June 28, 2011, a ground-breaking ceremony was held in Incheon for the construction of the main Games stadium (see Figure 11.2). This, however, was accompanied by increasing awareness of the host city's shaky finances. Incheon's mounting debt was the main source of contention in the 2010 local election, which saw the defeat of Mayor Sang-soo Ahn by the opposition party candidate Young-gil Song, whose election pledges included the reduction of metropolitan debt, including a reduction in expenditures for the Asian Games. He even considered giving up the Asian Games altogether, although this turned out to be damaging for his political reputation. An alternative plan was to refurbish an existing stadium (which had been incurring operational losses at the time) instead of building the brand new one originally pledged by the previous mayor. However, the news of canceling the construction of a new stadium provoked severe complaints from those residents and businesses who had vested interests in the proposed new site and Mayor Song gave in and agreed to resume the construction of a new stadium.

Over the years, Incheon's financial situation had been aggravated as the metropolitan government's drive to realize its growth ambition was put into high gear. The city's debt level, known to be manageable until the mid-2000s, rose rapidly, largely due to the promotion of mega-projects and the preparation for the 2014 Asian Games.[49] While the total amount of municipal bonds issued was 1.41 trillion Korean Won (KRW) by the end of 2007, it soared to reach 2.33 trillion KRW in 2009, and then 3.26 trillion KRW in 2014.[50] Accordingly, the ratio of total municipal debts to the annual budget also surged over the years, recording 26.9 percent in 2007, 29.8 percent in 2009 and 37.5 percent in 2014, dangerously approaching the 40 percent ceiling, a threshold defined by the Local Finance Act to identify local government's fiscal crisis.[51] Out of the 3.26 trillion KRW

Figure 11.2 Main stadium for the Incheon Asian Games; photographed by the author in 2014.

of municipal debts by the end of 2014, nearly one-third (31.8 percent) resulted from the bonds issued to finance the construction of the Asian Games facilities (see Table 11.1 below). The direct costs of the Asian Games preparation related to the Games facilities were effectively debt-financed.[52]

Another 5 percent (121 billion KRW) of the total debt was due to the project to construct the second line of Incheon's urban rail network. The project was originally scheduled for completion before the opening of the Asian Games, to showcase Incheon's public transportation. However, the project saw various delays and is now to be completed by mid-2016. According to a report provided by the Incheon Asian Games Organizing Committee in 2011 for the Incheon Metropolitan Council, the total costs of the Games preparation were expected to reach 2.74 trillion KRW, which would have been a little more than two-fifths of Incheon's total annual budget in 2011. These included the costs of constructing Games facilities (1.90 trillion KRW) as well as the operational costs of the organizing committee and other supporting offices. Of all the Games preparation costs, the metropolitan government was to undertake 71.9 percent while the central government was to cover only 19.4 percent of the total costs.[53]

Incheon's financial situation was further aggravated by its use of a municipal development corporation, Incheon Development & Tourism Corporation (hereafter IDTC), to pursue a number of infrastructure and real-estate projects as set out in the Incheon Urban Master Plan. Although the debt incurred by the IDTC was kept separate from the aforementioned metropolitan debt, the Incheon Metropolitan Government was ultimately responsible for the accrual of debts by the IDTC. Financing the IDTC projects was funded through bond issues and reliance on project financing, but this eventually placed a financial burden on the municipality. The total amount of financial debts owed by the IDTC increased from 401.3 billion KRW in 2006, surged to 1.5 trillion in 2007, and reached in 3.5 trillion in 2009. During the next four years, the financial debts doubled again, reaching 7.0 trillion KRW in 2013.[54] About 90 percent of all the financial debts as of the end of 2013 were from the metropolitan government's real-estate projects, especially centered on mega-projects such as the Yeongjong Sky City land development and the Geomdan new town development, located west and north of Incheon's historic core respectively. These two mega-projects were designed to be new sub-centers of Incheon, aimed at contributing to the diversification and invigoration of Incheon's economic activities and land use.

However, the heavy upfront costs poured into the land assembly, as well as compensation for property owners in the process of land expropriation, meant that the IDTC had to bear a substantial degree of financial pressure. In particular, the land development of the Yeongjong Sky City site was accompanied by a lack of business interest in land purchase: the rate of land sales was only 24 percent—far below the expectation of the metropolitan government, and therefore preventing it from recovering costs and raising profits that were meant to go into other development projects, especially the redevelopment of Incheon's historic center. The Geomdan new town development has also been substantially delayed since the announcement of compensation measures for existing property owners in October 2009.

Table 11.1 Total debts of Incheon Metropolitan Government.

	2011	2012	2013	2014	2015	2016	2017	2018	2019
Balance	**2,740**	**2,802**	**3,159**	**3,258**	**3,171**	**3,008**	**2,796**	**2,542**	**2,228**
General account	1,150	1,111	1,130	1,064	1,042	936	795	654	515
Asian Games facilities	585	685	1,023	1,035	1,008	948	883	798	692
Urban rail construction	116	154	170	188	190	193	170	158	121
Other urban transport projects	2	2	0	0	0	0	0	0	0
Sewerage projects	164	150	134	118	98.1	78.5	60.5	45.4	31.6
Regional Development Bonds	626	611	626	648	637	668	714	723	725
Incheon Free Economic Zone (IFEZ) Project	97.6	89.5	75.5	206	195	185	174	163	143
Debt level (percent)	37.7	35.1	35.7	37.5	37.7	38.2	36.6	32.7	29.0

Source: Incheon Municipal Government website.

Note: Unit is Billion Korean won. For 2015–19, the numbers refer to estimations.

The financial debts incurred by these two mega-projects constituted about 56 percent of total financial debts as of the end of 2013.[55]

It is difficult to see how these grim situations may change in the near future. The designation of a number of inner-city redevelopment projects, in particular, were hit not only by the global financial crisis in 2007–08, but also by the emphasis on real-estate projects in the IFEZ. As the section chief responsible for urban redevelopment in the Incheon metropolitan government said

> If inner-city redevelopment projects are to succeed, there should not be other new-build apartment projects nearby. Certainly, the new-build projects in the IFEZ and the Asian Games village have become a hindrance to the inner-city redevelopment, as those are more sought after by buyers who are from Seoul or neighboring provinces.[56]

Conclusion

Once awarded, mega-events have their own momentum, due to unavoidable deadlines and the host city's ambition to showcase itself to global and domestic spectators. The need to stage a highly visible and recognizably impressive event, under time and budget constraints, creates a sense of urgency, and induces a high level of concentrated investment in the built environment (e.g., Games facilities, transport infrastructure, beautification, etc.). As this chapter shows, mega-events are often embedded in larger plans to transform the built environment and promote the global reputation of the host city and country. In both Guangzhou and Incheon, preparation for the Asian Games was actively incorporated into their overall urban development plans. The two mega-events reflect each host city's ambition to achieve increased global visibility and prominence. In Guangzhou, the city was focused on consolidating its position as the "dragon head" in South China and, at the same time, rising to become an international regional center. Incheon also aspired to become an international regional center, aided by its free economic zone and its international airport. Both cities witnessed a heavy emphasis on expanding the investment in the built environment in the form of promoting urban redevelopment, new town construction, infrastructure provision, and so on.

Incheon's local state entrepreneurialism was evident in its promotion of various booster projects that aimed at transforming the city-scape through real-estate projects and infrastructure construction, as well as the promotion of the central state-endorsed free economic zone, one of the first of its kind in South Korea. As discussed elsewhere,[57] Incheon made efforts to make use of land reclamation as a means to expand its land-asset basis, which could then be sold to developers and other private businesses to raise revenues that would in turn be used to finance other imperative developmental projects. For Incheon, the promotion of a large number of development projects encompassing both infrastructure and real estate produced a deepening speculative urbanization process, which was built on a dangerously high level of local debts incurred by both the metropolitan government and its public corporation. In essence, Incheon's state entrepreneurialism was driven by debts.

For Guangzhou, the event-led development proved to be useful in both times of inflationary expansion (when the central government actually cautioned against excessive investment) and of recession, all of which characterized the economic climate during the Asian Games preparation period between 2005 and 2010. During the former inflationary period, while the central government warned local governments not to make excessive investments, the Asian Games preparation was an excuse for Guangzhou to justify further investments. In times of economic recession after the global financial crisis, the Asian Games preparation was also useful for Guangzhou to minimize, if not overcome, negative impacts of the crisis on the city and on the PRD region as a whole. Guangzhou also exhibited the usual "land-based accumulation," which makes proactive use of land-related extra-budgetary revenue for financing fixed asset investments.[58] This practice is built on the local state acting as a de facto landlord, the power endowed in the local state by the central state-led reform to commodify land assets and let local states administer land (use right) transactions.[59] The Guangzhou municipal government turned out to be excessively indebted, a shared feature in mainland China among local governments. Such indebted conditions have become a source of major concern more recently, as China's economic growth is expected to slow down in comparison with previous years' growth records.

In conclusion, despite the apparent differences in the political economic structure of the two cities, the ways in which both Incheon and Guangzhou pursued their entrepreneurial state agenda present a lot of similarities, especially in terms of how the state-led investment in the built environment had been largely debt-driven in both cities, and how this process was facilitated by the mega-event preparation. Incheon's high level of local debts resulting from issuing municipal bonds was a source of concern, especially during the final phase of its Games preparation. Guangzhou's debt level also came to the attention of the general public more recently, raising doubts about the effectiveness of China's local governments' unrestrained investment in fixed assets. Recently, the central state implemented a pilot scheme to allow key local governments such as Zhejiang, Guangdong, Shanghai, and Shenzhen to experiment with the issuing of municipal bonds.[60] This was expanded in May 2014 to cover ten local governments: Shanghai, Zhejiang, Guangdong, Shenzhen, Jiangsu, Shandong, Beijing, Qingdao, Ningxia, and Jiangxi. From September 2014, all local governments were given the go-ahead to issue bonds to finance their development without having to face restrictions as before.[61] The true effect of this new scheme is yet to be seen. While the scheme has been designed to allow local governments to find an alternative avenue of raising funds for development and depend less on land resources, it is highly possible that without diminishing development aspiration and GDPism, the practice of speculative and debt-driven development is likely to continue in the foreseeable future in China.

Acknowledgments

The author acknowledges the financial support from the LSE Annual Fund/ STICERD New Researcher Award (2009–11) and the National Research

Foundation of Korea Grant funded by the Korean Government (NRF-2014S1 A3A2044551). The author also thanks the assistance from Soojin Chung and Doyoung Oh with regard to the research on Incheon. Many thanks are also due to Rick Gruneau and John Horne for their constructive editorial suggestions. The usual disclaimer applies.

Notes

1 Shin, "Urban Spatial Restructuring."
2 Duckett, "Bureaucrats in Business"; Wu and Phelps, "(Post) suburban development and state entrepreneurialism."
3 Pirie, *The Korean Developmental State.*
4 Park et al., *Locating Neoliberalism in East Asia.*
5 See Liew "China's engagement with neoliberalism"; and Park et. al., *Locating Neoliberalism in East Asia.*
6 Harvey, "The Urban Process under Capitalism"; see also Shin, "Unequal Cities of Spectacle and Mega-events in China."
7 Castells, "Four Asian Tigers with a Dragon Head"; and Glassman and Choi, "The *Chaebol* and the US Military-Industrial Complex."
8 Jessop and Sum, "An Entrepreneurial City in Action," 2295.
9 See Cochrane et al., "Manchester Plays Games."
10 Oi, "The Role of the Local State," 1132; and Oi, "Fiscal Reform and the Economic Foundations."
11 Oi "The Role of the Local State," 1137, original emphasis.
12 Ibid., 1140.
13 Duckett, "Bureaucrats in Business"; and Duckett, "The Emergence of the Entrepreneurial State."
14 Shin, "Residential Redevelopment and Entrepreneurial Local State"; and also see Lin et al., "Strategizing Urbanism"; and Hsing, *The Great Urban Transformation.*
15 Wu and Phelps, "(Post) suburban development and state entrepreneurialism," 427.
16 Hsing, *The Great Urban Transformation.*
17 Ibid., 104.
18 Burbank et al., 2001, *Olympic Dreams*, 29.
19 Cochrane et al., "Manchester Plays Games."
20 See Xu and Yeh, "City profile of Guangzhou," 365–8.
21 See Shin, "Urban Spatial Restructuring."
22 Ibid., and Cheung "The Points of Regional Cooperation."
23 Huang, "Guangzhou Old City Redevelopment."
24 *Nanfang Daily*, "For the First Time."
25 Personal interview, September 17, 2009. As per the mid-market rate as of December 31, 2010, US$1 was equal to 6.6 yuan. See "Current and Historical Rate Tables," XE: http://www.xe.com/currencytables/.
26 Shin, "Envisioned by the State."
27 Incheon Metropolitan Government, *Incheon Statistical Yearbook 2013.* The share of the secondary sector (manufacturing, construction, mining, electricity, gas and water supply) had been a little more than one-third of the gross regional product between 2007 and 2012. The share of agricultural production, forestry and fishing was 0.5 percent or less during the same period.

28 Kositchotethana, "South Korea hopes to beat out Delhi."
29 Chen, *Shanghai Pudong*.
30 Shin, "Envisioned by the State."
31 Ghawi, "Incheon Free Economic Zone."
32 Interviewed on December 12, 2011.
33 Lee, "Incheon's Development Promises," 73–4.
34 Ibid., 89; and Incheon Metropolitan Government, *Draft Incheon Urban Master Plan 2025*.
35 Incheon Metropolitan Government, *Draft Incheon Urban Master Plan 2025*, 2.
36 Ibid., 23.
37 See Shin, "Envisoned by the State."
38 "Introducing the fields of the 2014 Incheon Asian Games in Songdo," Songdo IBD: http://songdoibd.tistory.com/721.
39 Shin, "Residential Redevelopment."
40 Interviewed on September 16, 2009.
41 Qiu, "Budget for Asian Games."
42 Interviewed on September 16, 2009.
43 Lin et al., "Strategizing Urbanism."
44 Anderlini, "China Opens Debt Window"; and Sweeney, "China's Parliament."
45 Qiu, "Budget for Asian Games."
46 Yang, "Guangzhou Reveals Details."
47 Zhang, "The Status of Budget Implementation."
48 Wang, "Guangzhou Nears Debt Red Line."
49 Kim, "Fiscal Crisis of Incheon: Its Status and Prospect."
50 Ibid., 262; Incheon Metropolitan Government, "Debt Status." As per the mid-market rate as of December 31, 2009, US$1 was equal to 1170.5 Korean Won. As of December 31, 2014, US$1 was equal to 1092.0 Korean Won. See "Current and Historical Rate Tables", XE: http://www.xe.com/currencytables/.
51 Incheon Metropolitan Government , "Debt Status."
52 Kim, "Fiscal Crisis of Incheon and the Asian Games," 59–60.
53 Part of the reasons behind the municipality's undertaking of heavy investment in the Asian Games facilities was the less-than-expected support from the central government. This becomes evident when compared with the experience of the 2002 Summer Asian Games hosted by Busan, which received government subsidies to cover 35.9 percent of all the Games preparation costs. See Kim, "Fiscal crisis of Incheon and the Asian Games," 60.
54 Incheon Metropolitan Government, *Report on Plans to Reduce the Debts*, 6.
55 Ibid., 7.
56 Interviewed on December 12, 2011.
57 See Shin, "Envisoned by the State."
58 Hsing, *The Great Urban Transformation*; and Lin et al., "Strategizing Urbanism in the Era of Neoliberalization."
59 Shin, "Residential Redevelopment and Entrepreneurial Local State."
60 Anderlini, "China Municipalities to Issue Bonds."
61 Sweeney, "China's Parliament."

Bibliography

Anderlini, Jamil. "China Municipalities to Issue Bonds." *Financial Times*, October 20, 2011: http://on.ft.com/pZ5tbu.
———. "China Opens Debt Window for Local Governments." *Financial Times*, May 21, 2014: http://on.ft.com/1nnQxg0.

Beijing Statistics Bureau. *Beijing Statistical Yearbook 2011*. Beijing: Beijing Statistical Bureau, 2011.

Burbank, Matthew J., Gregory D. Andranovich, and Charles H. Heying. *Olympic Dreams: The Impact of Mega-events on Local Politics*. London: Lynne Rienner Publishers, 2001.

Castells, Manuel. "Four Asian Tigers with a Dragon Head: A Comparative Analysis of the State, Economy, and Society in the Asian Pacific Rim." In *States and Development in the Asian Pacific Rim*, Richard P. Appelbaum and Jeffrey W. Henderson (eds.), 33–70. Newbury Park, CA: SAGE, 1992.

Chen, Yawei. *Shanghai Pudong: Urban Development in an Era of Global-local Interaction*. Delft: IOS Press, 2007.

Cheung, Peter T.Y. "The politics of regional cooperation in the Greater Pearl River Delta." *Asia Pacific Viewpoint* 53 (2012): 21–37.

Cochrane, Allan, Jamie Peck, and Adam Tickell. "Manchester Plays Games: Exploring the Local Politics of Globalisation." *Urban Studies* 33 (1996): 1319–35.

Duckett, Jane. "Bureaucrats in Business, Chinese-style: The Lessons of Market Reform and State Entrepreneurialism in the People's Republic of China." *World Development* 29 (2001): 23–37.

———. "The Emergence of the Entrepreneurial State in Contemporary China." *Pacific Review* 9 (1996): 180–98.

Ghawi, Samir. "Incheon Free Economic Zone Putting S. Korean development into high gear." *McClatchy – Tribune Business News*, April 29, 2007: http://search.proquest.com/docview/459369030?accountid=9630.

Glassman, Jim, and Young-Jin Choi. "The *Chaebol* and the US Military-Industrial Complex: Cold War Geopolitical Economy and South Korean Industrialization." *Environment and Planning A* 46 (2014): 1160–80.

Harvey, David. "The Urban Process under Capitalism: A Framework for Analysis." *International Journal of Urban and Regional Research* 2 (1978): 101–31.

Hsing, You-tien. *The Great Urban Transformation: Politics of Land and Property in China*. Oxford: Oxford University Press, 2010.

Huang, Jian. "Guangzhou Old City Redevelopment to be Piloted on Enning Road." *China Real Estate News*, May 28, 2007. [In Chinese.]

Incheon Metropolitan Government. "Debt Status." February 5, 2015: http://www.incheon.go.kr/posts/49/91?curPage=1. [In Korean.]

———. *Draft Incheon Urban Master Plan 2025* [In Korean]. Incheon: Incheon Metropolitan Government, 2009.

———. *Incheon Statistical Yearbook 2013* [In Korean]. Incheon: Incheon Metropolitan Government, 2014.

———. *Report on Plans to Reduce the Debts of the Incheon Development & Tourism Corporation – Submitted to the Incheon Metropolitan Council in April 2014* [In Korean]. Incheon: Incheon Metropolitan Government, 2014.

———. *Revision of the 2025 Incheon Urban Master Plan* [In Korean]. Incheon: Incheon Metropolitan Government, 2012.

Jessop, Bob, and Ngai-Ling Sum. "An Entrepreneurial City in Action: Hong Kong's Emerging Strategies in and for (Inter) Urban Competition." *Urban Studies* 37 (2000): 2287–313.

Kim, Myung-Hee. "Fiscal Crisis of Incheon and the Asian Games." *Welfare Trend* 150 (2011): 59–62. [In Korean.]

———. "Fiscal Crisis of Incheon: Its Status and Prospect." *Hwanghae Culture* 75 (2012): 260–77. [In Korean.]

Kositchotethana, Boonsong. "South Korea hopes to beat out Delhi for 2014 Asian Games." *McClatchy - Tribune Business News*, March 17, 2007: http://search.proquest.com/docview/462591435?accountid=9630.

Lee, Hee-Hwan. "Incheon's Development Promises Throwing Lives into an Empty Future: The Cases of the Global Fair & Festival and Urban Redevelopment Projects." *Architecture and Society* 19 (2010): 72–91. [In Korean.]

Liew, Leong. "China's engagement with neoliberalism: Path dependency, geography and party self-reinvention." *Journal of Development Studies* 41 (2005): 331–52.

Lin, George C.S., Xun Li, Fiona F. Yang, and Fox Z.Y. Hu. "Strategizing Urbanism in the Era of Neoliberalization: State Power Reshuffling, Land Development and Municipal Finance in Urbanizing China." *Urban Studies* 2014: doi: 10.1177/0042098013513644.

Nanfang Daily. "For the First Time, Guangzhou Municipal Office of Three Olds Redevelopment Responds to Hot Spots: The Government Never Expects to Make Money." April 24, 2010. [In Chinese.]

Oi, Jean C. "Fiscal Reform and the Economic Foundations of Local State Corporatism in China." *World Politics* 45 (1992): 99–126.

———. "The Role of the Local State in China's Transitional Economy." *The China Quarterly* 144 (1995): 1132–49.

Park, Bae-Gyoon, Richard Child Hill, and Asato Saito. *Locating Neoliberalism in East Asia: Neoliberalizing Spaces in Developmental States*. Oxford: Wiley-Blackwell, 2011.

Pirie, Iain. *The Korean Developmental State: From Dirigisme to Neoliberalism*. London: Routledge, 2008.

Qiu, Quanlin. "Budget for Asian Games on the way, says city official. *China Daily*, February 25, 2011: http://www.chinadaily.com.cn/china/2011-02/25/content_12075209.htm.

Shanghai Statistics Bureau. *Shanghai Statistical Yearbook 2011*. Shanghai: Shanghai Statistical Bureau, 2011.

Shin, Hyun B. "Envisioned by the State: The Paradox of Entrepreneurial Urbanism and Making of Songdo City, South Korea." In *Mega-Urbanisation in the Global South: Fast Cities and New Urban Utopias of the Postcolonial State*, Ayona Datta and Abdul Shaban (eds.). London: Routledge, forthcoming.

———. "Residential Redevelopment and Entrepreneurial Local State: The Implications of Beijing's Shifting Emphasis on Urban Redevelopment Policies." *Urban Studies* 46 (2009): 2815–39.

———. "Unequal Cities of Spectacle and Mega-events in China." *City* 16 (2012): 728–44.

———. "Urban Spatial Restructuring, Event-led Development and Scalar Politics." *Urban Studies* 51 (2014): 2961–78.

Sweeney, Pete. "China's Parliament Authorises Local Governments to Issue Bonds." *Reuters*, September 1, 2014: http://reut.rs/1niEksv.

Wang, Jing. "Guangzhou Nears Debt Red Line, Its Figures Show." *Caixin Online*, July 31, 2013: http://english.caixin.com/2013-07-31/100563494.html.

Wu, Fulong, and Nicholar A. Phelps. "(Post) suburban development and state entrepreneurialism in Beijing's outer suburbs." *Environment and Planning A* 43 (2011): 410–30.

Xu, Jiang, and Anthony G.O. Yeh. "City profile of Guangzhou." *Cities* 20 (2003): 361–74.

Yang, Chen. "Guangzhou Reveals Details of Local Government Debt." *Global Times*, December 27, 2012: http://www.globaltimes.cn/content/752518.shtml.

Zhang, Jieming. "The Status of Budget Implementation in 2010 and a Draft Budget for 2011 in Guangzhou." March 24, 2011: http://zwgk.gd.gov.cn/007482532/201103/ t20110331_32416.html. [In Chinese]

12 Mega-events of the future

The experience economy, the Korean connection, and the growth of eSport

Michael Borowy and Dal Yong Jin

Introduction

Over the last decade, competitive digital gaming (eSport) has grown rapidly with increasing attention from media, institutions, and governments as viewership and prize numbers grow year after year. Electronic sports leagues, in which players compete through networked games and related activities, have existed since the early 1980s.[1] However, the increasing popularity and monetization of the activity in the twenty-first century has led the gaming industry to promote and support large-scale events resembling major sporting competitions. By promoting gaming as a sport-like activity, the digital gaming industry has sought to elevate the economic and cultural status of gaming. In so doing, they have transformed gaming from something done privately or semi-privately in living rooms or arcades, or more collectively in online networks, to a more publicly visible form of spectacular entertainment. While eSport competitions have yet to reach the scale, levels of investment, and sizes of audience found in sport mega-events such as the Olympics or World Cup, or even that of second-tier events such as the Pan American or Commonwealth Games, they are moving rapidly in this direction.

Consider, for example, that the 2013 *League of Legends* Season 3 World Championship sold out the Los Angeles' Staples Center in just one hour. A year later, the same Championship attracted over 40,000 fans to a former World Cup soccer stadium in Seoul.[2] *The International 2014*, a major *Defense of the Ancients 2 (DotA 2)* tournament also sold out its approximately 10,000 tickets at Seattle's Key Arena in an hour. Tickets were subsequently being sold on eBay for up to five times (US$500) the original sales price. The event featured a grand prize of over $5 million (won by China's team Newbee) with over $10 million in prize money overall. Online spectatorship for the *International 2014* approached 950,000 even before the final match, in comparison to 1.1 million simultaneous online viewers for the 2014 Superbowl, and a peak of 1.7 million simultaneous online viewers for the 2014 FIFA World Cup.[3] Online (concurrent) viewing grew to well over a million viewers for the Electronic Sports League's (ESL)[4] *One Frankfurt* (Dota 2) tournament in 2015, which featured (sold-out) finals scheduled in the Commerzbank Arena, a former site of the 2006 World Cup.[5]

This chapter provides an overview of the growth and development of eSport events as public spectacles on a global scale. While the first indications of professionalized, competitive digital gaming aspiring to become a legitimate sport were witnessed in American arcades in the 1980s, it was not until the late 1990s when digital gaming underwent a process of "sportification," leading to its reconceptualization as "eSport."[6] South Korea (hereafter Korea), in particular, played a major role in the sportification of gaming, not coincidentally due to a unique conjuncture of social and technological developments associated with Korea's hosting of the 1988 Summer Olympics in Seoul. During the 1990s, Korea formally recognized digital gaming as an official national sport.

By examining the evolution of eSport from arcade games, and private forms of amusement, into larger-scale sport-like events, held in concert halls, arenas, and stadiums, we witness the transition of a competitive play activity into a form of global capitalist spectacle. This transition is usefully situated in a broader discussion of the growth of "the experience economy" around the world. In developing this analysis, we argue that the rise of public gaming spectacles has had the effect of repositioning players and fans within new promotional chains that organize synergies between competitive play, public events, spectating, marketing, and business strategy. The growing popularity of large-scale gaming event also has also worked to integrate gaming more tightly into the entrepreneurial ambitions of countries and cities that strive to present themselves as "world-class" centers of digital industry, technological innovation, tourism. and entertainment.

eSport in the economy of experiences and events

Scholars have found eSport to be a difficult activity to define. While traditional sporting events, such as football and baseball, have been looked to as forerunners by eSport organizers, competitors, and fans, eSport is a new social entity, a bridge between sport, electronic gaming, media, and entertainment event.[7] Hutchins offers one of the earliest systematic attempts to interpret the complicated relationship between digital play, sport, and the media by analyzing the Korean-founded World Cyber Games (WCG).[8] In his view, the key point about eSport is the impossibility of disassociating media from the production of the event. The WCG event proved that Internet-enabled technologies of production, spectatorship, and dissemination, as well as the notion of "sport" and digital gaming as a form of media content, merge to create a novel hybrid entity. The result is a "gaming, computing, media and sports event all at once; familiar in its presentation format but unfamiliar in its content."[9]

Hutchins' recognition of the quintessentially mediated nature of eSport raises questions about the experiences eSport provides its participants and the increasing valorization of these experiences in modern life. It is more than a coincidence that digital gaming emerged during a time in the late twentieth, and early twenty-first centuries, where more and more areas of human experience have become commodified. This has occurred so broadly and intensely that some economists have referred to the growth of an international "experience economy." The idea of the experience economy emerges from macro analyses of global economic changes over the last few millennia (for instance, transitions from agricultural to industrial, and then to services production). A greater penetration of the economy into the realms of leisure, culture, and self-expression has accompanied these changes, resulting in a widespread "culturalization" of economics, associated with the growth of a late twentieth-century consumer culture, and the increasing prominence of media, design, and advertising industries. With the emergence of so-called "post-industrial," "postmodern," or "post-Fordist" social transitions, the production of events takes on a greater role in processes of capitalist accumulation.

These broad trends are often evaluated from significantly different political orientations. Examples can be found in the work of writers as diverse as Daniel Bell, Kaname Akamatsu, Alvin Toffler, and David Harvey.[10] However, the origin of the specific phrase "experience economy" lies in the work of the business historians, Pine and Gilmore, who used the phrase to refer to a new phase of economic development beyond post-industrialism.[11] Although Pine and Gilmore acknowledged that the consumption of experience has been a driver of economic growth through various sectors (the arts, cuisine, sports, travel, etc.) throughout much of history, they argued that the marketing of experience commodities in the late twentieth century had become the primary source of capital accumulation, accentuating the non-utilitarian aspects of consumer goods.

After Pine and Gilmore's business-oriented, and largely uncritical, analysis of this apparent global economic shift, a number of other authors set out to more precisely define the phrase. For example, Poulsson and Kale saw commercial experience as "an engaging act of co-creation between a provider and a consumer wherein the consumer perceives value in the encounter and in the subsequent memory of that encounter."[12] Although the "experience economy" could be a part of the service sector, there are significant differences between "services" and "experiences," that the concept fails to account for. For example, a service entails something that is done *for you*, and an experience is a product that does *something to you*, leaving you with a significant memory. In fact, they argue that experience is exemplified by an intensified consumption phase; the *act of consuming* is the product. In a related discussion, Darmer and Sundbo go on to add that, although an experience can consist of a product (they give the example of a theater play), it can also be a supplement to a product; the experience becomes the entirety of the package, including the consumer's state of mind.[13] They reiterate that experiences include connotative elements, including place of consumption, décor, design, marketing, usage, and symbolic values and associations that constitute the experience, which could be applied to everything from shoes to vacations. Furthermore, experiences can be physical or nonphysical, mentally demanding or not, passive or active. Importantly, they also note that experiences can be visited (the primary goal of tourism), or the experiences can come to the consumer (such as ordering a film from Netflix). We would go on to suggest that public events in the experience economy, and mega-events in particular, provide sites for experiencing levels of emotion and enjoyment typically unrivaled in many other areas of life, and this—often connected to the social distinctions that come from consuming "world-class" experiences—underwrites both their popularity and their economic value.

In analyzing the nature of game experiences in consumer societies, Kocurek saw the rise of coin-operated games as "an introduction to the spending practices essential to the emergent consumer economy . . . correspond[ing] with a shift in consumer spending away from durable goods and toward [more ephemeral] forms of cultural goods and entertainments."[14] She saw these shifts as likewise suggesting a transition from Fordist manufacturing and consumption to post-Fordist/postmodern forms. These factors were particularly important for the emerging digital gaming industry of the 1970s and 1980s in North America, which arose in a climate of audience fragmentation and economic deregulation, matched with conditions where a concern for moral regulation often remained strong. As gaming grew in prominence, critics argued that gaming was harmful to youth and needed stronger regulation. Arcade operators and game producers responded by promoting the idea of a unified, gamer culture with shared interests (e.g., against regulation) and by advertising public gaming spaces as sites where the new gaming community could come together. More importantly, the promotion of a unified gamer culture created a large block of consumer/player/audiences whose shared wants and experiences could be more effectively valorized. These linkages between gaming community, cultural experience, consumption, and lifestyle were critical as they established a shared gamer *identity*, with players meeting together in distinctive physical spaces to play games and discuss the newest industry happenings.

A combination of community and media interest fast-forwarded the staging of digitally mediated quasi-sporting competitions, as these events were soon relived in gaming fanzines, newspapers, and news reports on television. The gaming connection to sport seemed both logical and inevitable. Sport has served as an example of successful entertainment-based event marketing in a mediated culture where play was to become both an involved, performance-centric experience as well as a spectatorial one. Sporting events became experiential commodities during the nineteenth and twentieth centuries, so it seems hardly surprising that promoters soon adopted a similar model in the digital gaming industry. Sporting competitions, with individuals or teams advancing through brackets to a final, provided a readily available model of organizing gaming competitions. Moreover, there was an established and growing gaming community around electronic games, based on soccer, football, and hockey, as well as a burgeoning business in fantasy sports teams and leagues online, run essentially as digital versions of competition at the highest levels of the actual sports. The result has been stronger linkages between conventional sports and their traditional sponsors, and competitions involving digital gaming. An example is the development of the *FIFA Interactive World Cup*, which recently featured nearly 2 million players, as well as significant involvement by Sony.[15]

Still, from a marketing standpoint, there is something unique about staging events in fixed sites. As Johansson and Näslund note, "staged events" in singular physical spaces "provide a powerful way to reach customers—not only those that take part, but also others who will learn about it afterwards through media."[16] To solidify gaming competitions, both as aspiring sporting events and novel constituents of the experience economy, media reporting was centrally important for the early development of eSport, particularly during the formative years of the early 1980s.

The rising significance and financial potential of eSports as promotional events became synonymous with the intensification of the experience economy. At the core of the event is a commercial product, sold on a global scale, where expertise in the event can be put on spectacular display. The marketing of spectacle would soon take the lead among numerous other aspects of event marketing, and, with this, the elevated degree to which the packaging and focusing of the event as a significant business activity became apparent. On this point, Johansson and Näslund note how the production of the promotional eSport event became more dependent on theatricality, in the sense that companies implemented techniques from theater that attempted to construct a distinctive brand. Because "the postulation of the experience economy favors theatrical presentation over reality," they assert, "in accordance with a fascination for spectacle, the theatrical and the spectacular have been hailed as key value creating qualities of the experience economy."[17]

As Pine and Gilmore were developing their thesis on the experience economy in the 1990s, *event marketing* was quickly taking shape as the leading promotional tool for many companies, an instrument whose growth rate was exceeding all other promotional methods. Integrating corporate sponsorship of an event with various other marketing elements, including advertising, sales promotion, and public relations, event marketing in the 1990s would grow to $12 billion annually by mid-decade, growing at a rate of approximately 17 percent per year.[18] By 1998, this number had jumped to $17.4 billion worldwide.[19] The growth in eSports was part and parcel of this broader trend toward integration through event marketing. As this occurred, eSport events became even more reliant on conventional sport as a template, not least because conventional sport had been undergoing important changes of its own in sales and marketing practices in the 1980s and 1990s. As Gruneau and Whitson have pointed out, during this time an unprecedented wave of corporate media-sport synergies began to remake major league sports in Europe and North America.[20] In addition, sports mega-events such as the Super Bowl, the Olympics, and the World Cup began to evolve into global entertainments, and global marketing phenomena, on an unprecedented scale.

The Olympic Games arguably best illustrate this evolution. The changing scope of the Games' relationship with commodified audiences, corporate interests, and prevailing media (all driving components of event marketing) were especially transformed after the Los Angeles Olympics in 1984, which symbolized the growing ascendance of a neoliberal worldview, where countries promoted free markets, dropped their protectionist walls, and declared themselves "open for business."[21] The LA Games were the first instance of a profit-making Olympics, and they "rewrote the formula for staging the global sports spectacle" for subsequent generations.[22] By establishing a new standard whereby public events would be expected to feature spectacular ceremonies, "the showbiz spectacle pre-empted the sports festival right from the start."[23]

These changes coincided significantly with the growth and evolution of television broadcasting. During the second half of the twentieth century, television went from being barely significant in staging the Olympics to one of its key components. For example, during the 1960 Rome Games, 1 out of every 400 dollars of the cost of hosting the Olympics was returned by television. By the 1984 Games, television provided 1 of every 2 dollars.[24] An important aspect of this transition had to do with technological and economic developments within the television industry itself, which expanded potential to reach global audiences and created greater competition between networks. For instance, the spread of cable and satellite delivery systems in the 1980s were significant features that increased the value of Olympic audiences for advertisers. At the same time, the deregulation of broadcasting systems in many parts of the world facilitated bidding wars from both public and private networks for the biggest and most popular sporting events. International broadcasters jockeyed for comparative advantage, promising larger fees, and more hours of coverage, with higher production values. Meanwhile, the Olympic Games came to be seen as a bonanza for civic image making and urban entrepreneurialism because it put the host location at the center of the world for a brief period of time, as well as expediting urban development through investments in infrastructure.

The trajectory followed by the Olympics, from notable international event, to a highly mediated, money-producing, global spectacle, became a model for almost all other large-scale sporting events. Over the past three decades, sporting mega-events have become more designed for consumption and marketing. This transition has accelerated since the 1990s as digital technologies have created previously unimagined possibilities for commodifying audiences to sell to prospective advertisers. With its endless capacity for providing content for newspapers, radio, television, mobile communication, and the Internet, an early twenty-first century "digital-media-sport complex" has become one of the world's most influential market powers.

The eSport Korean connection

Asian countries began to host digital game tournaments as early as the 1970s. At one early event, the *All Japan TV Game Championships* in Tokyo, sponsored by arcade manufacturer Sega, 16 finalists were selected from a pool of 300 local champions throughout Japan. The *Vending Times* newspaper reported that an official for Sega had already realized "the importance of such tournaments to foster better business relationships between the maker-location customer and create an atmosphere of competition on TV amusement games."[25] Even at a time when the ideas of event marketing and the experience economy were just beginning to take shape, game developers and arcade administrators were able to use associated strategies to harmonize the primordial gaming community by establishing an event linking game creators, public gaming proprietors, and digital game consumers, irrespective of whether they were casual or competitive players. The embryonic conditions for a mediated form of entertainment to gain a sport-like quality were present for decades in Asia prior to the twenty-first century.[26]

However, during the 1990s, it was in Korea where sharp-eyed government officials, corporate executives, and entrepreneurs began to recognize the deepening international confluence of sport, media, and event marketing in the experience economy. As interest in digital gaming grew in Korea, the idea of eSport emerged as an appealing combination of culture, play, and (potentially) labor. Professional gaming soon became a job category in Korea along with attendant new job-market roles such as team manager, analyst, and eSport play-by-play commentator (called a "caster"). The growth of these new high-tech, information economy jobs helped to fulfill governmental mandates calling for higher employment levels in the face of the 1997 Asian financial crisis. Government policies and laws that subsidized and were favorable to new technologies, especially those involved with the Internet, became a fundamental basis for the growth of eSport and the game industry. The Korean government explicitly endeavored to make Korean technology-driven businesses the cornerstones of the national market. An important step in this process was enacting the "Long-term Promotion Plan of the Game Industry" in 2004, with the goal of increasing Korea's market size in the sector to $10 billion, and employing 100,000 people. In the early years of the twenty-first century, the Korean government was spending over $100 million annually to promote, research, and develop the industry.[27]

One of the most important results of Korea's investment into competitive gaming was the Korean-founded World Cyber Games (WCG) (now defunct since 2014). Games' CEO and President Hyoung Seok Kim declared that "2010 marks 10 years of World Cyber Games, in that time we have brought together more than 10 million people from 90 nations to celebrate the achievements and triumphs of nearly six thousand players."[28] Beyond acting as an international forum for the promotion of eSport globally, the annual WCG was a hotbed of corporate marketing, investment, and synergy. For example, in 2010, Samsung, the event's main sponsor, demonstrated products that were focused on the spectator demographic (a new 7-inch Galaxy Tab, a new monitor and cell phones), donated $122,000 worth of computer monitors to the Los Angeles County Education Foundation to encourage technology education, and purchased carbon offsets to cover "everything from the electricity used at the tournament to the airline emissions of the players traveling from all over the world."[29]

Among the legacies of the World Cyber Games was its global reach; indeed, the WCG frequently bounced between the "West" and the "East." Between 2000 and 2003, WCG was hosted in South Korea. In 2004, the annual event was staged outside Korea for the first time, in the US. The subsequent competitions were played out in Singapore, Italy, the US, Germany, China, the US, Korea, China, and then China once more as the WCG's final showing in 2013. In the end, only five of the 14 annual events were held in Western countries. Furthermore, the event with the highest overall prize payout (approximately $500,000) occurred in Chengdu, China in 2009. However, despite the early successes of these events, and although qualifiers occur globally in today's leagues, most major finals in the 2010s (such as the championships for Major League Gaming and The International) take place in Western countries. The 2014 League of Legends World Championship, held in South Korea, is one notable exception.

The long history of investment by the Korean government, technology corporations, and the public was meant to sustain and to amplify economic incentives through the convergence of old and new media. In order for Korea to become a global leader, it had to finance the media and telecommunication markets, of which the hyper-experiential eSport industry was a leading mover. Many large corporations sought to capitalize on the convergence of telecommunications and broadcasting and the gaming industry provided unique opportunities to mix content, broadcasting (such as eSport), and telecommunications. The tangible benefits reaped by Korean companies became palpable almost immediately. For instance, only two years after it had become involved in the online game sector, SK Telecom, the largest mobile service provider in Korea, announced that it was no longer just a telecommunications company but a new media group, including gaming. The company rapidly changed its corporate image from a mobile telecom company to a new media- and content-driven media group.[30]

The Korean eSport industry itself continues to grow. As of December 2013, there were nine professional eSport leagues in Korea, including for 1) *League of Legends*; 2) *StarCraft 2*, 3) *Sudden Attack*, 4) *Dungeon & Fighter*, 5) *FIFA Online 3*, 6) *DOTA 2*, 7) *Counter-Strike*, 8) *KARTRIDER*, and 9) two amateur leagues. In total, prizes amounted to approximately US$3.4 million. With the rapid growth of eSport, many spectators regularly watch these games, and therefore, since 2012, some leagues have started to sell tickets ($15–25 per ticket).[31]

There is a strong tie between the growth of eSport in Korea and the 1988 Summer Olympics hosted in Seoul. Exemplifying a growing trend for mega-events to be staged outside of Western countries, these Olympic Games were timely for the nation, as Korean elites expressed their desire to be recognized on the global stage. Most notably, Seoul 1988 occurred in the context of Korea's telecommunication revolution, which has largely been attributed to television coverage of the Games that "coincided with the rise of the nation's electronics and telecommunications industry to the position of leading exporter and most strategic economic sector."[32] This would position Korea as among the most technologically developed nations in the world. It also occurred during the rapid growth of the newly commercialized and spectacularized Olympic Games, as well as the proliferation of "global television"; the awarding of the Olympics to Korea was seen as a political, economic, and cultural catalyst primarily because of the large television and media presence. As it relates to the Olympics, the Korean case is especially salient for eSport because it helped to legitimize the country in the international eye, showcasing its newly found technological prowess and paving the way for digital games to become one of the nation's most significant national sports. The Korean-based World Cyber Games and the various Korean pro leagues were built on structural and ideological foundations that originated in not only the Olympics in general, but the Seoul Olympics in particular.

Public contests and institutional supports for eSport

Kennedy and Hills have argued that

> Our experience of sport is inevitably informed by the sport media, and an understanding of the way the media constructs meanings around sport and identities among its audience is central to a critical engagement with sport. As a phenomenon, however, media sport is forever moving, constantly reconfiguring sport in relation to changing social contexts and values.[33]

When sport and media amalgamated fully with the rise of the video game industry and public competition, eSport arose as a product of this environment, especially in Korea. In other words, as sport and technology became more and more fused during the last few decades of the twentieth century, it should have come as no surprise that soon the media themselves would become sport-like.

The competitive physicality of sport is importantly not private—it was a showcase for others to partake in, to watch, and to discuss. From the Greek Olympics and the Roman Colosseum, to the Renaissance and medieval knightly tournaments, and from sport throughout colonial gentlemen's play and now the mass-mediated commercial spectacle of contemporary sport, one key thread is clear: the presence of the audience. eSport organizers in Korea quickly realized that to build a new sport-like activity, audience engagement and participation would be critical. The recognition of the importance of theatricality and spectacle has been one reason that eSport has proliferated and maintained its growth: organizers have been able to capture youth imagination and expand youth interest. In conventional sport, junior leagues, trading cards, and endless memorabilia helped youth demographics remain absorbed as participants. Similarly, with eSport, the conscious effort to sustain economic relevance has led to many marketing initiatives aimed at young player/consumers. While game marketers have always successfully targeted young players, this trend has become even more prevalent and pronounced when it comes to competitive gaming.

Further contributing to the proliferation of competitive gaming as both a growing event spectacle and a new career path for youth are educational and institutional involvements. For example, starting in 2014, George Mason University in Virginia began to offer minor degrees for "Sport and Computer Game Design," combining the school's sports management and computer design programs. Among the applications and selling points was a more concise understanding of how sport and gaming are merging, offering students options where they can not only use gaming tools for analysis, training, and teaching,[34] but as a foundation for formalizing the relationship between sport and gaming as a new kind of media event.

In 2014, Robert Morris University in Illinois was the first US university to offer eSport scholarships (35 in total), complete with varsity jackets, five coaches, and the support of university administration. Pro gaming teams have become part of the school's athletics department, with RMU investing $100,000 to turn its computer lab into an eSport arena.[35] The teams play against other college teams in what has become a considerable network of college and university clubs competing in leagues across North America, Europe, and Asia. Tellingly, secondary schools are also beginning to offer institutional supports for students wishing to pursue competitive gaming. In British Columbia, Canada, the Vancouver School Board recently endorsed a new eSports league, with eight teams (as of November 2014) representing local high schools competing.[36] These kinds of supports were pivotal during the rapid growth of sports such as baseball and football during the nineteenth and twentieth centuries, and the growing integration of competitive gaming with schools, businesses, and complementary social events will continue to insulate the emergent eSport industry.

Another major theme contributing to eSport as a major public showcase is the longevity of players in the community after retirement (which for pro gamers is typically mid-twenties). Even after their time in the spotlight, professional gamers have been leveraging their successes in eSport toward the promotion of arcades, PC cafés, and new gaming stadiums as meccas of competition, as has happened with professional sport more broadly throughout the twentieth century. Achievement has played a large role in furthering the notion that certain gaming-oriented spaces could become nodes of (cyber)athletic tourism. US pro arcade gamer Leo Daniels, who earned five national records and coached other players (including two other national champions), recognized at an early point that his competitive feats at the arcade could be a major drawing point for business, beyond training and coaching other players. Daniels manages the Light Years Amusement Center in North Carolina, where eight of the state's records had been set. He related that attempts had been made to attract attendees and spur centralized competition at this particular arcade by issuing challenges: "When we opened, we advertised for people to come down and try to break records or challenge me."[37] The promotion of competition, borrowed from sport, whereby the champions of the past are mentoring future pro gamers (as team coaches, for example), is helping to sustain the continuing growth of the activity.[38]

As eSport experiences unprecedented growth in the West after many missteps in the late 1990s and early 2000s, Asia's leading role in eSport continues in 2015, not only as a region that produces teams winning tournaments for many of the most popular games (including *League of Legends*, *DotA 2*, and *StarCraft II*), but as a place where game consumers are experiencing and contributing to the continued success of eSport events. Notably, China's Hengqin Island, adjacent to the massive entertainment and experience hub of Macau, will soon see a 15,000-seat arena devoted to eSports. With more than 500 million people playing digital games in China (and about 145 million playing more than an hour per day), the venture made economic sense for Hong Kong's Lai Fung Group, which is developing the arena as the centerpiece of an almost $3 billion gaming theme park.[39] This new arena joins ones already in place in Asia, such as Intel's stadium in Chengdul, China, as well as newly developing ones such as those in Santa Ana, California, and Columbus, Ohio. As eSport events continue to attract attention from fans, institutions, business, and government, professional gaming's status as one of the newest players in the mega-event landscape will push ever more toward the vanguard of experiential commodification and event marketing.

Conclusion

The eSport experience of the 1990s was rooted in a confluence of formative factors specific to Korea's expanding role in global affairs and as a new site for public event consumption. Korea's eSport legacy was built on the infrastructure, knowledge, and capacity that were largely guided by the country's hosting of the 1988 Olympics games and other spectacular urban events as well as easy access to low paid manufacturing labour in the region. The adoption of a new public, competitive event that emphasized technology (and especially gaming), sport, and media was timely, as Korean elites looked to position the nation at the forefront of the global economy championing convenience, commoditized experience, and computerization as its guiding attributes.

During the 1990s and 2000s, professional gaming competitions continued to be organized and sanctioned as public contests complete with title sponsors, audiences, and even media coverage. These eSport events became vehicles for promoting media platforms and linked sport and technology. Recent eSport contests have become indicative of a shift in the way events are witnessed, from the traditional televised spectacle to an increasingly popular digital online viewership model. In this sense, competitive gaming as a key feature of overall gamer culture also demonstrates the changing nature of public-event consumption as a leading product of what has become known as the experience economy.

The eSport event originates as merely one response to historical developments when it comes to public sites of entertainment, such as the amusement park, circus, or carnival. However, we argue that it is also an extension of the mediated sports spectacle within the digital market economy. Gaming events provide an important opportunity for the mass marketing and promotion of the digital industries as part of a broader transposition of competitive play within the experience economy. Sport has served as an example of successful entertainment-based event marketing in a mediated culture where play has become an involved, performance-centric experience as well as a spectatorial one. Public gaming in fixed spaces, and modeled along the lines of conventional sport, repositioned players and fans within a promotional chain that organized synergies between competitive play, public events, spectating, marketing, and business strategy. This has increased the attractiveness of eSport to urban elites searching for promotional ventures that can be associated with image building and the marketing of cities as centers of excellence in the digital media, advertising, and design fields. The world's cities have not yet embarked on bidding wars to attract major eSport events. But, as global audiences grow, and economic synergies continue to develop around such events, there is every reason to believe that eSports will become global mega-events of the future.

Notes

1 Jin, *Korea's Online Gaming Empire.*
2 Breslau, "The International 2014"; and Kain, "The International 'Dota 2' Championships."
3 Burns, "eSports Can Now Drop the e."

4 ESL is currently the world's largest eSports company. The company has a global reach with offices in Germany, Russia, France, Poland, Italy, Russia, China and the US.

5 Cilliers, "ESL brings eSports to World Cup Stadium"; Jamias, "DOTA 2 Tournament."

6 Borowy and Jin, "Pioneering eSport."

7 Jin, *Korea's Online Gaming Empire.*

8 Hutchins, "Signs of meta-change."

9 Ibid., 852.

10 See Bell, *The Coming of Postindustrial Society*; Akamatsu, "A historical pattern"; Toffler, *Future Shock*; Harvey, *The Condition of Postmodernity.*

11 Pine and Gilmour, *The Experience Economy.*

12 Poulsson and Kale, "The Experience Economy," 270.

13 Darmer and Sundbo, "Introduction to experience creation."

14 Kocurek, "Coin-drop capitalism," 205.

15 Cilliers, "ESL brings eSports."

16 Johansson and Näslund, "Artisans of the spectacle," 158.

17 Ibid., 157.

18 Avrich, *Event and entertainment marketing*, 132.

19 Taylor and Cunningham, "Event marketing," 425.

20 Gruneau and Whitson, "Upmarket continentalism."

21 See Gruneau and Neubauer, "A gold medal."

22 Tomlinson and Young, "Culture, politics, and spectacle in the global sports event." 10.

23 Tomlinson, "Olympic spectacle: Opening ceremonies and some paradoxes of globalization," 590.

24 Real, *Super Media*, 230.

25 "Sega Sponsors All," 69.

26 Borowy and Jin, "Pioneering eSport."

27 Hua, "Video game players score big money in South Korea."

28 World Cyber Games, "Globe's Best Gamers Converge in Los Angeles."

29 Ibid.

30 Jin, *Korea's Online Gaming Empire.*

31 Ministry of Culture, Sports and Tourism, *2014 Guide to Korean Games Industry and Culture.*

32 Larson and Park, *Global Television and the Politics of the Seoul Olympics*, xvi.

33 Kennedy and Hills, *Sport, Media and Society*, 6

34 Makuch, "Virginia university to offer the first degree combining game design and sports."

35 Sanserino, "Video games gain new ground with athletic scholarships."

36 Kieltyka, "Vancouver schools foster new generation of virtual athletes."

37 Associated Press, "Making it in the world of video."

38 Borowy and Jin, "Pioneering eSport."

39 Brustein, "Huge video game stadium coming to Macau's neighbourhood."

Bibliography

Akamatsu, K. "A historical pattern of economic growth in developing countries." *Journal of Developing Economies* 1(1) (1962): 3–25.

Associated Press. "Making it in the world of video." *The Globe and Mail*, October 12, 1982: 17.

Avrich, B. *Event and Entertainment Marketing: A must guide for corporate event sponsors and entertainment entrepreneurs.* Chicago, IL: Probus, 1994.

Bell, D. *The Coming of Post-Industrial Society: A Venture in Social Forecasting.* New York: Basic Books, Inc., 1973.

Borowy, M. and Jin, D.Y. "Pioneering eSport: The Experience Economy and the Marketing of Early 1980s Arcade Gaming Contests." *International Journal of Communication* 7 (2013): 2254–75.

Breslau, R. "The International 2014 sells out in an hour." 2014: http://www.ongamers.com/articles/the-international-2014-sells-out-in-an-hour/1100-1182/.

Brustein, J. "Huge video game stadium coming to Macau's neighbourhood." 2014: http://www.businessweek.com/articles/2014-04-25/hengqin-near-macau-to-host-the-worlds-first-video-game-stadium.

Burns, T. "eSports Can Now Drop the e." *Aljazeera*, July 26, 2014: http://www.aljazeera.com/indepth/opinion/2014/07/esports-can-now-drop-e-2014724112549724248.html.

Cilliers, H. "ESL brings eSports to World Cup Stadium with largest Dota 2 event to date." 2014: http://www.mweb.co.za/games/ViewNewsArticle/tabid/2549/Article/11806/ESL-brings-eSports-to-World-Cup-Stadium-with-largest-Dota-2-event-to-date.aspx.

Darmer, P. and J. Sundbo. "Introduction to experience creation." In J. Sundbo and P. Darmer (eds.). *Creating Experiences in the Experience Economy.* Cheltenham: Edward Elgar, 2008, pp. 1–12.

Gruneau, R. and Neubauer, R. "A gold medal for the market: the 1984 Los Angeles Olympics, the Reagan era, and the politics of neoliberalism." In *The Palgrave Handbook of Olympic Studies*, Helen Lenskyj and Steven Wagg (eds.). London: Palgrave Macmillan, 2012.

Gruneau, R. and Whitson, D. "Upmarket continentalism: Major League sport, promotional culture, and corporate integration." In *Continental Order: Integrating the North American Continent for Cyber-Capitalism*, Vincent Mosco and Dan Schiller (eds.). Boulder, CO: Westview Press, 2001, pp. 235–64.

Harvey, D. *The Condition of Postmodernity.* Malden, MA: Blackwell Publishers, 1990.

Hua, V. "Video game players score big money in South Korea." *San Francisco Chronicle*, December 18, 2006: A1.

Hutchins, B. "Signs of meta-change in second modernity: The growth of eSport and the World Cyber Games," *New Media and Society* 10 (6) (2008): 851–69.

Jamias, Michael "DOTA 2 Tournament At ESL One Frankfurt draws In 1 million viewers." *MMO Games Connection*, 2015: http://mmo-play.com/rpg-games/dota-2/news/dota-2-tournament-esl-one.

Jin, D.Y. *Korea's Online Gaming Empire.* Cambridge, MA: MIT Press, 2010.

Johansson, M., and L. Näslund "Artisans of the spectacle: Entrepreneurship in the event industry." In *Entrepreneurship and the Experience Economy*, D. Hjorth and M. Kostera (eds.). Copenhagen: Copenhagen Business School Press, 2007, pp. 155–79.

Kain, E. "The International 'Dota 2' Championships will be televised on ESPN, boasts biggest prize ever." 2014: http://www.forbes.com/sites/erikkain/2014/07/17/the-international-dota-2-championships-will-be-televised-on-espn-10-8-million-prize-biggest-in-gaming-history/.

Kennedy, E. and L. Hills. *Sport, Media, and Society.* Oxford: Berg, 2009.

Kieltyka, M. "Vancouver schools foster new generation of virtual athletes." 2014: http://metronews.ca/news/vancouver/1212335/vancouver-schools-foster-new-generation-of-virtual-athletes/.

Kocurek, C.A. "Coin-drop capitalism: Economic lessons from the video game arcade," In *Before the Crash: Early video game history*, M. Wolf (ed.). Detroit, MI: Wayne State University Press, 2012, pp. 189–208.

Larson, J.F. and H. Park. *Global Television and the Politics of the Seoul Olympics*. Boulder, CO: Westview Press, 1993.

Makuch, E. "Virginia university to offer the first degree combining game design and sports." 2014: http://www.gamespot.com/articles/virginia-university-to-offer-the-first-degree-combining-game-design-and-sports/1100-6419811/.

Ministry of Culture, Sports and Tourism. *2014 Guide to Korean Games Industry and Culture*. Naju: KOCCA, 2014.

Pine, J., and J. Gilmore. *The Experience Economy*. Boston, MA: Harvard Business School Press, 1998.

Poulsson, S.H.G., and S.H. Kale. "The experience economy and commercial experiences." *Marketing Review* (4) (2004): 267–77.

Real, M.R. *Super Media: A Cultural Studies Approach*. Newbury Park: SAGE, 1989.

Sanserino, M. "Video games gain new ground with athletic scholarships." 2014: http://www.post-gazette.com/business/tech-news/2014/11/23/Video-games-gain-new-ground-athletic-scholarships/stories/201411230082.

"Sega sponsors all Japan TV game championships." *Vending Times* (14) (1974): 69.

Taylor, S.F., and P.H. Cunningham. "Event marketing." In *The Advertising Business: Operations, creativity, media planning, integrated marketing*, J.P. Jones (ed.). Thousand Oaks, CA: SAGE Publications, 1999, pp. 425–36.

Toffler, A. *Future Shock*. New York: Bantam Books, 1970.

Tomlinson, A. "Olympic spectacle: Opening ceremonies and some paradoxes of globalization." *Media, Culture, & Society* (18) (1996): 583–602.

Tomlinson, A., and C. Young. "Culture, politics, and spectacle in the global sports event: An introduction," In *National Identity and Global Sports Events: Culture, politics, and spectacle in the Olympics and the Football World Cup*, A. Tomlinson and C. Young (eds.). Albany, NY: SUNY Press, 2006, pp. 1–14.

World Cyber Games. "Globe's best gamers converge in Los Angeles for the World Cyber Games 2010 Grand Final Videogame Competition and Festival." September 30, 2010: http://www.prnewswire.com/news-releases/globes-best-gamers-converge-in-los-angeles-for-the-world-cyber-games-2010-grand-final-videogame-competition-and-festival-104090553.html.

Index

Lightning Source UK Ltd.
Milton Keynes UK
UKOW04n1057260716

279211UK00009BA/78/P